Alchemists of Revolution

WITHDRAWN

ALCHEMISTS

OF

REVOLUTION

TERRORISM IN THE
MODERN WORLD

Richard E. Rubenstein

Basic Books, Inc., Publishers   New York

The following publishers have generously given permission to use extended quotations from copyrighted works:

From *Against Individual Terrorism,* by Leon Trotsky. Reprinted by Pathfinder Press. Copyright © 1974.

From *The Terrorism Reader,* by Walter Laqueur. Copyright © 1978 by Walter Laqueur. Reprinted by arrangement with New American Library.

From "State Sponsored Terror Called a Threat to U.S.," by Thomas L. Friedman, reprinted by permission of the New York Times Company. Copyright © 1983 by the New York Times Company.

Library of Congress Cataloging-in-Publication Data

Rubenstein, Richard E.
    Alchemists of revolution.

    References: p. 237.
    Includes index.
    1. Terrorism—History. I. Title.
HV6431.R83 1987   303.6'25'09   86–47740
ISBN 0–465–00095–9 (cloth)
ISBN 0–465–00094–0 (paper)

For Brenda Libman Rubenstein

L'espoir déçu s'habille en bombes.

(Hope betrayed arrays herself in bombs.)

Graffito, 1977

Université de Provence

CONTENTS

ACKNOWLEDGMENTS

THIS BOOK has been a ten-year project. In completing it, I have been aided and emboldened by many friends, including my former colleagues and students at Roosevelt University in Chicago; the administration of that University, which provided valuable research support; the Franco-American Fulbright Commission and my colleagues at the Université de Provence; and the students, faculty, and administration of Antioch School of Law in Washington, D.C. I appreciate the help proffered by librarians and staff members of the U.S. Library of Congress, the Regenstein Library of the University of Chicago, and the Lauinger Library of Georgetown University.

I owe particular debts of gratitude to the following individuals, none of whom bears the slightest responsibility for any errors of perspective or fact contained in this volume: Roderick Aya, Betty Bernstein, Cornelia Bowman, H. Russell Cort, Richard Curtis, Rodney Estvan, Regina Holloman, Isaac C. Hunt, Jr., Dr. Jerome I. Katz, Bessie C. Minnick, Frank Munger, Alice Robinson Palmer, Edward L. Palmer, William A. Pelz, Matthew Rubenstein, Francia Salas, Michael W. Schwartz, Joseph Seymour, America Ugarte, and Frank Untermeyer. Special thanks go to Darcy S. Jaffee for helping prepare the manuscript for publication, to Ronald L. Goldfarb and Gail Ross for their splendid representation, and to Steve Fraser of Basic Books for his sensible and valuable editorial suggestions.

RICHARD E. RUBENSTEIN
Washington, D.C.
May 1, 1986

INTRODUCTION

DURING the mid-1960s, when American cities were struck by a wave of violent racial uprisings, an explanation commonly offered was that a handful of fanatical outsiders—in President Lyndon Johnson's words, "a few mean and willful men"—were responsible for instigating the violence. Congress responded by passing legislation that made it a crime to cross state lines with the intention of provoking a riot; the Federal Bureau of Investigation initiated its now infamous COINTELPRO campaign to "penetrate and disrupt" allegedly seditious groups; and the police took on the Black Panther party.

Unlike most cases of terrorism, however, the ghetto uprisings took place in our own backyard. Its participants (seen nightly on television) were people we knew, or might have known but for the familiar realities of racial segregation and economic exclusion. We did not really need a National Advisory Commission on Civil Disorders to tell us that the "outside agitator" theory of racial disorder was a sham and a diversion, or that the underlying causes of the rioting were to be found in our own social history . . . and in our own hearts. Thus the rage for retaliation was soon dampened. The nation searched its soul, and while it did not solve the problems of racism and poverty, at least, for a time, it tried.

Terrorist violence evokes a very different sort of reaction; we approach it essentially as outsiders. The terrorists live in far-off lands, reflect alien cultural values, embrace incomprehensible religious and political ideologies. They are the products of a history with which we are unfamiliar and which we think does not implicate us. Furthermore, the type of violence they perpetrate has few parallels in our own domestic experience. Racial rioting we understand, just as we understand violent strikes, confrontational demonstrations, prison riots, and political assassinations committed by deranged loners. But systematic terrorism—the calculated use of small-group violence to generate mass mobilization for political change—has been a determining factor in American history only once: when the Ku Klux Klan and kindred groups used it to restore white supremacy to the South after the Civil War.

As we will see, the triumph of the original KKK has much to tell us about the conditions for success of terrorist movements. But the memory of that group's violent reign has faded or been repressed, and nothing in our more recent history has prepared us to understand the dynamics of a serious indigenous terrorist campaign. Therefore, as Americans around the world become targets of terrorist violence, we find ourselves responding with a combination of anger, fear, and naiveté, a state that makes us particularly vulnerable to manipulation by demagogic politicians and pseudoscientists, the purveyors of "outside agitator" theories of terrorism and quick-fix retaliatory cures.

Item: In May 1981, a Turkish fascist named Mehmet Ali Agça attempts to kill the Pope. Immediately, a clutch of right-wing terrorism experts, cheered on by U.S. government officials and the mass media, announces that this is the result of a Soviet-Bulgarian plot to eliminate papal support for the Polish Solidarity movement. Unfortunately for the "Red Network" theorists, Agça proclaims at his trial that he is Jesus Christ, and suggests that he was told to finger the Russians and the Bulgarians by agents of SISMI, the Italian version of our Central Intelligence Agency. The "Pope plot" collapses, the Bulgarians arrested on Agça's say-so are released, and we are left knowing virtually nothing about the organization of which he was actually a member: Turkey's fascist Grey Wolves.

Item: In October 1983, a truck bomb driven by a Lebanese Shiite guerrilla blows up the American garrison at Beirut Airport, killing hundreds of GI's. This time, we are informed by the experts, the real villain is the government of Iran—or perhaps the government of Syria—since the ignorant, fanatical Shiites could not possibly have the technical expertise and material needed to construct such a weapon. But again the evidence of outside manipulation vanishes in the morning mist. Again the urge to retaliate is provoked, then frustrated. And again we are left in ignorance of terrorism's *internal* causes. Indeed, the notion that Shiite fighters are suicidal robots programmed by foreign manipulators to kill Americans—what might be called the "Manchurian Candidate" theory of terrorism—ensures that we will *not* understand their history, their motives, or their reasons for making us their targets.

Item: In October 1985, the cruise ship *Achille Lauro* is hijacked and an American passenger killed by members of the Palestine Liberation Front, an ultranationalist group operating on the fringes of the Palestine Liberation Organization. And in December, the Fatah Revolutionary Council, a group headed by Yasir Arafat's sworn enemy, Palestinian terrorist Abu Nidal, is credited with two ferocious bombings at the Rome and Vienna airports. The United States announces that because the Libyan government has given moral and material support to the terrorists, Libya is responsible for these attacks. It is clear that many governments, including that of Muammar Khaddafi's Libya, have supported Palestinian fighters and may be said to bear a share of moral responsibility for their actions. (The United States's responsibility for Israel's invasion of Lebanon, and Israel's for the massacres at Sabra and Shatila, are equally clear.) But support is not control, and if the history of terrorism teaches us anything, it is that terrorist movements with an indigenous political base generally call their own shots and develop their own sources of supply.

Who outside the American South "sponsored" the original KKK? What sinister "network" supplied the most effective terrorists of the 1970s, the urban guerrillas of Uruguay and Argentina? Who now "manipulates" the Irish Republican Army Provisionals, France's Direct Action, or, for that matter, the neofascist movements proliferating so rapidly throughout Western Europe? All of these organizations obtained support where they could. None were the creatures of outside sponsors, so dependent on external sources of supply that they could be eliminated by turning off some spigot. It is well known, for example, that the IRA Provisionals raise a good deal of money by soliciting contributions from Irish Americans. Yet who would be so foolish as to think that IRA violence in Northern Ireland could be ended by severing the "American connection," or so callous as to believe that the British would be justified in bombing South Boston in retaliation for the killing of British troops in Londonderry? Ironically, the closer to home terrorism strikes and the more we recognize that terrorists, no matter how culpable, are people like us, the less likely we are to accept quack theories of foreign "sponsorship" and the necessity for massive retaliation against alleged sponsors.

What the terrorism experts should understand—but apparently do not wish to acknowledge—is that retaliation based on the principle of collective responsibility for terrorist actions follows precisely the adversary's script. When President Ronald Reagan sent a U.S. task force across the "line of death" in March 1986 to confront the Libyans in the Gulf of Sidra, Abu Nidal smiled. And when American bombers based in England attacked Tripoli in April, killing some forty Libyans, including Khaddafi's adoptive infant daughter, in retaliation for the bombing of a Berlin discotheque frequented by American GI's, he rejoiced. Indeed, if Reagan did not exist, it would be necessary for Abu Nidal to create him. Let us see why this is so.

Mention terrorism, and most people immediately think of specific forms of violence like assassination, hijacking, kidnapping, and the bombing of public facilities. Nevertheless, it seems to me, a more useful definition of terrorism is this: it is politically motivated violence engaged in by small groups claiming to represent the masses. Although illegal, terrorism is not simply crime; mere criminals rarely purport to act on behalf of an entire nation, class, religion, or ethnic group, nor do they ordinarily accept martyrdom. And although political, it is not really warfare either, since the number of active combatants is small and their relationship to mass groups questionable. Terrorism, if you like, is a kind of crime that aspires to become warfare. Its goal is to link a small vanguard of militants to the resigned, timid, or corrupted masses—to awaken these oppressed sleepers and lead them to power.

How is this to be accomplished? The key lies in the truism that there is no force more terroristic than a national state at war. What terrorist assassination campaign compares with the CIA's "Phoenix Program," which resulted in the liquidation of at least ten thousand suspected Communists during the Vietnam War? What kidnapping operation can match the "disappearances" engineered since the mid-1970s by government-sponsored death squads in Guatemala, El Salvador, or Argentina? And what modern terrorist bombing can compete with the annihilation of entire cities in World War II? Obviously, state terrorism is immeasurably more destructive and indiscriminate than small-group violence. In terrorist theory, this simple fact has the impact of Newton's falling apple; for if small-group attacks can provoke powerful governments to retaliate against the terrorist's suppliers, sympathizers, and ethnic brethren, the state itself will accomplish the terrorists' main task. The sleepers will awaken, the cycle of retaliation will continue, the struggle will go forward.

That is why Abu Nidal laughs as U.S. jets stream in over Tripoli, blowing up women, children, and the French Embassy in addition to designated military targets. He knows that the invasion of Lebanon, triggered by his own group's 1982 attempt to kill Shlomo Argov, the Israeli ambassador in London, was a disaster for Israel that created a new front-line enemy on that nation's northern border. Why should the "Israelification" of American policy prove any less disastrous for the United States?

We will see in the pages that follow that terrorism is generated not only by grievances, but by the political weakness of militant intellectuals unable either to organize mass violence or to attract reliable allies to their cause. This disconnection of the intelligentsia, I will argue, is a primary internal cause of terrorism, dictating to a large degree its philosophy, tactics, and consequences. Only under certain circumstances is small-group violence an effective method of overcoming the militants' social and political isolation; but retaliatory responses that inflame a population already aroused by nationalist passion, and that drag third and fourth parties into the arena of conflict, surely constitute one of these circumstances. The most effective terrorist act in world history (to take an extreme example) was the assassination of Austria's archduke Ferdinand at Sarajevo in June 1914 by "Young Bosnia" terrorists who were struggling to liberate the Balkans from Hapsburg control—an act supported, if not instigated, by the Serbian Black Hand organization. The Austrian decision to treat this as an act of war requiring retaliation against Serbia triggered the mobilizations that led directly to World War I; and that war *did* destroy the Austro-Hungarian Empire, freeing the Slavs from foreign domination. To the rest of the world, perhaps, Sarajevo represents the beginning of a long nightmare. To modern Yugoslavs, it is the cradle of liberty.

This example may be extreme, but it is not irrelevant. Three lessons seem particularly notable. First, a policy of massive retaliation against terrorists, their suppliers, and their sympathizers is a war policy. Indeed, in the case of the United States it is part and parcel of a defense strategy increasingly based on offense: a nuclear first-strike capability, war-fighting readiness, the supply of sophisticated weapons to anti-Communist guerrillas, and a plan (made public by President Jimmy Carter) to "decapitate" the Kremlin leadership in the first moments of World War III by striking at what the Pentagon calls "C^3I"—command, control, communications, and intelligence. The attempt to debilitate Libya by bombing Colonel Khaddafi's headquarters was a particularly chilling indication of this correspondence. Those who consider the Middle East to be the Balkans of the modern era would do well to ponder the lesson learned too late by the Austrians.

Second, terrorism alone virtually never accomplishes the task of igniting a general conflagration. "Revolutionary" terrorism more often obstructs social revolution than produces it. Social revolutionaries aim to set class against class, overthrow the class in power, and reconstruct society—tasks for which small-group violence is unsuited even when it provokes excessive retaliation. Nationalist terrorism has a more explosive potential, in part because of the relative modesty of its goals. Nationalists hope to unite all classes of natives against the foreigner, to make occupied territory ungovernable, and to achieve recognition by other states. Small-group violence alone does not fulfill these hopes, but if the foreigner cooperates by retaliating against all natives and by attacking other states, anything is possible.

Third, to conceive of terrorism as the mere product of outside manipulation, created by the machinations of this government or that, makes it impossible to understand either its causes or its consequences. A front-page article in the *New York Times*** asked, "Is this terrorism motivated by political grievances, or has it simply become another tool of international relations for some states?" Most often, the answer is *both.* Terrorism is not mass violence, and foreign powers have long tried to use it for their own ends. But a terrorist movement with staying power, a movement capable of serving a destabilizing function, is not just a stage play produced by foreign intelligence agencies. It has historical antecedents, roots in a certain social milieu, relationships with other local organizations; it has its own sense of grievance and philosophy of remediation, its own modus operandi and contradictions. The surest way to misunderstand a terrorist organization, even if one considers it illegitimate, is to deny its local authenticity. The Soviets do this when they brand the Afghan rebels "bandits." And the *New York Times* does it by suggesting that terrorists like Abu Nidal are "hired guns" because they accept support from foreign governments.

Indeed, when foreign powers aid local terrorists, it is impossible to decide who is using whom, and for what purposes, without a strong sense of the rebel organization's political weight. What are its local social and political connections? In what ways (if any) does it reflect the wishes or satisfy the needs of larger groups? How rational is its program, and how capable is it of

*Thomas L. Friedman, "Loose-Linked Network of Terror: Separate Acts, Ideological Bonds," *New York Times,* 28 April 1986, A1.

using the leverage provided by more powerful allies or opponents? What social changes strengthen or undermine its position? Terrorism is a notoriously unreliable tool, as the Russian Czarists discovered in 1909, when their chief "mole" in the terrorist underground turned out to be the underground's chief assassin! This is because it is the product of internal forces, not just external manipulation. It has a life of its own.

That life is the subject of this book. Moreover, in my view it is no more reducible to grievances than to manipulation. Grievances have been with us always, but the history of modern terrorism spans little more than one century. What we want to know is why this form of violent politics was revived with such force in the late 1960s and early 1970s, and why it persists. Furthermore, small-group violence seems an exceedingly dangerous and ineffective way of redressing grievances. What impels young people to embrace it as a way of life? Under what circumstances, if any, does it work? And what are its unintended consequences?

In attempting to answer these questions, I have used a comparative method. Because terrorist movements are locally based and conditioned, they exhibit great diversity from group to group, country to country, and generation to generation. Nevertheless, their common features are particularly striking. Terrorist violence, we will find, is a response to a certain kind of social crisis. Widely divergent groups, politically speaking, share important structural similarities in their thinking, organization, and practice. This suggests that there is a logic of terrorist action that has a good deal to do with determining the outcome of diverse struggles and that may produce results unimagined by any party. To describe and illustrate this logic is one of our principal goals.

This, then, is the plan of the study. I begin by exploring the psychology of terrorism and by attempting to free the subject as a whole from misleading stereotypes and metaphors (part I). Then, in part II, I offer an explanation of terrorism's social causes, describing the typical situation that seems to produce terrorist movements at various times and places. Part III compares the theories and practices of the major schools of modern terrorism: anarcho-communist, nationalist, and fascist. Finally, part IV investigates the relationship between terrorism and social revolution, and part V defines the roles played by terrorists in modern struggles for national liberation. The overall purpose of this analysis is to provide the reader with an insider's feel for the subject—an understanding of terrorism as a historical and a human activity rather than as some mysterious, satanic force. My theme, let it be noted, is neither "Exterminate all the brutes!" nor "Sympathy for the Devil." One need have very little sympathy for terrorists to insist that they are neither brutes nor devils, but people in many ways like us.

PART I

THE POLITICAL IMAGERY OF TERRORISM

Chapter 1

The Bogeyman,

the Hero, and

the Guy Next Door

IT IS HARD to write at all dispassionately about terrorism. In our grandparents' day, the figure of the black-coated anarchist with his bomb became an archetype of the sinister—a popular bogeyman evoking dread, revulsion, and anger. Since then, the terrorist image has altered. In Western eyes, it now wears an Arab headdress and carries an AK–47 submachine gun or a grenade. But it remains a nightmare figure: shadowed, inscrutable, evil. We don't really "see" the terrorist. One does not stare the bogeyman in the face.

The distinguished psychologist, Lawrence Z. Freedman, has

observed that terrorism terrifies primarily because of its unex-
pectedness.[1] Suddenly, in the midst of peace, in the heart of
normalcy, violence explodes. The unforeseen explosion is
shocking enough, but its impact is magnified by the revelation
of an unexpected fanaticism, an apparently malevolent will, in
the bosom of society. Far more than traffic accidents or most
common crimes, terrorist acts make observers feel like victims
or survivors: at first shocked and passive, then fearful, then,
finally, enraged. Terrorists bank on provoking righteous wrath
—an emotion that, translated into policy, virtually guarantees
official overreaction to their deeds.

One century ago, for example, someone threw a bomb into
a squad of policemen trying to break up an anarchist rally in
Haymarket Square, Chicago. In what is now recognized as a
legendary miscarriage of justice, the leading organizers of the
rally were selected for prosecution; seven were convicted, and
three were hanged. Those arrested were leaders of the movement for an eight-hour workday, the subject of the rally. Although they espoused the cause of social revolution, there was
no evidence that they had planned or suspected a bomb attack
on the police.[2] On the other hand, hindsight is easy. Those who
considered themselves potential victims soon felt like hanging
judges, and leaders were duly punished for the sins of their
followers. At the time, few voices were raised to defend those
now remembered as the Haymarket martyrs.

Or consider the Palmer Raids of 1919–20, when more than
four thousand alleged radicals were arrested by order of U.S.
Attorney General A. Mitchell Palmer. Many were badly beaten,
and several hundred aliens were placed on ships and deported
to Russia without trial.[3] Surely a textbook case of state terror
and injustice. What motivated these excesses, however, was a
tangle of real and imagined plots, terrifying to the average
citizen, which culminated in the mailing of bombs to Wall
Street financiers by persons unknown. The skulking figure with
the bomb had reappeared, and someone had to be held responsible.

It is impossible, I think, to understand terrorism from the

perspective of either victim or judge. We need to suspend judgment, however provisionally, in order to define the phenomenon and to study its causes and effects in history. Better yet, why not try through imagination to see the world through terrorist eyes before reassuming one's own identity? It is not true, as the French proverb says, that to understand all is to forgive all. In *Eichmann in Jerusalem,* Hannah Arendt showed us that a victim of Nazi terror could refuse to play the judge, at least temporarily, in order to gain a better understanding of the executioner.[4] Behind the Nazi bogeyman she discovered an ordinary man who had dehumanized himself in the service of bureaucratic gods. The howls of outrage that greeted the work when it first appeared in the pages of *The New Yorker* magazine were not a response to any attempt to rehabilitate Adolf Eichmann's reputation; clearly, Arendt offered him neither a literary apologia nor forgiveness. The protests were a response to her discovery that we are not just the potential victims of some new Holocaust but its potential perpetrators.

Question: who is the terrorist? Answer: someone more like us than we ordinarily care to admit. The urban guerrilla is likely to be a young adult of more than average education, fervently committed to a political cause, and driven by a combination of hope and desperation to commit acts of violence in its service.[5] Most terrorists are no more or less fanatical than the young men who charged into Union cannonfire at Gettysburg or those who parachuted behind German lines into France. They are no more or less cruel and coldblooded than the Resistance fighters who executed Nazi officials and collaborators in Europe, or the American GI's ordered to "pacify" Vietnamese villages. And they are generally no crazier than you or I might be if some implacable authority robbed us of our land or turned our dream of a better life into ashes.

This has nothing to do with justifying terrorism. It seems to me that political violence is justified only when it ends oppression, and that (to lay a few early cards on the table) terrorist violence is a singularly ineffective method of ending oppression. Nations and social classes are sometimes liberated through violent means, but it is a mass movement that does the job, not a small-group conspiracy. Those who succeed in connecting themselves with a mass movement generally escape the label "terrorist." We call them revolutionaries, soldiers, and, in some cases, statesmen. Those who fail and give up the struggle are considered realists. The terrorist is one who, because of popular indifference, state repression, or both, fails either to mobilize the masses or to quit. Hope compels these rebels to continue, desperation to continue alone.

Thus there is no such thing as "the terrorist personality." As Lawrence Z. Freedman notes,

> A psychological profile of a model terrorist cannot be drawn. The personalities are disparate. The context and circumstances within which terrorism, both political and ecclesiastical, has been carried out are diverse in chronology, geography, and motive.[6]

People who declare war on the state may be quite sane or seriously disturbed. They may be expressing repressed hatred of their parents or they may not. They may harbor intense suicidal impulses or may simply have decided, like good soldiers, to take unusual risks for a cause they believe in. Certainly, most of them scarcely resemble the stereotypical villains of television and motion picture drama: enraged lunatics, mercenary hit men, or emotionless robots. Terrorists are often possessed by political ideas, but their ideas, like ours, float in a sea of feeling. Their very diversity of personality suggests that they are more human, more familiar than we care to admit. An informative article on Italian terrorism by a Chicago journalist was headlined, "Red Brigades: Like the guy next door."[7]

Lacking a psychological profile, we nevertheless know something about these "people next door," especially those who consider themselves social revolutionaries. We know, for example, that they tend to be young adults ranging in age from eighteen to thirty-five, that they are primarily male but include a large number of females in leading roles, and that they generally come from middle-class or upwardly-mobile working-class families.[8] We understand that many have been college students, professionals, or white-collar workers, and that, before becoming terrorists, most were involved in nonviolent political activity on the fringes of the mainstream parties.[9] Finally, we know quite a lot about their political ideas and activities, and even something (from memoirs, interviews, and witnesses' testimony) about their private hopes and fears.[10] Reasoning from this data with a little imagination, it is possible to describe not a terrorist personality but a *sensibility*, or system of interrelated feelings, common to diverse personalities.

An early attempt to describe such a sensibility was made by Leon Trotsky, who believed that the two emotions central to "heroic" terrorism were vengeance and despair. Noting that anarchist assassination attempts had become frequent in Western Europe and North America, he remarked that these acts "always come after some atrocity committed by the government—the shooting of strikers or executions of political opponents."[11] The most important psychological source of terrorism was "the feeling of revenge in search of an outlet." This desire for revenge, Trotsky insisted, "has its rights," but unleashing it against state officials rather than against the capitalist system disorganizes and demoralizes the revolutionary opposition more than it does the state.[12] Furthermore, if terrorists are driven to attack the state alone, this is the result of despair. They have lost faith in the masses' capacity to act in their own best interests. For these activists violence is often a noble gesture, a means of satisfying honor or dying bravely, rather than a step toward some predictable social transformation. Despair thus describes the state of mind of radical intellectuals cut off from both their middle-class brethren and their proletarian or peasant clients. Combined with the desire for revenge, it provides the emotional basis for substituting their own heroism for that of the unawakened masses.

This is a useful starting point. Vengeance and despair are still powerful factors in motivating terrorist action; yet the matter is more complex than Trotsky recognized. The Ulrike Meinhoff Kommando, a West German terrorist group, may have been created, in part, to avenge the Red Army Fraction (RAF) leader's death in prison, but what sort of revenge was the popular, influential Meinhoff herself seeking when she helped create the RAF? To the urban guerrilla, vengeance is not simply a matter of tit for tat—you killed our leader, so we kill yours; it flows from a more generalized sense of injury, a feeling verified, not created, by state violence against comrades. The psychology of the vendetta no doubt plays some role in any violent struggle that is at all protracted, but most modern terrorism is subjectively far more like warfare than like a Hatfield-McCoy feud.

Similarly, although "despair" certainly helps explain why intellectuals like Meinhoff abandoned their earlier commitments to nonviolent politics, it does not explain their conviction that violence could be an effective organizing tool. Most terrorist youths are not John Wilkes Booths, striking one last symbolic blow for a lost cause. It would be more accurate to say that they are unreasonably hopeful—that, having lost faith in the masses' capacity to mobilize in response to words, they have embraced an even more passionate faith in action. "We have lost all faith in words," said the founder of Russian terrorism, Sergey Nechayev, in 1869. "For us the word is only of significance when the deed is sensed behind it and follows immediately upon it."[13] And what is a deed or action? Not a speech, a political discussion, or a vote; not even a demonstration, strike, or sit-in; but "something which destroys something absolutely."[14]

What sort of sensibility does this suggest? Nechayev's profound disenchantment with words is the end-product of a process that began with enchantment. His bitterness is that of the young intellectual who discovers that the words he has worshipped are false idols, impotent to reorganize society. He is a lapsed reformist, having lost the faith that noble ideas, expressed in political debate or acted out nonviolently, can alter the hierarchy of power. The modern terrorist—another lapsed reformist—is also betrayed, and the impact of this betrayal divides his or her world in two. On one side, he or she ranges all of the talkers: the politicians, priests, labor leaders, armchair radicals, and publicists whose words and "wordy" acts, no matter how seemingly radical, induce people to obey unjust authority. On the other side, separated from all talkers by the great gulf of outlawry, are the disillusioned ones—those who, having once been tricked by words and gestures, have decided never to trust them again.

Among terrorists, nonviolent activity is considered a form of "words" because it is experienced as essentially deceitful. The overt purposes of conventional political activity (including conventional radicalism) seem to mask a far more powerful covert effect. Opposition short of violence maintains a shared sense of social possibilities and inevitable limitations that keeps both rulers and ruled in place. Political language and nonviolent acts are inherently ambiguous; they confirm this false reality even as they appear to challenge it. But violent action—"something that destroys something absolutely"—can rend the fabric of illusion, or so the guerrillas think. What is most important for their emotional formation, however, is that they experience the betrayal of hope personally, not as analysts but as victims.

Examine their personal histories. This one was a pacifist certain that the appeal of nonviolence would prove irresistible even to rulers with guns. That one was a reformer convinced that fiery speeches and clever political maneuvering would surely rally the masses to her cause. A third was a Communist Youth League member who believed in the Party's devotion to the workers, and a fourth a patriot who trusted his leaders to preserve the nation's honor. If they now feel like victims of deception, this is because they began adult life so trustingly, believing in their message of hope, their power to deliver it, and the capacity of others to listen and respond. Their failure to be heard is not just a disappointment; it is an identity-shattering blow. It suggests that, in a world of promises and excuses, equivocation and lies, only violence is unambiguous and trustworthy.

Youth plays a role in explaining the intensity of this reaction.

Erik Erikson has pointed out not only that "youth tends to think ideologically," but that "the particular ego-quality which emerges with and from adolescence" is fidelity.

> Fidelity is the ability to sustain loyalties freely pledged in spite of the inevitable contradictions of value systems. It is the cornerstone of identity and receives inspiration from confirming ideologies and affirming companions. . . . When Hamlet, the emotional victim of his royal parents' faithlessness, poses the question, "To be or not to be," he demonstrates in word and deed that to him "to be" is contingent on being loyal (to the self, to love, to the crown) and that the rest is death.[15]

Of course, Hamlet is no terrorist. The shock of betrayal does divide his world into hostile hemispheres of words and deeds; but unlike the terrorist, Hamlet remains trapped in words, unable to reconstitute his identity by taking his just revenge. The betrayal is too personal for that. He can avenge his father only by destroying his mother, and so *he* becomes the traitor, failing to honor the ghost's request until action is forced on him. By contrast, what permits terrorists to act is the impersonality of their victimization. Their deceiver is not a person against whom vengeance is taboo, but an oppressive system that happens to be represented by people. Modern terrorists are thus free, as Hamlet was not, to be implacable—that is, to act like soldiers.

Far more is involved here, obviously, than mere disenchantment with words. Revolutionary terrorists are not only young adults; they are morally ambitious intellectuals, and failure is as shattering an experience for them as it is for any other middle-class person who invests his or her identity in a career. Words are an intellectual's stock in trade, but they are only means to an end, which is to "move" people. Success means communicating with a selected audience (readers, clients, students, patients, constituents) in such a way that they are changed by the experience. Failure suggests a defect in either the message or the medium. Terrorists are communicators who have lost faith not in their message but in their ability to affect the audience using nonviolent language. In a sense, they are twice betrayed—first by the ruling class (especially by reformers who make radical change within the system seem possible), then by the masses themselves. Words and conventional actions prove impotent not only to disarm the powerful but to arm the powerless. Manipulated by threats and promises, suckered by advertising, divided against themselves by prejudice, and lied to persistently and successfully by government, they seem enmeshed in illusion—unable to visualize a better society, much less act to achieve it. Even the witness of "secular saints," even the violent deaths of martyrs, leave them unmoved. One might almost define a terrorist as someone who has decided to avenge his own dead, since neither the state nor the people will strike that blow.

The failure of lower-class groups to respond even to sacrificial nonviolence creates the "despair" that Trotsky described as an emotional foundation of terrorism. Those entirely disenchanted with reform may still retain a commitment to mass action. For example, they can become hard-line Marxist-Leninists without for a moment accepting the legitimacy of small-group violence. But the twice-betrayed no longer believe that political organizations of any stripe can tear through the web of illusion. Only a military organization, they insist, can accomplish that task. This position gives their pronouncements and explanations a hard-edged, realistic tone. The jilted lovers of words now speak only in communiqués. Nevertheless, the radical distinction they like to draw between words and deeds and between political and military action ought not obscure the fact that, for them, violence is still a means of communication. It is a last-ditch effort to break out of isolation, to be heard by others, and so to give their own ideas and values historical significance.

Terrorist acts, like acts of religious faith, stop just *short* of despair. Paradoxically, the faith they affirm, despite their anti-intellectual form, is the belief that ideas transform society. Here are the thoughts of Ch'en, a Chinese terrorist, as he prepares to blow up Chiang Kai-shek's limousine following the massacre of Communists in Shanghai. (Ch'en is a fictitious character created

by novelist André Malraux, who had met his real-world counterparts in China.)

> The problem was not to maintain the best elements among the
> oppressed masses in their class in order to liberate it, but to give a
> meaning to their very oppression: let each one assume responsibility
> and appoint himself the judge of an oppressor's life. Give an imme-
> diate meaning to the individual without hope and multiply the
> attempts, not by an organization, but by an idea: revive the martyrs.
> Pei, writing, would be listened to because he, Ch'en was going to
> die: he knew how much weight an idea acquires through the blood
> that is shed in its name.[16]

In some respects Ch'en is not a modern terrorist, since he seeks
absolute solitude and sees no purpose in surviving to fight
another day. Future terrorists would be more likely to destroy
the generalissimo's car with a remote-controlled bomb than to
throw themselves upon the wrong vehicle, as Ch'en did, "with
an ecstatic joy."[17] They are more soldierly than he, less suicidal,
and more confident of their ability to influence events in a
predictable manner. Ch'en's formal education was Christian;
theirs (in a broad sense) is scientific, and their attitude toward
violence reflects the modern intellectual biases toward technical
rationality, experimentation, and control. The notion that small
doses of violence (graduated down to "kneecappings" and
bombing empty buildings) can be used over a long period of
time to undermine authority and create a guerrilla army is a
typically modern fantasy of "scientific management." Ch'en's
götterdämmerung is far too romantic for terrorists in the age of
technique.

Nevertheless, like Ch'en's, their fantasy remains an isolated
intellectual's dream of efficacy. Where the old-style terrorist
sought a glorious death, the modern urban guerrilla pushes
buttons—calculating effects with all of the care of a laboratory
technician . . . or a public relations man. But both strategic styles
reflect the same basic drive: to reconnect the activists with
society, and therefore with history. Since the late 1960s, the
Western intelligentsia has been facing a crisis similar to that

which confronted European youths toward the end of the last century. This crisis of *social disconnection,* to be described in more detail a bit later, shows no signs of abating. The Red Brigadist, like Ch'en and Nechayev, is a person unwilling to join the oppressors and unable to lead the oppressed—an intellectual attempting to shoot his way out of isolation. Tragically, for all concerned, in most instances the attempt is doomed to fail. Violence, in the end, turns out to be no more trustworthy than words.

Terrorists derive their exaggerated respect for violent action, in large part, from the state itself—the modern, "progressive" state that emits an endless stream of words while bludgeoning its enemies into submission. Their perception, by no means irrational, is that the words pronounced in parliamentary debates and legislation, press conferences and international negotiations, derive their real meaning and potency from the jails and missiles prepared for those who will not listen to reason. Their error, however, is to imagine that what works to maintain state power also will work to overthrow it. Social disorganization and the absence of solidarity among oppressed groups make state terror effective. These same factors generate oppositional terrorism, but in the way that a disease generates a fever. So long as they persist, small-group violence remains impotent—a form of petty crime incapable of dislodging the great criminals in power.

Part II of this study describes how the social foundations for the construction of terrorist movements are laid when rapid, uneven economic development severs the connections between social classes, preventing the intelligentsia from fulfilling its customary role of social intermediary and springing loose idealistic, ambitious youths for independent action. The political preconditions for terrorism exist when a mass-based movement of nonviolent reform collapses, or when it becomes clear that such a movement cannot begin to reorganize society. Psychologically, the stage is set for terrorism when young intellectuals experience their isolation as betrayal, and when violence seems the only alternative to shameful silence. We must bear in mind, of course, that only a few hundred people supported by a few thousand sympathizers need feel this way in order to unleash a serious terrorist campaign.

Nevertheless, it seems to me that a sharp increase in revolutionary terrorism is probably not on America's short-term agenda. This is not because young intellectuals in the United States have been reconnected with upper-class patrons and lower-class clients, or because satisfying careers appear to be within their reach; and it is certainly not because any mass-based political movement has attracted their energies. On the contrary, the American intelligentsia as a whole, and particularly those sectors oriented toward public service, has become so isolated, so politically impotent and vulnerable to economic pressures, that its members have temporarily lost hope in the possibility of social reconstruction. They feel victimized, but not betrayed; demoralized, but not morally outraged. Their struggle to survive in a period of soaring deficits and impoverishment of the public sector, intensified job competition and lowered expectations, has deprived them, for the time being, of the taste for risk-taking. For a large portion of the American intelligentsia, the recession that began in the mid-1970s has not yet ended; nor has radical hope—personal or social—yet been reborn.

At the same time, it seems clear that we are incubating terrorists in the United States. For when hope does begin to rise—and with it rage against the persistence of inequality, injustice, and war—what will prevent educated and ambitious young people from taking the terrorist road? A wealth of useful social service careers? As government "goes private" we are annihilating these opportunities. A viable movement of social reform? The traditional party of reform continues to fragment, reflecting the fragmentation of its mass base. Militant mass organizations dedicated to racial and economic justice? They do not exist, except in the minds of small groups of militants. Even now, should some untoward event ruffle the placid surface of American politics, the probability of increased terrorism is high, if only because of the absence of alternative means of expressing hope and anger. Rapid economic growth in the United States, coupled with radical inequality in the distribution of its benefits, could raise this probability to near certainty. And in a nation that tends to distribute benefits according to the race or ethnicity of recipients, nationalist violence is a particularly disturbing possibility.

Certainly, U.S. authorities are behaving as if they believed an increase in domestic terrorism were imminent. Millions of dollars are spent annually on counter-terrorist research, and on the training, equipment, and operation of special counter-terrorist forces, both military and industrial. Under President Ronald Reagan, the FBI has been unleashed to infiltrate and spy on "enterprises prone to terrorism," free of the restrictions that had been imposed by Jimmy Carter on the Bureau's political intelligence gathering.[18] A steady drumbeat of hearings, proposed legislation, and right-wing propaganda emanates from the U.S. Senate Subcommittee on Terrorism and Internal Security, and public buildings in Washington, D.C., are bunkered like fortresses against possible car-bomb attacks. There is about this activity a certain Maginot Line quality, since the assumption made is that terrorist attacks are most likely to be the work of known enemies: hostile governments like those of Libya or Iran, existing terrorist organizations like the Puerto Rican Front for National Liberation (FALN) or Islamic Jihad, or domestic extremists of the far Left and far Right. It is surely not irrational for America's rulers to fear that the growing wave of attacks on their diplomats, civilian travelers, and soldiers abroad will tumble onto domestic shores. But experience suggests that while everyone guards the front door against known enemies, the unknown terrorist slips in the back.

Concrete bunkers may have their uses, but they cannot protect a society against the violence of its own alienated youth. In a time of economic uncertainty and lowered political expectations—a period in which private concerns seem to overwhelm public aspirations—it is easy to underestimate the craving of young intellectuals for lives of social significance. Nevertheless, this need exists, and persists, despite all efforts to ignore or repress it. Young people hunger for morally satisfying careers, for linkage with the oppressed, for lives that have meaning outside of the narrow circle of family and friends. And if other opportunities to satisfy this ambition do not exist, some of them will attempt to create their own linkages through violence. This is why the most effective counterterrorist device yet discovered is a popular mobilization for significant change. Domestic terrorism can be averted, in the long run, only when there are mass-based organizations capable of linking the youthful intelligentsia to the people.

Chapter 2

Terrorism as Crime

or as Warfare

TO CALL an act of political violence terrorist is not merely to describe it but to judge it. Descriptively, "terrorism" suggests violent action by individuals or small groups. Judgmentally, it implies illegitimacy. These meanings are closely related, since there are very few situations in which assassinations, bombings, kidnappings, or bank robberies seem justified. By contrast, wars and revolutions are frequently considered not only justifiable but holy.

Political language divides along the fault line separating mass violence from individual or small-group violence. Organized political violence involving the participation of large numbers of people is generally recognized as war or revolution, with combatants designated as "soldiers," "guerrillas," "commandos," or "freedom fighters." These terms imply that their activities reflect the will and advance the interests of some large social group—a class, race, religion, or nation. Individual violence, on the other hand, is frequently associated with madness or crime. To call its practitioners "terrorists" implies that, like lunatics or criminals, they constitute an isolated minority rather than representing a mass constituency. According to this under-standing, mass violence may sometimes be justified, individual violence virtually never.

The difficulty is that one cannot distinguish mass from indi-vidual violence simply by counting heads. In 1958, there were far more young men in Cuban dictator Fulgencio Batista's army than there were Fidelista "terrorists" in the mountains; yet in a very short time, the Fidelistas were the ones leading a popular revolution, while those who had commanded the Cuban army were plotting to assassinate the new premier, Fidel Castro, with the help of the CIA and the Mafia.[1] Conversely, when thou-sands of young Argentine guerrillas began attacking govern-ment officials, business enterprises, and army outposts in the early 1970s, some political analysts decided that they could not be "mere terrorists" because there were so many of them. But deciding whether politically motivated violence is a revolution or a terrorist campaign requires more than an adding machine. The decision reflects a complex judgment, an interpretation of facts based on one's own commitments and perspectives.

To the defenders of a particular regime or social order, any politically motivated disobedience (even mass resistance) smacks of terrorism. When the South African government an-nounces the arrest of a "terrorist criminal," we do not know whether the police have captured a student protestor against apartheid, the editor of an illegal newspaper, a trade union organizer, or an armed guerrilla fighter. And on the other hand, a regime in power is considered terrorist by those who deny its legitimacy even if they are but a handful and their opponents legion. Nobody wants to be called a terrorist; ter-rorism is what the *other* side is up to. This is why, as one authority puts it, "there is no satisfactory political definition extant or forthcoming . . . no common academic consensus as to the essence of terror and no common language with which to shape a model acceptable to political scientists or social psychologists."[2]

This situation has not been improved by recent definitions focusing on terrorism's scariness: its intention to intimidate civilians.[3] *All* political violence, including war, revolution, and everyday enforcement of criminal law, involves the intimidation (or "deterrence") of civilians. Sad to say, direct attacks against defenseless civilian targets are as much a part of mass warfare as of small-group terrorism. Clearly, no such definition will tell us whether the kidnappers of Israeli athletes at the 1972 Munich Olympics were "terrorist criminals" or "heroic freedom fighters," or which terms best describe today's Nicaraguan Contras. Where there is political consensus, people speak a common language, and problems of definition seem merely academic. Where there is none, definitions crystallize differences, and dissensus can be fatal.

Consider, for example, Argentina's "dirty war" against the urban guerrilla groups of the 1970s. At that time, Argentine attitudes toward terrorism were spread along a broad political spectrum, ranging from vigilantism in defense of the established order to armed attacks against the state. Most of the larger parties of the Left considered the ruling junta illegitimate. Nevertheless, they condemned attacks on business people and government officials by urban guerrilla groups like the People's Revolutionary Army and the Montoneros. Similarly, although the forces of the moderate Right generally considered the regime legitimate, they opposed the actions of the Argentine Anti-Communist Alliance, a secret military organization that specialized in arranging the "disappearances" of leftists and liberals. Because the generals in power were more inclined to seek out and punish leftist terrorists than those of the Right, a number of moderates, including high church officials, accused the government of complicity in terrorism. For its part, the junta banned most of the nonviolent parties of the Left, charging that *they* were aiding or abetting terrorists. Meanwhile, thousands died or disappeared in Argentine civil strife, most of them victims of right-wing violence.[4]

Given the absence of political consensus in world society, it is not unusual for definitional questions to be settled at gunpoint. Even so, discussing terrorism coherently presents unusual difficulties. Problems of political definition are commonly generated by multiple claims to an honored title: Is the United States, or is the Soviet Union, truly "democratic"? Is the homeland of "socialism" the U.S.S.R., or is it the People's Republic of China? Even where a word is most often used as a term of abuse—"fascist," for example—the ideas and practices of groups claiming the title can help reestablish its meaning. But to my knowledge, the last group to openly call itself terrorist was the People's Will *(Narodnaya Volya)*, a Russian student organization that disappeared in the 1890s. Since then, the word has become an epithet meaning "one who practices illegitimate violence." It is a rarity in political discourse—something very close to a universal term of abuse.

As a result, terrorism has an aura of mystery. In his book *Transnational Terror,* political analyst J. Bowyer Bell describes terrorism as "a condition known implicitly to most men, but which is somehow beyond rigorous examination."[5] But it is not really *that* occult. Insofar as we use the word to describe particular forms of political violence, it is known. Insofar as we use it to judge the moral and political validity of such violence, it seems beyond rigorous examination. The fulcrum of analysis, then, is the point at which description and judgment merge.

Assume, for example, that a group of IRA Provisionals shoots a British soldier stationed in Northern Ireland. What does it mean to call this action terrorist? To begin with, it means that the action is violent and that it violates local law or custom. Although violent and illegal, the shooting is not simply a criminal act; it is also politically motivated. Nevertheless, some people are bound to say, "Those terrorists are nothing but criminals." For them, the shooting lacks political and moral justification, with the result that its subjective side—the political motive—is canceled out. The political intentions of the assassin are not considered substantial enough to take the violent act out of the category of individual crime. Of course, the IRA fighters contend that they are soldiers representing a mass group—the Catholic population of Northern Ireland—in a war against the British and their local Protestant allies. To those who reject this claim, however, justification for what they consider a heinous crime is nonexistent. The attack on the British soldier is therefore a murder rather than an act of war.

This reasoning leads some politicians and analysts to characterize terrorism as crime pretending to be politics or madness wearing an ideological mask. "A crime is a crime is a crime," intoned Prime Minister Margaret Thatcher in 1981, defending Britain's refusal to grant political prisoner status to imprisoned IRA activists. But to characterize an act as criminal rather than military is to imply the existence of a generally accepted, minimally effective legal system embracing the attacker, the victim, and the judge. The IRA hunger strikers' suicide by starvation represented their ultimate rejection of criminal status and the legal system that confirmed it.

When IRA prisoners insist that they are not criminals, but soldiers, they deny their membership in the legal community represented by Thatcher, and affirm their adherence to another community—one that as yet lacks the power to impose criminal sanctions on its members but that they believe may establish its authority through violent struggle. How, they ask, can shooting a soldier be considered criminal when the act is committed on behalf of the Irish people against the illegitimate, British-supported government of Northern Ireland? Indeed, from the IRA perspective, to recognize the Ulster government's authority to define crimes and punish criminals is to accept the division of Ireland and the continuation of British rule, whereas violating that authority realizes, at least symbolically, the concept of a united Ireland. Therefore, one who denies that the shooting is criminal affirms the supremacy of the act's political content over its personal or legal content: it is an act of war rather than a murder. Similarly, calling the killer a soldier (or commando, urban guerrilla, freedom fighter, brigadist, etc.) represents a repudiation of the equation terrorism = crime. It is a way of asserting that the assassin is not a common criminal acting on his or her own, but a warrior whose actions reflect the wishes and advance the interests of a much larger group.

There seems little possibility at first of distinguishing objectively between acts of terrorism and acts of internal or external war. "One man's terrorist is another man's freedom fighter" seems as far as the inquiry can go. Nevertheless, the two equations already noted—terrorism-as-crime and terrorism-as-warfare—may help us reach higher ground. I call these definitions metaphors because it seems clear that political terrorism is sui generis—a specific form of violence distinguishable from both crime and warfare, although bearing a family resemblance to both. Exposing both images to closer analysis is one way of disentangling terrorism from misleading associations in order to bring its unique characteristics into clearer focus.

It is not difficult to understand why so many people see a close resemblance between terrorism and common crime. Like most other crimes, political kidnappings, hijackings, and assassinations are ordinarily perpetrated by individuals or small groups, not by masses of armed civilians or a large military force. Furthermore, in most instances terrorist acts take place on property or territory claimed and policed by an established government, not in a war zone, "liberated area," or other territory contested by some rival state authority. Finally, the terrorists' immediate targets are persons and property normally protected by the laws of that government. Usually there is no question of them attacking a state's armed forces in conventional battle or of their attempting directly to seize state power —nor could there be, since the terrorists are few and their enemies control the territory. Therefore, while rebellious activists may call themselves commandos or freedom fighters, the common understanding among observers unsympathetic to their politics or methods is that they are criminals with a political axe to grind.

Common language reflects this understanding. Just as the

shooting that the IRA describes as an act of war is assimilated to a familiar category of domestic crime (murder), the capture of prisoners is considered kidnapping, and the seizure of property (termed "expropriation" by terrorists) robbery. The armed fighters' adoption of military organization titles (Red *Army* Fraction, Red *Brigade*) seems a mere conceit or fantasy intended to disguise their real isolation—hence, their real criminality. This pretension is most apparent when the fighters' number is small, but even when several thousand take the field, we still call them terrorists if they appear to be acting without mass participation or support. In ordinary usage, the acts most likely to be considered terrorist are those that combine a high level of political motivation with a low level of mass participation. Where confusion reigns is on the borderlines, when there is doubt as to the sincerity or rationality of the activists' motives or the extent of their mass support. For example, one hesitates to call Charles Manson and his "family" terrorists, despite their apparent intention to provoke a racial war in southern California, since they seem to have been merely psychopathic. More to the point, one hesitates to call the twenty thousand U.S.-supported Contras in Central America anything *but* terrorists, since the extent of their mass support in Nicaragua is so thin.

This suggests that there may not be as much disagreement over the definition of terrorism as has been thought. The disagreement—and it is critical—is about how to apply the definition in particular cases. During the 1960s, for example, American officials eager to minimize the mass revolutionary aspects of the Vietnamese insurgency termed the activities of the National Liberation Front terrorist; but NLF supporters insisted that although acts like the assassination of village officials may have *resembled* individual terrorism, actually they were dictated by the needs and desires of a genuine mass movement. Similarly, contemporary observers of the violence in Northern Ireland describe it as terror, gang warfare, or civil war, depending on their estimate of the level of mass participation and organization in that struggle. In any particular conflict situation, there is not *that* much disagreement (although there is often some) about the numbers of combatants involved. Approximate figures for the number of IRA guerrillas, Red Brigadists, or members of the Palestine Liberation Front are pretty well accepted by both critics and sympathizers of these groups.[6] There is more dispute about the breadth and activism of their popular support and, most of all, about their capacity to mobilize and lead a mass movement. The gist of the disagreement, in other words, is qualitative. It is about the extent to which a relatively small number of armed fighters "represents" a much larger group.

The metaphor of terrorism-as-crime answers this question of qualitative involvement by focusing attention on the present level of armed struggle. If the masses are directly involved in violence against their own government or against a foreign state, they are not terrorists. If a few activists who claim to act for the masses begin blowing up police stations and shooting politicians, they are. Unfortunately, matters cannot be settled this simply. There is no doubt that in some respects, terrorism resembles common crime—that an airline hijacking for the release of political prisoners, for example, resembles a hijacking for money. Nevertheless, in a vital sense the resemblance is misleading, for the political hijacker and his or her confederates rarely act for themselves alone. Usually they are members of a larger political organization that has ordered the act or that approves of it. Furthermore, the hijacking itself is ordinarily not an isolated event, but part of a campaign that includes nonviolent actions and that is intended to achieve some political goal. Most important, in conducting this campaign, both the hijackers and their organization claim to represent a social class, racial or ethnic group, or nation, and to act on this mass group's behalf. This is precisely why they consider themselves not political criminals involved in individual violence, but revolutionary soldiers or patriots conducting a mass campaign.

Of course, this claim may be utterly unjustified, in which case the crime metaphor seems an accurate enough description; the terrorist, like the criminal, is acting essentially on his own. But what if it is the numbers game that is misleading? Clearly, mass struggles have sometimes been anticipated, even ignited, by the violence of small, apparently isolated vanguards.[7] (When this occurs, historians discover that the vanguard was not really isolated, thus clearing its members ex post facto of the charge of terrorism!) We cannot simply *assume* that small-group violence is unrelated to a mass movement. The claim of representation raises concrete questions that ought not be decided summarily or by definition: what is the relationship between the violent group and the masses it claims to serve, in particular cases and in general? In what respects, if any, does the self-proclaimed vanguard act for the more passive mass? Does a campaign of terrorism ever advance the interests of larger groups? If so, under what circumstances and with what results? What are the unintended consequences of such a campaign, and what are its long-range political effects?

These questions, so interesting and important, are quite beyond the reach of those committed to establishing a numerical distinction between individual crime and mass warfare. The understanding of terrorism is not advanced by terminology that summarily dissociates behavior from motivation, and that begs the question of terrorism's long-range political impact. Thus there is a tendency, especially on the part of angry opponents, to assume that terrorist ideology is merely a rationalization for criminal behavior. Political motivation is the occult, the subjective factor existing inside the activist's head, whereas mass participation is objectively measurable. As a result, terrorists are isolated from the masses by definition, and are assumed to be politically (and very likely personally) irrational—to suffer the delusion of being representatives of the masses when they really represent only themselves and a handful of fellow fanatics.[8] Of course, this is question-begging with a vengeance. The activists' isolation is not proved, it is assumed on the basis of a theoretical framework in which the only form of group solidarity recognized is the temporary aggregation of individual interests. From this perspective, not only the terrorist group but *any* would-be vanguard organization appears isolated and irrational, except where the masses have elected it their legal representative or where they immediately follow it into battle.

American social science has some difficulty analyzing questions of representation that cannot be answered by studying election results or taking a public opinion poll. The very notion of a political vanguard is alien to many of our scholars, in part because it implies that significant changes in mass political consciousness can occur during periods of social upheaval, elevating what seemed an isolated, extremist sect to the position of popular representative of an entire class or nation. Those biased toward social stability frequently confuse vanguardism with terrorism, even though the most successful vanguard organizations (for example, the Russian Bolsheviks) generally avoided small-group violence, condemning attempts to substitute "heroic" terrorism for mass action (see detailed discussion in chapter 11). Even if one focuses on violent vanguardism, however, it is clear that under certain circumstances, groups apparently isolated from their mass base or defeated by a superior force have been able to make good their claim to mass representation.

An example is the French Resistance to Nazi occupation during World War II.[9] Resistance, unlike terrorism, suggests mass violence. It is consistent with the contention that the French anti-Nazi movement was actively supported by the majority of French citizens as well as by the Allied armies actually responsible in 1945 for France's liberation. Nevertheless, this is the winner's version of a far more uncertain prior reality. In 1941, with the French army destroyed, the Germans occupying northern France, and a collaborationist government ruling the south, it was not at all clear that a few thousand Resistance fighters—a great many of them Communists—actually represented the French people. Nor was it clear that the self-exiled General Charles De Gaulle was, as he so confidently claimed, the "incarnation" of the French nation. Alone in besieged London, De Gaulle was well aware that his views were not at first shared by the French people, many of whom accepted fascist domination with more equanimity than was later admitted.[10] His claim was therefore vanguardist. It stated, in effect, "The minority that now organizes violence against the state will become the majority. I speak and act in the name of this future majority." The question is *how one tests the validity of such a claim.*

How, indeed? For if all political violence that does not command immediate mass support is automatically deemed terrorist, there is no way to distinguish between true and false claims of representation other than to await the verdict of history. De Gaulle's claim, for example, could not be verified until it became clear that the Allies would survive the German *blitzkrieg* and invade France. In other words, the head-counting approach leads us into a trap; if we accept it, we cannot predict whether ostensibly isolated terrorist acts will evolve in the direction of mass action or remain on the level of individual crime. Politically, this produces a most peculiar result. Initially, the metaphor of terrorism-as-crime reflects conservative assumptions: that the terrorist is isolated, irrational, and doomed to fail. But since this judgment may be reversed by the court of history, it must always be provisional. Today's isolated extremist may become tomorrow's legitimate leader. Yet this is precisely what terrorists themselves maintain—that they are the statesmen and women of the future! Ironically, therefore, conservative usage leads by an indirect route to the radicals' favored definition: terrorist is a name the provisional winners of a war or revolution use to describe the provisional losers.

From the point of view of, say, the Popular Front for the Liberation of Palestine, the similarities between the PFLP commando and the French Resistance fighter are decisive. Although both have performed acts resembling common crime, this is really the result of a temporary balance of forces in war. Acts of war become crimes when the balance is tipped so strongly against certain combatants that their actions are necessarily conducted in small groups on enemy or neutral territory and directed against people or property normally protected by domestic law. Therefore, from the PFLP's perspective, behavior that seems criminal is not at all incongruous with their claim to represent the Palestinian people. The forms of representation appropriate to defeated, disorganized, and unrecognized groups are different than those adopted by their victorious adversaries.

Of course, the French too were defeated; but De Gaulle was never expelled from England as Arafat was from Jordan and Lebanon. Their resistance was never shattered by continual defeat into a dozen warring sects. And their foot soldiers were never compelled to fight on the territory of distant nations using urban guerrilla tactics. To the PFLP, the primary difference between French and Palestinian fighters is *quantitative:* the Palestinians have been so badly defeated that they have lost both their homeland and the support of their former allies. Naturally, the "civilized world" considers their armed representatives madmen and criminals for continuing a hopeless struggle. Presumably, had Germany and Japan won World War II, the partisans of free France might even today be hijacking commercial airlines and shooting diplomats while the world recoiled in horror from such fanaticism, such criminality. The winners of an armed conflict always seek to legitimize their victory and make it permanent by declaring that the war is over; their interest is to make the distinction between small-group violence and mass violence *qualitative.* But for the losers, defeat is temporary and terrorism merely the continuation of mass struggle under adverse conditions and by other means.

In contrast to the crime metaphor discussed earlier, this approach views terrorist activity as a type of warfare: as class war, interstate war, or a combination of the two (for example, a war of national liberation). This description is actually a prediction: it foretells the gradual transformation of irregular warfare, fought by a vanguard with limited, largely passive civilian support, into a conventional war or revolution that mobilizes the masses to defend their interests directly. As the balance of forces changes, the challengers may move from what appears to be individual terrorism through a series of stages that culminate in a mass insurrection or conventional war. For the incumbents, the process is reversed. The scenario goes something like this:

in the initial stage of conflict, those who hold state power attempt to maintain order by normal law-enforcement methods in the face of outbreaks of crimelike violence. At this point, since the incumbent regime enjoys both a near-monopoly of armed force and a high degree of mass support, sporadic, localized, and individualistic violence by opponents is likely to pose, at most, a problem for regular police or local army units. This characterization of small-group violence as a police problem persists, for propaganda reasons, even in cases where anti-regime activities become better organized and enter the phase some call "armed struggle" (which could also be called the phase of sustained or escalated terrorism).

One indication that this stage has been reached is a shift in the focus of rebel attacks from symbols of authority, like businesspeople and high government officials, to more strategic economic, military, and political targets, such as arsenals, army patrols, transport and communications facilities, and factories. The intensified level of struggle means that the regime's usual order-maintenance forces are no longer capable of coping with violent dissent. By this time, the authorities already will have begun to practice unusual forms of repression, for example, by transferring control of antiterrorist operations to the regular army, suspending or altering normal criminal law procedures, banning hostile organizations, or mobilizing progovernment vigilante groups. Nevertheless, it is precisely now that the authorities will insist most passionately that their opponents are "terrorist criminals," for to characterize them in any other way would be to admit that civil violence was in the process of evolving into civil war.

Civil war itself can be divided into two phases, as Vietnam's master strategist, General Vo Nguyen Giap, suggested: guerrilla warfare and conventional war.[11] In the guerrilla phase, the rebel army uses irregular tactics, including hit and run attacks, "expropriations" of arms and money, and selective assassinations, to tie down the regime's forces and hamper its recruitment efforts. Simultaneously, the rebel leadership labors to convert mass sympathy into representative institutions of "dual power": committees of workers, farmers, and soldiers linked to a central political organization. Success on the political level provides (among other things) a stable base for military recruitment and the ability to finance and conduct a conventional war against the army of the regime.

It is important to note that guerrilla warfare, properly defined, is a method of moving from large-scale rebellion to revolution. It requires a high level of mass participation, a potent, centralized political leadership, and a professional fighting force. Terrorists who call themselves guerrillas are expressing a hope rather than a reality—the hope that their small groups will become a unit (or nucleus, to use the more ambitious term that is popular in Europe) of a mass-based guerrilla army. Even the participants in long armed struggle campaigns, like the pro-Castro M–16 movement in Colombia, the Basque Land and Liberty (ETA), and the IRA Provisionals, have not yet succeeded in creating guerrilla armies, while, by contrast, the rebels of the FMLN (Farabundo Marti Front for National Liberation) in El Salvador did succeed (in 1980–81) in moving from the phase of armed struggle to that of guerrilla warfare.[12] If El Salvador's regular army should collapse or be defeated on the plane of conventional warfare, then (in the absence of U.S. intervention) armed resistance to the new regime might well be reduced to the level of armed struggle and, finally, to that of terrorism.

The virtue of the terrorism-as-warfare metaphor is that it allows for the possibility of change—shifts in the balance of power, changes in the level of struggle, and reversals of roles between groups in and out of power. The fact that such changes are possible, and that the world knows them to be possible, accounts for the extraordinary impact of Yasir Arafat's appearance before the United Nations in 1974, clothed in the costume most Westerners associate with Arab terrorism. The costume seemed a dramatic (or terrifying) symbol of the possibilities of political transformation in a changing world: yesterday a terrorist, today a diplomat; today a pillar of law and order, tomorrow a vengeful Contra. As if to top even the irony of Arafat's United Nations appearance, the Israeli general election three years later brought to power a man who had made his reputation in the 1940s as a terrorist chieftain: Menachem Begin, former leader of the Irgun. Indeed, the terrorism-as-warfare metaphor accounts so well for the possibility of political change that one may be tempted to embrace the relativistic definition that it implies: terrorism is a word used by "ins" to describe the violence of the "outs."

This definition is not so much incorrect as insufficient, since, like the crime metaphor discussed earlier, it assumes what needs to be proved. Terrorism-as-crime assumes that an evolution of terrorism into mass struggle will not take place: once a terrorist always a terrorist. Terrorism-as-warfare simply reverses the assumption. By picturing various types of small-group violence as stages in a process of mass mobilization, it assumes either that the actions in question presently command mass support, or that they are undertaken in the interests of the masses and one day will command their support. (The very concept of evolution implies inevitability.) As stated earlier, however, this is exactly what cannot be settled by definition. The historical evidence suggests that most groups engaging in terrorism never reach the stage of armed struggle, and that most that do are defeated before conflict escalates to the level of civil war. This is true, for example, of the best-known Latin American insurgents of the 1960s and early 1970s, the Uruguayan Movement for National Liberation (Tupamaros) and the Argentine Montoneros. Moreover, armed struggle may be counterproductive for activists in the sense that it immobilizes the masses, reducing them to the role of spectators, or even advocates of law and order, while a small minority does battle in their name.

These problems have not gone unrecognized by advocates of revolutionary terrorism. Since history's verdict is always after the fact, some have argued that it is necessary to "do the experiment"—to strike out at the regime in the hope that the masses will rally to the cause. But what if they do not? What if the odds are overwhelmingly that the would-be vanguard will remain isolated from its mass base and be destroyed? Even then, the argument goes, it is better to resist than to collaborate. A movement needs martyrs as well as victors; sooner or later, one's daring, sacrificial deeds will inspire a mass revolt. John Brown, a veteran of armed struggle against slave owners in Kansas, declared war on the slave system in 1856 by seizing Harpers Ferry and calling on southern slaves to rebel. A terrorist act? Surely; but events four years after his execution seemed to prove him both martyr and prophet: "John Brown's Body" became a *casus belli* and Abraham Lincoln completed what Brown had, in a sense, started.[13] Similarly, some modern terrorists have compared themselves to the Narodniki, the educated youths who attacked Czarist officials with bombs a generation before revolution overthrew both czarism and capitalism in Russia. "We may not be the revolution itself," they have said in various ways, "but we are its precursors."

In one sense, it is impossible to disprove the precursor theory, for sometime in the future the masses may rebel and honor long-dead terrorists as heroes and martyrs. On the other hand, in many cases, terrorist attacks have inhibited mass organization and have seriously injured the revolutionary or national cause. Again, the tragic example of the Tupamaros is instructive. Having succeeded in destabilizing Uruguayan politics, but not in mobilizing effective mass support for their cause, the urban guerrillas in that country backed an electoral coalition whose defeat provoked a coup by the Right.[14] Today, more than a decade later, political life in Uruguay is just beginning to recover from the trauma. One day, perhaps, its people will install a government controlled by wage-workers and farmers, as the Tupamaros had hoped. In that event, however, what should be honored is their self-sacrifice and faith, not their strategy for revolution.

The Cuban war cry, *Venceremos!*—we will win—is a meaningful political slogan when the time frame implied for the emergence of mass struggle is reasonably short. Fidel Castro's breathtaking speed in moving from armed struggle to state power in only three years infected a whole generation of Latin American revolutionaries with unreasonable optimism. More realistically, where such evolution occurs at all, it is likely to consume a period of ten to twenty years. To project a revolution in one generation may not be unrealistic, but an infinitely long-term prediction—*Venceremos* someday—is more akin to religious belief than to political prediction. It is a statement of faith rather than a proposition connecting a cause (small-group violence) with an effect (the mass uprising). Whether in any particular case an act of violence is primarily a form of bearing witness or a prelude to mass struggle is a question that cannot be answered a priori or, for that matter, by "doing the experiment." It can be answered, if at all, only on the basis of careful, open-minded analysis.

The chief defect of the terrorism-as-crime metaphor was its failure to admit the possibility of a continuum linking terrorism and armed struggle to mass violence. The chief defect of terrorism-as-warfare is its failure to admit that the continuum has frequently been frozen or reversed, condemning small-group fighters to isolation or martyrdom, either heroic or absurd, depending upon one's point of view. Terrorism is not just a behavior or set of behaviors capable of being defined empirically as political crime; but neither is it merely a name that the provisional winners of a power struggle call the violence of the provisional losers. To assert that a violent act is essentially criminal is to have concluded that it is *not* integral to a process of legitimate political transformation. To assert that it is essentially an act of war implies that it reflects the desires or advances the interests of the masses and is strategically rational; hence, that it *is* integral to the mass struggle. The dispute in any particular case is not really about the meaning of "terrorism." It is about whether the violence in question is capable of liberating or empowering a class, nation, or other significant group.

This, then, is the issue that will concern us: the relationship of terrorism to group liberation. To avoid prejudging the matter, I use the word "terrorism" not as a term of abuse, but in a "cold" sense, to denote *acts of small-group violence for which arguable claims of mass representation can be made.* This definition accepts the observation that terrorism resembles crime; but it also accepts the possibility that it may represent an early stage of mass mobilization, the opening salvo in a war of group liberation. I hasten to add that focusing attention on the violence of smaller groups does not imply any preference for that of the state; for if terrorism simply means frightening, insensate, or illegitimate violence, national states are clearly the greatest terrorists of all.

Chapter 3

From Terrorism

to State Terror

CHANGES in political imagery signify alterations of political attitudes. Following the devastating attacks on the U.S. and French garrisons in Beirut by Lebanese Shiites in 1983, one noticed a new use of the terrorism-as-warfare metaphor in the United States. For the first time, it was those under attack rather than the guerrillas who referred to terrorism as "a new form of warfare," insisting that the handful of activists who had been launching suicide missions against military and diplomatic targets were not isolated fanatics but well-connected representatives. Whom did they represent? Not their own people, Americans were told, but hostile foreign regimes using terrorists as proxies and tools.

Clearly, this is not the sort of representation the guerrillas themselves claim! On the contrary, to assert that they are mere pawns in some other nation's game is a way of dismissing their pretensions to local leadership, of reducing the mass struggle they claim to lead to a kind of shadow play produced by external actors.

The new warfare rhetoric performs two functions: it denies the terrorists' connection with an authentic rebellion, and it places ultimate responsibility for their acts on the governments that supply, train, or succor them. Local terrorism, in this view, becomes an irrelevant or illusory "epiphenomenon." The reality is manipulative action by hostile states. Thus, the U.S. government declared in 1985 that the bombings of the Rome and Vienna airports by members of the Fatah Revolutionary Council represented acts of war by Libya, one of the nations that sheltered and condoned Abu Nidal, the Council's leader. In fact, no evidence demonstrating Libyan complicity in these attacks was ever produced. Calling this episode of terrorism "war" was primarily a frustrated response, signifying acceptance of the principle of collective responsibility: if we cannot find and punish the perpetrators, we will punish their suppliers and sympathizers.

Like the common crime and civil war metaphors, the metaphor of interstate war substitutes assumption for argument. Militarily, it reflects the questionable premise that drying up the terrorists' external sources of supply will terminate their activities. Morally, it is intended to justify retaliation in which innocent civilians get hurt. And politically, it ends the search for indigenous social causes of terrorism, preferring to view local violence as a product of policies formulated in some foreign capital.

Of course, there are instances in which this sort of reductionism is justified. The old Macedonian terrorist group IMRO (Inner Macedonian Revolutionary Organization) clearly degenerated to the point that it became a mere pawn in Balkan power struggles, a gang of thugs for sale to the highest bidder. But to assert that such figures as Abu Nidal, George Habash of the PFLP, or the leaders of the Islamic Jihad are creatures of the Libyan, Syrian, or Iranian governments is another matter entirely. Ever since the nineteenth century, the great powers, as well as a large number of middle-sized powers, have financed terrorist groups, meddled in their politics, and attempted to use them to achieve some fancied advantage over their adversaries. Far more often than not, however, this alleged "weapon" blows up in the sponsor's face. Life would be much simpler if the states that supported terrorists directly or indirectly also controlled them. Then the "enemy" would be openly exposed instead of hidden in shadow, and would be vulnerable to conventional military attack. But as we shall see, the great bulk of the available evidence suggests that operational control of terrorist activities by foreign states is the exception, not the rule. Terrorism cannot be wished away by defining it as state terror.

The tendency to equate terrorism with state terror, or to view the former as the bad seed that produces the latter, is characteristic of one type of conservative analysis. "For the conservative critics of revolution," political scientist Mark Hagopian states, "radicalism, dictatorship, and the Terror are three ways of saying the same thing."[1] Thus, the historian Albert Parry asserts in *Terrorism: From Robespierre to Arafat* that terrorist violence is "double-edged":

> It is the terror used to achieve the overthrow of the existing government. It is also the terror employed when these very same terrorists, having tasted victory and seized the state, wield their new-found power to victimize their opponents, both real and imagined.[2]

If Parry is talking only about the mass terror of civil war, this statement is unexceptional. Civil wars frequently do bring harsh and repressive regimes to power (although the regimes overthrown may have been worse). But Parry's intention is more ambitious than this. It is to convince us that there is no substantial difference between small-group terrorists, successful revolutionists, and practitioners of state terror. Terrorism, in this view, is state terror in embryo, and the state terrorist an urban guerrilla who made good.

This produces a remarkable theoretical muddle. On the one hand, Parry labels Lenin a terrorist even though the Bolsheviks' success was based in no small part on their *refusal* to practice small-group violence. Assassination, anathema to the Leninists, was the principal weapon of their chief competitors, the Russian Socialist-Revolutionaries.[3] On the other hand, since genuine terrorism rarely reaches the level of sustained "armed struggle," much less revolutionary civil war, Parry and other conservatives characterize it as common crime, madness, or sheer evil. As a result, the notion that state terror is the product of small-group terrorism remains unproved. Moreover, it seems unprovable. Terrorism sometimes *provokes* state terror, as when a government suspends normal legal procedures or declares martial law in order to hunt down its enemies. But it does not *become* terror, like a naughty child growing into a hardened criminal. Terrorists are rarely at home with revolutionary regimes in power. More often, they become its enemies or its victims.

More sophisticated conservatives have attempted in recent years to distinguish "good" terrorists, like the Nicaraguan Contras, from "bad" terrorists, like the IRA Provisionals, presumably on the ground that the former profess anticommunism and the latter do not. This represents an adaptation of liberal theory to conservative purposes, for the good terrorist/bad terrorist distinction was originally developed by liberals concerned about distinguishing healthy antiauthoritarian violence (for example, classical tyrannicide) from totalitarian revolutionary violence.

According to philosopher Albert Camus, for example, the good terrorist "kills only once and pays with his life"; the bad terrorist "justifies thousands of crimes and consents to be rewarded with honors."[4] Individual resistance to unjust authority is glorified so that mass revolutionary violence may be condemned. Thus, says Camus, the good terrorist takes personal responsibility for his or her deeds, even to the point of accepting compensatory punishment for them. For him, "murder is identified with a suicide. A life is paid for by another life, and from these two sacrifices springs the promise of a value."[5] Revolutionary "priests and bigots," on the other hand, do not trade their lives for those of their enemies. They "accept the risk of death, but will also agree to preserve themselves as far as they can for the sake of serving the revolution." Thus, losing all sense of the relationship between means and ends, bad terrorists, "who place the revolution and the Church of Man above themselves," end by rationalizing genocide.[6]

Camus's aim is to defend the right to revolt against conservatives, who see all violent rebellion as state terror in embryo, and against Marxists, who approve the mass violence necessary to overthrow capitalism while opposing individualistic terrorist adventures. Liberal analysts from John Locke to Hannah Arendt have attempted to justify rebellions against despotic political authority (e.g., the American Revolution) while condemning revolutions that aim to overturn an entire social order (e.g., the Russian Revolution).[7]

The good terrorist is therefore either a martyr to the cause of liberal democracy or a fighter for national independence. The Russian militant who blows himself and his victim to kingdom come with the same bomb is a hero to Camus, notwithstanding that such attacks arguably hindered the development of an effective mass movement against the czar. Similarly, the Moslem rebels currently battling Soviet and Afghan forces for control of Afghanistan are considered freedom fighters in the West, even though the social system they fight to maintain is both precapitalist and predemocratic. Bad terrorists, on the other hand, aim to bring about a social transformation through violence. In going beyond the limited goals of national independence and resistance to tyranny, in attempting to organize the violence of one class against another, they are deemed to be implicitly totalitarian.

Thus before 1960, Fidel Castro, who seemed to be struggling for national independence within the limits of a capitalist democracy, was reported to be a good terrorist even by the *New York Times*. After expropriating the major North American corporations doing business in Cuba, after instituting a planned economy, and after allying his country with the Soviet Union, he was discovered to have been a bad terrorist all along![8]

But in fact, the attempt to distinguish good terrorists from

bad is fruitless. Consider, for example, the critique made by the
eminent scholar Bernard Avishai of the work of American analysts J. Bowyer Bell and Jan Schreiber. Bell and Schreiber have
argued that since terrorism is endemic in a revolutionary age,
democratic states ought not sacrifice their liberal institutions on
the altar of counterterror.[9] To Avishai, this sort of softness is
nothing short of immoral. While admitting that terrorists may
sometimes be forgiven for attacking a dictatorship, "a cruel
foreign imperial regime . . . or police acting brutally for an
intolerant majority," he insists that:

> Terror is clearly a moral violation in democratic societies, in which
> libertarian constitutions and practices make violence superfluous to
> the pursuit of dissenting political objectives.[10]

Or, putting the case more clearly:

> What makes terrorists bad is not merely that they resort to violence,
> but also that they use violence against forms of political life that
> have been devised to abolish violent intellectual and moral repres-
> sion.[11]

Therefore, Avishai argues, when it comes to dealing with terrorists in democratic nations, there is no reason either to consider them freedom fighters or to be oversolicitous of their
rights. Democratic institutions "are not now so fragile that they
cannot be defended without being destroyed, as Bell and
Schreiber suggest."[12]

What makes this a peculiar argument is that it seems, at first
glance, to justify terrorism of the commonest sort, so long as the
violence does not take place in the societies Avishai considers
democratic. For Palestinians living under Israeli military occupation on the West Bank or in the Gaza Strip, terrorism against
Israel is precisely a form of protest against "a cruel foreign
imperial regime." For Catholics living under Protestant rule in
Northern Ireland, terrorism against the Ulster constabulary is
no more or less than an attack on "police acting brutally for an

intolerant majority." Presumably, Avishai, whose cousins were killed by Palestinian terrorists, does not mean to exonerate either the PLO or the IRA Provisionals. He would undoubtedly argue, therefore, that Israel and Ulster are democratic societies compelled to defend themselves by undemocratic but necessary means against terrorism. Nevertheless, to make it perfectly clear who are the good terrorists and who are the bad, Avishai adds two further criteria that terrorists must meet in order to be considered morally acceptable. First, they must "convincingly be seen as working for a society in which one form of violent repression will not be replaced by another." And second, they must not attack innocent civilians.[13]

The intention of this formulation is clearly to limit the scope of good terrorism to bourgeois tyrannicide—the liberals' favorite form of political violence. Assassins like the Swiss hero William Tell, or those who plotted the 1944 murder of Hitler, do not intend to reconstruct society or empower a new class to rule, but simply to liberate their people from an oppressive government. They do not attack civilians, only top officials. And they do not mobilize mass violence, they act on behalf of the masses, and in their place. For Avishai, nonrepressive seems to be a code word for non-Communist. He apparently prefers regimes that guarantee political liberty while maintaining economic inequality to regimes that have eliminated gross inequality while restricting political rights. This kind of reasoning, by implication, grants a moral seal of approval to the Mafia hit men who accepted a CIA contract to kill Castro, while it condemns violence against the South African regime by members of the pro-Communist African National Congress. An Israeli militiaman who, after attacking PLO camps in Lebanon, returns to his settlement on the occupied West Bank of Israel is evidently to be considered an innocent civilian, whereas children undergoing guerrilla training in those same camps are not!

The problem is that, from the perspective of nationalism, there are no innocent civilians. One cannot justify terrorism in the name of a single nation's self-determination without opening the door to competing applications of the same principle by terrorists representing other nations. And if violence in defense of political liberty is legitimate, what of violence in defense of the right to eat? Avishai believes it possible to distinguish the democracies, where political violence is "superfluous," from the dictatorships, where terrorism is permissible because there are no other means of political expression. But this is singularly unconvincing. In the first place, terrorism is ordinarily useless against a well-entrenched dictatorship.[14] How, then, can it be permissible? Furthermore, in liberal democracies, even moderate reforms like recognition of trade unions have seldom been secured without considerable violence.[15] Business elites in democratic states are no less inclined than Stalinist bureaucracies to crush opposition movements that seriously threaten their power. Would Avishai say, then, that the destruction of Chilean democracy in 1973 by Augusto Pinochet and his generals justifies assassinating the generals? Perhaps he would, but only if the assassins were working for a nonrepressive society —in other words, if they were Western-style liberals!

Terrorism is unacceptable in liberal theory to the extent that it leads to social revolution. But the idea that it *can* lead to social revolution is the primary article of faith of the terrorists themselves. One who declares that bad terrorism produces revolutionary terror is agreeing (though disapprovingly) with the idea that armed attacks by a small vanguard group can instigate a mass uprising and detonate social revolution. When critics like Schreiber suggest that contemporary urban guerrillas are following the example of revolutionaries like Mao Tse-tung[16] and Ho Chi Minh, they accept the dubious assumptions that Mao and Ho began as isolated terrorists, that it is possible to expand an armed struggle nucleus into a Red Army, and that attacking police officers and kidnapping businesspeople in the city are comparable to rural guerrilla warfare. Even left-leaning analysts like Edward Hyams declare that terrorism "often succeeds," thereby confusing nationalist violence with social revolution.[17] Terrorism does sometimes work to rid a territory of foreign occupation. Frequently, it assists conservative nationalists to seize and maintain state power. However, only under highly unusual circumstances does it help to promote social revolution.

Surprisingly—or so it may seem—those who insist most strongly that terrorism and revolution are radically different strategies for social change are the Marxists. At least to those espousing orthodox views, terrorism, while perhaps understandable, is never justified; but there *are* "good" and "bad" forms of mass terror. Thus, Leon Trotsky defended the violence of the Russian Revolution on the grounds that it represented "the state terror of a revolutionary class."[18] Marxists do not believe that violence is good because the enemy is evil and the terrorist's heart pure, or that violence is bad because it leads to mass terror (that is, to social revolution). The converse is true. They hold that political violence is justified only when it results in mass liberation; and mass liberation requires mass action, not the delegation of war-making power to some violent elite.

What is bad about terrorism, from the Marxist point of view, is that it does not lead to revolution. Most often it provokes repressive measures that rather than "radicalizing" the people, reduce their role to that of helpless spectators. Trotsky stated:

> In our eyes, individual terrorism is inadmissible precisely because it belittles the role of the masses in their own consciousness, reconciles them to their powerlessness, and turns their eyes and hopes toward a great avenger and liberator who some day will come and accomplish his mission.[19]

This effect, Lenin maintained, has a cause: small-group violence does not represent the lower classes. Terrorism is the violence of the intelligentsia, not of the proletariat. It is a form of "single combat" that reflects the individualistic world-view of the small trader, student, or professional person—a view hostile to mass-based workers' revolution.[20] Therefore, unlike liberals and conservatives, Marxists do not recognize the category of "good terrorist." They condemn not only the terrorism of their adversaries but that of potential allies as well. When a Jewish terrorist named Herschel Greenspan assassinated a high Nazi official in Paris (an act satisfying Avishai's criteria for good terrorism), Trotsky responded:

> We Marxists consider the tactic of individual terror inexpedient in the struggle to liberate the proletariat as well as the oppressed nationalities. A single isolated hero cannot replace the masses.[21]

On the other hand, Marxists have laid themselves open to the charge of being soft on terrorism because of their refusal to equate the acts of a Herschel Greenspan—or for that matter, an Ulrike Meinhoff—with the violence of the ruling class. Greenspan's deed was a disaster for German Jewry, for it gave the Berlin dictatorship the excuse it had been waiting for to launch a new campaign of state terror against the Jewish community. Meinhoff's Red Army Fraction provoked a far milder, but nonetheless illiberal, reaction on the part of the postwar German government, and sacrificed a generation of young militants for no apparent purpose.[22] Still, Marxists have insisted, the main enemy is the capitalist state, not its misguided opponents. Greenspan was not a fascist provocateur, declared Trotsky, even though his act played into the Nazis' hands. One might as well call Rasputin a Communist because he helped provoke discontent in Russia, or brand the Red Brigade fascist (as the Italian Communist party did in the late 1970s), because the effect of its activities was to strengthen the Right. It is always necessary, when criticizing terrorism, to recognize what Trotsky termed "the inevitability of such convulsive acts of despair and vengeance."[23]

> Our open moral solidarity with Greenspan gives us an added right to say to all the other would-be Greenspans, to all those capable of self-sacrifice in the struggle against despotism and bestiality: Seek another road! Not the lone avenger but only a great revolutionary mass movement can free the oppressed.[24]

In one important respect, however, the Marxist perspective, like those of liberals and conservatives, begs the question. Its focus on individual violence, on the "lone avenger," does not deal directly with the questions posed when larger numbers of fighters claiming to represent a mass movement (and sometimes claiming to be Marxists!) declare war on the state. Particularly in view of Lenin's insistence that a revolutionary mass movement must be catalyzed and led by a relatively small number of disciplined professionals—a party of the political vanguard —how do Marxists distinguish between terrorism and revolution prior to receiving history's verdict? Clearly, the "lone avenger" is another metaphor, one that uses singularity to symbolize the false vanguard's isolation from the working class. For even when the lone Greenspan was replaced by thousands of resistance fighters, their violence, too, could be characterized as essentially terrorist: understandable and noble in intention, but impotent to liberate Europe from fascist tyranny.

Despite its defects, I find the Marxist perspective more useful as a framework for analyzing the causes and consequences of terrorism than any of its competitors. First, it is relatively free of pacifist cant. Marxists do not pretend that violence is the sole prerogative of groups in power, or that good terrorists can be distinguished from bad on the basis of their ideological preferences. Second, it insists that political movements, including violent ones, manifest changes in the relationships between and within social classes. This opens the door to a theory of the social causes of terrorism, which our liberal and conservative analysts have had difficulty generating. And third, it does not assume that terrorism is crime, warfare, or revolution in embryo, but invites us to explore the relationship between small-group violence and mass action.

It is time to accept that invitation. We begin by surveying the varieties of modern terrorism in Latin America, Europe, and the Middle East, hoping to discover in the contemporary record some clues to a mystery. Why, in the late 1960s and early 1970s, did terrorism suddenly reappear in the West as a significant form of political violence? And why, despite apparently crushing defeats and reversals, does it persist even into the late 1980s?

PART II

CAUSES AND
NONCAUSES
OF TERRORISM

Chapter 4

The Noncauses of

Modern Terrorism

IN MARCH 1976, at the height of the urban guerrilla explosion in Latin America and western Europe, the U.S. State Department sponsored a conference on terrorism. One might expect the two hundred foreign and American specialists in attendance to have done some serious thinking about the causes of terrorism—in particular, the social and economic causes that so often set the stage for political action. Instead, what the conference revealed was the profound aversion to social theory of those concerned exclusively with suppression of the urban guerrillas. Political scientist A. Chalmers Johnson summarized the results:

> Most conference participants believed that the direct causes of terrorism [that is, the socio-economic causes] had remained relatively constant in recent times and that the rise in transnational terrorist

incidents was due almost entirely to changes in the permissive causes [foreign sponsorship, availability of publicity, etc.]. . . . Many members of the conference doubted that the direct causes of terrorism could be discovered in political or socio-economic conditions. They were skeptical of the argument that the way to stop terrorism was to "remove its causes," particularly when in concrete cases the causes seemed more psychological or pathological than socio-political.[1]

What this really means is that most of these experts did not *care* to inquire more closely into the socioeconomic causes of terrorism, either because they believed that the inquiry was fruitless or because they felt that to identify causes might be to identify grievances, and thus provide terrorists with excuses. The academic formulations cited by Johnson barely conceal the commonest sort of conservative prejudices. That terrorism's "direct causes" have "remained relatively constant" means, I suppose, that the poor are always with us (or perhaps, that students will be students), while to assert that the "permissive causes" of the rise in terrorist acts have changed only restates in academic jargon the hoary outside-agitator theory of civil violence. Similarly, the reference to "psychological or pathological," rather than "socio-political," causes suggests the assumption that terrorists are simply fanatics, unreasoning and unreasonable, reproducing in history the essential disorder of their own minds. If this were true, the only form of analysis that would illuminate the subject is psychoanalysis. Fortunately, no less an authority on terrorist behavior than the historian Walter Laqueur has pointed out the uselessness of the search for a "terrorist personality":

Given that men and women at certain times and at various places have engaged in political violence, throwing bombs and firing pistols, does not necessarily prove that they had more in common with one another than have rose growers or stamp collectors. . . . That their members have been young is the only feature common to all terrorist movements, and that hardly requires explanation.[2]

What does require explanation is why young people have thrown bombs and fired pistols at certain times and in certain places rather than others and, further, what the consequences of such behavior have been. Why, in particular, has there been such a significant increase in urban guerrilla activity in the industrialized nations since 1968? According to official sources, more than five thousand terrorist acts were committed worldwide in the decade of the 1970s, of which approximately 40 percent took place in western Europe, 25 percent in the urbanized Latin American nations, and 10 percent in the United States.[3] Although the total number of direct participants in urban guerrilla attacks is not very large (4,500 is a generally accepted ballpark figure), the number of terrorist organizations active in urbanized nations is startling: approximately forty in Latin America, and more than two hundred in Europe.[4] These figures tended to decline in the early 1980s, among other things because of defeats suffered by the larger, more ideological groups (the Argentine People's Revolutionary Army [ERP], Uruguayan Tupamaros, Italian Red Brigade, and West German Red Army Fraction), but they have again risen sharply. In part, this reflects the generation of new causes and the formation of new groups; in part, it demonstrates the capacity of shattered terrorist organizations to spawn third- and fourth-generation offspring. What interests us, then, are both the immediate causes of modern terrorism and the longer-term causes that help to explain its persistence into the late 1980s.

Among American scholars and journalists, two explanations have achieved a certain currency: the "Red network" theory favored by many conservative writers, and the "permissive society" theory advocated by a number of centrists and liberal commentators.[5] Each theory expresses a modest truth that becomes an untruth when stretched too far. Thus, conservatives are certainly justified in believing that there exists a terror network or "terrorist international"—a number of cooperating organizations supported directly or indirectly by the Soviet

Union and/or its allies. In fact, there seem to be several such networks, both "Red" and "Black," although American analysts have been far more interested in the former than in the latter. However (for reasons we will explore shortly), they are not justified in considering the existence of such networks to be a primary cause of terrorism. Similarly, although it is correct to assert that terrorists generally have an easier time of it in democratic societies than under effective dictatorship, to make a great deal of this distinction is surely misleading. How can democracy be a cause of terrorism, when small-group violence afflicts only certain democracies at certain times? And what makes some dictatorships more effective than others in avoiding or suppressing terrorism?

Confronting these hard questions means paying attention to terrorism's internal causes: the constellation of economic, social, political, and psychological factors that have the effect, in a particular society, of inciting young people to engage in conspiratorial violence. Unfortunately, it is the fashion nowadays to explain terrorism exclusively in terms of external causes—for example, outside sources of training, supplies, planning, or ideological inspiration. In *The Terror Network,* Claire Sterling goes to great lengths to prove the existence of "an international terrorist circuit, or network, or fraternity" financed and assisted by Soviet bloc forces.[6] Sterling's terminology is deliberately vague. What is a "network"? Not an organization, evidently, since Sterling concedes that the evidence "does not prove a closely planned and centrally commanded worldwide conspiracy."[7] But she insists nevertheless that Communist states acting as external sponsors are primarily responsible for the wave of terrorism that has swept the Western World since the late 1960s. Sterling's thesis is as contradictory as it seems, for if the Soviets and their allies are not in command of a planned conspiracy, then at most their role is to provide advice or material assistance either to terrorists or to groups that supply terrorists. And a source of supply (however else it may be judged) can hardly be considered a primary cause of terrorism. As we know, determined combatants usually find material support somewhere, managing at times to milk both the Communist and Capitalist cows.

The intellectual villain here is the network concept, which, although lacking evidence of central control, is used to imply that terrorists are mere puppets of their suppliers. Sterling shows, for example, that the notorious Ilyitch Ramirez Sanchez ("Carlos"), who carried out a series of effective terrorist operations in Europe during the mid-1970s, worked at times with the German June 2d Movement, a small anarcho-communist group whose members trained with the PFLP, which was supported by Syrian and Libyan agencies, which cooperated frequently with the Soviet KGB. There is little reason to doubt these findings. The German RAF, IRA Provisionals, and Japanese Red Army were also wired into this network, and cooperative enterprises like the attack on Lod Airport in Israel (1972) and the kidnapping of the OPEC oil ministers (1977) have been well documented. But the problem is not that terrorist groups sometimes cooperate; it is that in many nations they exist, and persist, despite efforts to destroy them by shutting off their sources of supply. Conversely, when terrorists are uprooted and defeated, this is generally not because some network has been disrupted or because their foreign sponsorship has been terminated, but because they have been deprived of their base of support at home. In fact, the most powerful terrorist groups of modern times, such as the Argentine ERP and Italian Red Brigade, have also been the least dependent upon external suppliers.

Similarly oversimplified is the one-sided emphasis on a single terrorist network. Conservative analysts, for the most part, choose not to analyze the right-wing network, supported directly or indirectly by the United States and its allies, which has spread havoc from Turkey and Lebanon to Central America.[8] Thus, Claire Sterling has nothing to say about the joint CIA-Mafia attempts to assassinate Castro during the 1960s, the assassination of Chilean diplomat-in-exile Orlando Letelier in Washington, D.C., in 1976 by anti-Castro Cubans financed by the Chilean Agency for Intelligence and National Defense

(DINA), or the Central American death squads, Nicaraguan Contras, South Korean Central Intelligence Agency (KCIA), Israeli Central Institute for Intelligence and Security (MOSSAD), and the South African-backed guerrillas now operating throughout Southern Africa, all of which are linked with the CIA and, to some extent, with each other. "Linkage," an intentionally blurry word, can mean anything from active sponsorship of a specific terrorist act to unintentional complicity in extremist violence. The U.S. government, for example, denies that it had advance knowledge of or control over the plot against Letelier, although it admitted to having maintained extensive contacts with both DINA and the Cuban right-wing organization Omega 7.[9] A linkage between the CIA, DINA, and Omega 7 clearly exists: at worst, we could assume that the connections between the three organizations are intimate, that they take place at all organizational levels, and that the CIA exercised direct control over the Letelier operation. But, at least on the basis of evidence presently available, this would be an overstatement.

By the same token, although one can discover connections aplenty between "Carlos," the RAF and June 2d groups, the PFLP, the Libyans, and the KGB, it is impossible to state with conviction that any "Carlos" operation was performed under the orders or with the advice of the KGB. This is not to say that the Soviet Union and the United States are free of moral responsibility for the acts of their protégés' protégés; it is simply to affirm that the farther one moves down the chain of linkages from superpowers like the United States or the Soviet Union to relatively unpowerful extremist groups, the more questionable becomes the hypothesis of a tightly controlled network. *That* is why network theorists like Sterling have been unable to find concrete evidence of a "closely planned and centrally commanded" conspiracy. Moral responsibility may exist when the creature one has assisted to live runs amok, however indirect the assistance. And certain terrorist operations are surely undertaken with the connivance of outside sponsors. But network theory is not really a theory of terrorism at all. It is an avoidance mechanism: an invitation to consider internal causes as being of little consequence and external sponsorship as all-determining. Modern terrorologists are fascinated by *technique*—sophisticated weapons in the hands of underground grouplets, types of bombs, elaborate schemes for obtaining false papers, and the like. That is, they are fixated on supply, when what most requires explaining is demand—not the sources of terrorist matériel, but the sources of terrorism itself.

An object lesson in the danger of using linkage to imply control is the attempted assassination of Pope John Paul II in May 1981 by Ali Mehmet Agça, a member of the Turkish fascist group the Grey Wolves. After his capture, Agça confessed that he was acting under the control of Bulgarian intelligence, which, everyone knows, is under the influence of the KGB. "Russian Plot to Kill Pope!" cried respected journals and respectable politicians.[10] Reading the Western press, one would never suspect the existence of a "Black network" of terrorism linking the Grey Wolves with Italian fascist groups like Ordine Nero, European fascist organizations with Latin American governments, and those governments with the CIA. A Black network does exist, however, and its members tend to be as intensely antipapal as those of any Communist or anarchist sect —especially if they are Moslem fascists.[11] Nor was it ever made clear what the Bulgarians, who have meddled in Turkish politics for generations, thought they were aiding Agça to do (assuming that Agça had contact with the Bulgarians, as he had claimed)—or what role, if any, the KGB normally plays in connection with Bulgaria's Byzantine operations in Turkey. Moreover, the rush to judgment in the Agça case caused the obvious to be overlooked: the Pope's would-be assassin was a Turkish nationalist participating in a powerful anti-Christian movement, and he was probably insane. Not even Lee Harvey Oswald believed that he was Jesus Christ! The inability of investigators in the United States to decide whether Oswald was a leftist conspirator, a rightist pretending to be a leftist, or a psychotic lone wolf should have taught us more about the dangers of constructing conspiracy theories that point unambiguously in one direction.[12]

People who want to make war on the state generally find the means to do so—a fact that would be too trite to mention had it not, apparently, been forgotten. At the turn of the century, anarchists armed with little more than knives, pistols, and homemade bombs terrorized Europe and North America quite effectively. In our own time, not just sporadic terrorist acts but extended violent campaigns have been fought with the weaker side relying largely on weapons taken from the enemy or obtained from curious sources. When one considers the whole range of civil violence, from individual acts of rage or martyrdom to civil war, supply appears to have increasingly more weight in determining the outcome as violence becomes more massive. Small groups have little need for exotic weapons; the European terrorists who obtained antiaircraft missiles during the 1970s never used one successfully, while the most devastating attacks of recent years have been made with car or truck bombs, submachine guns, and grenades.

Furthermore, the basic components of the terrorist infrastructure—terrorists' sources of forged papers, safehouses, transportation and communications links, personnel, and money, as well as weapons—are in plentiful supply locally. It is thus a myth that terrorist groups can be "crushed in the egg" by cutting off their external sources of supply. It is the local political base that makes the terrorist organization or breaks it. Politically isolated groups turn to banditry or disappear because of political weakness, not from a shortage of matériel. Others survive and expand, not because they have learned to master high technology, but because they generate their own sources of supply.

The failure to understand and apply this relatively straightforward proposition to incidents like the 1983 truck bombings of U.S. and French military garrisons in Lebanon has produced peculiar results. The Long Commission, a blue-ribbon panel of the U.S. defense department, reported early in 1984 that state-sponsored terrorism was responsible for the 1983 disasters.[13] The implicit conclusions: retrain American military units to engage in counterterrorist activity, and retaliate directly against alleged state sponsors. U.S. and Israeli experts agreed that, while there was no hard evidence of involvement in the truck attacks by the Syrian or Iranian governments, only "a government intelligence organization or something very similar to it . . . could have had the technical ability, manpower, experience, and financial resources to plan and organize such complicated and expensive attacks."[14] Israeli expert Ariel Merari's conclusion was typical. The United States and France, he asserted, "should think in terms of deterrence against the sponsoring nations. You don't kill a snake by cutting off its tail. You have to go for the head."[15]

This was very bad advice. The notion that the Lebanese truck bomb attacks were beyond the technical capacity of the Lebanese—an urbanized, technically competent people, despite their current poverty—was not only patronizing, it suppressed unpleasant facts. Fact One: the technical ability, manpower, and money necessary to mount Lebanese terrorist attacks were plentiful locally, because the Shiite nationalist fighters had an enormous political base. One would never suspect, reading the Long Commission report, that the slums of Beirut and the villages of southern Lebanon were largely inhabited by Shiite Moslems who were convinced that resisting Israeli occupiers and Lebanese Christians and their U.S. allies was a religious duty. Fact Two: even if Iran or Syria had aided the terrorists, attacking Teheran or Damascus would hardly have weakened this local resistance, because intense anti-Americanism could be "found not only among religious militants but also among students, shopkeepers and businessmen."[16] Recognition of these unacknowledged facts by foreign policy professionals may have served to deter American air attacks on known Shiite military bases.

By 1985, antiforeign violence in Lebanon had increased to the point that one hesitated to call it terrorism. It seemed rather to be an amorphous form of communal resistance to foreign occupation: mass violence without a unified command. This would explain the experts' observation that,

> by all indications, no single underground organization conceived, planned, organized and carried out these attacks. . . . There is no single terrorist group . . . to retaliate against, smash, or penetrate with intelligence agents.[17]

This being the case, Merari's advice to "go for the head" was singularly misconceived. A terrorist movement with popular support is not a snake but a Hydra: cut off one head, and two more will grow in its place. There is strong evidence that, in the wake of the Beirut disasters, a militant Christian group acting at the behest of the CIA and the Lebanese Christian intelligence agency, G–2, attempted to retaliate by car-bombing a building inhabited by sheik Fadlallah, a leader of the Shiite Hezbollah organization. Scores of civilians were killed, while the target escaped destruction.[18] Even if he had been assassinated, however, Hezbollah would not have been smashed; instead, it would have been incited to continue the cycle of revenge. And even if Hezbollah were gravely weakened by a series of counterterrorist attacks, what of the other groups operating under the umbrella of the Islamic Jihad?

Probably the most efficient counterterrorist organization in the world is the Israeli agency, MOSSAD, which has assassinated dozens of Palestinian guerrilla leaders during the past two decades.[19] The agency's overall ineffectiveness, however, is apparent. Counterterrorism works, if at all, only when it is part of a political strategy that successfully cuts off violent groups from local sources of supply. Supply-side experts and counterterrorist avengers put technology first and politics second, creating a reversed image of the truth. For propaganda purposes, governments frequently misrepresent the political strength of terrorist groups; but believing one's own propaganda can be fatal. Thus, the Bay of Pigs invasion of Cuba by anti-Castro terrorists did not fail because the invaders were deprived of U.S. air support, but because the vast majority of Cubans were prepared to repel any attack.

Years ago, Karl Marx pilloried the terrorists, calling them "alchemists of the revolution" who "throw themselves on discoveries which should work revolutionary wonders: incendiary bombs, hell-machines of magical impact," instead of mastering the more complex and subtle science of political organization.[20] Our terrorism experts, for the most part, are alchemists of the *counter*revolution. They hope to suppress terrorism, guerrilla wars, even social revolutions without recognizing the political and social conditions that produce them.

The liberal theory that attempts to correlate modern terrorism with "permissive" institutions has, at least, the virtue of looking for internal causes, although it hardly can be said to have found them. There are several variations on this theme. Some writers believe that democratic leniency encourages terrorism or makes it difficult to suppress, while others emphasize the prevalence of terrorism in inefficiently administered societies, be they democratic or totalitarian.[21] A number of commentators have focused on racial or ethnic conflict in such societies as a generator of small-group violence.[22] Still others connect the increase in terrorism with the uninhibited media coverage of terrorist acts and demands, or with the psychological appeals of extremism to affluent, permissively reared youths.[23] Like the Red network theory of the conservatives, all of these notions combine a small bit of truth with large doses of question-begging. To say that terrorism flourishes in permissive societies, or that it is encouraged by media publicity, really tells us nothing about the origins of the phenomenon. Rather, it implies that terrorist impulses are somehow loose in society, just waiting to be realized, and that they *will* be realized unless effectively deterred. Some analysts assign a cause to this assumed tendency: the prevalence of social injustice, or a high level of frustration among certain groups, or the decline of traditional inhibitors of personal violence. But none of these general explanations is satisfactory. Oppression, frustration, and aggression have been with us always, but terrorism—the violence of the intelligentsia—has erupted only under certain conditions.

Which conditions? Liberal commentators, by and large, have been no more inclined than have conservatives to develop a theory that would specify them. "It may be misleading to search for the root causes of terrorism,"[24] says Schreiber. And along the same lines, Laqueur explains that:

> Given the specific difficulties involved in the study of terrorism rather than political violence in general, it is not surprising that there has been no stampede to search for a general theory explaining the phenomenon.[25]

It seems to me that the reason for this uncharacteristic reticence is not just the inherent difficulty of the subject, but the fact that liberals are no less obsessed than law-and-order conservatives with the issues of short-term deterrence and control. The principal question, says Schreiber, is, "Who will bell the cat?"[26] One would like to know how the cat got loose in the first place —what relationship between social development, political institutions, and ideas generates modern terrorism—but governments and foundations that sponsor research in the field are looking for practical answers to immediate questions: how do you infiltrate a terrorist group? Do you or do you not negotiate in a hostage situation, and if so, under what guidelines? Should the mass media report the details of ongoing violent incidents? Should the government's antiterrorist activities be centralized? Officials are entitled to ask these questions and to pay for attempts to answer them, but the answers they get are necessarily limited by the narrow scope of the inquiry. Research that does not explain terrorism's origins cannot predict its likely course of development. Even worse, abandoning the search for social causes has the practical effect of substituting a theory of supply for a theory of causation. Foreign sponsorship (another evasive term, like "network") becomes the villain.

This does not mean that scholarship in the field of terrorism has been inaccurate or useless. Lacking a general theory, analysts have focused their attention on specific violent movements, thus providing us with a considerable amount of data on the history of the IRA, the political ideology of the Tupamaros, the psychological problems of members of America's Weather Underground, and so forth. Indeed, since 1976 a well-edited scholarly publication called *Terrorism: An International Journal* has been devoted primarily to this sort of empirical research, with results that are frequently enlightening. The major drawback of an approach that lacks a general theory, however, is a tendency to answer questions about the causes of terrorism by referring to the motivation of this or that group. The primary cause of Irish terrorism, for example, is sometimes said to be British policy in Ireland, sometimes Protestant or Catholic intransigence, sometimes the Irish personality, and even, on occasion, the alleged conversion of the IRA Provisionals to Marxism. While it is certainly true that one cannot understand behavior without appreciating its motivation, the underlying issue for social scientists is what *produces* the motivation both in particular cases and in general. The unfortunate result of the present theoretical impasse has been not only to "psychologize" the subject of terrorism but to fragment it. Each terrorist movement is considered in isolation from every other movement, except insofar as some foreign sponsorship or networking is judged to be taking place.

In his thoughtful article on terrorism in Northern Ireland, Alan O'Day remarks that,

Terrorism in Northern Ireland . . . has much to do with Irish history and is little inspired by movements elsewhere. It is a largely self-contained effort that reproduces its own heroic past and seeks ends that are entirely insular. The aims of the Irish are not at all like those of other groups engaging in terrorism; should the aims be achieved, other movements are unlikely to benefit from the success, except in the sense that their morale might receive a boost.[27]

All of this seems true enough; but whether the aims of the Irish are like those of other groups, and whether the IRA is supported politically or financially by other groups, are irrelevant to discovering the social causes and consequences of terrorism. The Irish cause is no more or less insular than that of the Basques in northern Spain, the Argentine Montoneros, the Palestinians, or, for that matter, more doctrinaire formations like the Red Brigade. No sizable terrorist movement can be comprehended in isolation from its own antecedents and its own society. Nevertheless, it is a fact that *all* of the groups just mentioned, as well as several hundred others, have engaged in significant campaigns of small-group violence during the past fifteen years. How do we account for this explosion of urban guerrilla activity in many nations, each with its own "insular" problems and history? When liberal scholars fail to explain this simultaneity—when they fail to demonstrate how similar social causes in diverse cultures can produce like effects—they leave the field to the conservatives, whose theories at least have the virtue of attempting to comprehend terrorism as a transnational phenomenon.

Similarly, rather than explore the consequences of terrorist violence with a view toward constructing a coherent social theory, most modern analysts focus on the effectiveness or ineffectiveness of official responses to the terrorist challenge. In general, liberal scholars have opted for more highly modulated responses to terrorism than conservatives. They caution against repressive overreactions that would weaken democratic institutions and emphasize the need "to reckon first with the subtler violence of legitimate power."[28] Interestingly, the analysts who make such statements are often those who live in nations with little experience of serious terrorism. Let the frequency and seriousness of attacks in their own country rise to the level of violence Argentina saw in the early 1970s or that occurred in Italy a few years later, and they are unlikely to object to "special measures" directed against terrorists, suspected terrorists, suspected supporters . . . and anyone else who might be connected with the violence.

The tendency of liberals to harden their line as terrorism escalates is attributable in part to specific acts directed against them—for example, the Red Brigade's kidnapping and execution of Italian liberal Aldo Moro—and in part to their deep identification (when push comes to shove) with the sociopolitical establishment. But it also suggests that the differences between soft and hard responses over the proper methods of combating and controlling terrorism were not profound to begin with. Many scholars start out searching for terrorism's social causes, but when the search produces unacceptably complex results (for example, results suggesting the need for significant social change), their focus shifts to what they think is doable: making the target less accessible, strengthening police and intelligence capabilities, cutting off sources of supply—in short, counterterrorism. If, in the end, liberal and conservative analysts appear to speak with one voice, this may be because they accept the same implicit dogma: terrorism, like sin, is mysteriously rooted in human nature. It cannot be ended, it can only be deterred or combated.

The inquiry that follows is designed to challenge this assumption in the most direct manner possible. Using major urban guerrilla campaigns of the past two decades as a basis for discussion, I consider terrorism as a specific social phenomenon, with describable origins and a predictable end. In focusing on the internal causes and consequences of modern terrorist movements, I do not mean to deny that they may be externally supplied and manipulated. Even the most dedicated network theorist must recognize, however, that for the Soviets, the Iranians, or for that matter, the Americans to have a substantial movement to manipulate, there must already be several hundred terrorists locally with a support base of several thousand sympathizers. Any foreign power can hire a local hit man or a small squad of saboteurs to do its bidding; but groups capable of mounting extended campaigns must be grounded in their own societies.

What has generated the formation of such groups, especially since the late 1960s? What results has terrorism achieved? And what are the prospects for the development of indigenous movements of the urban guerrilla in nations not yet severely afflicted by terrorist violence? Many experts have predicted an increase in state-sponsored terrorist activity, or violence by foreign-based organizations, within the United States. Lacking a coherent theory of internal causation, however, they have been unable to say whether or not we are to expect an indigenous version of the Red Army Fraction or the Red Brigade to appear on these shores. To offer even tentative answers to such questions requires moving beyond the immediate problems of deterrence and control. By analyzing the origins of modern terrorism, we may discover a basis for predicting its future.

Chapter 5

Origins of the

Urban Guerrilla

THE CUBANS had little need to export their revolution, there were so many willing imitators. The Fidelistas' remarkable success in overthrowing the dictatorship of General Fulgencio Batista sent a wave of hope throughout Latin America—and a wave of fear as well. Their success was especially inspiring to young intellectuals who saw a small band of dedicated guerrillas triumph over the moribund organizations of both the Right and the traditional Left and hold their own against Yankee pressure. In the eyes of militant youths, Castro's victory discredited not only the conventional practices of the Old Left parties, but also their philosophy—in particular, their distinction (nurtured by both Marx and Lenin) between small-group terrorism and mass revolutionary violence. Régis Debray, the young French theorist who became a follower of the guerrilla leader, Che Guevara, reasoned that totally committed activists could become the lever needed to move the great weight of social inertia, complacency, and intimidation. The *foco* (mobile guerrilla base) was the small force that would move the large force of society.[1] All over the continent, military schismatics embracing comparable political philosophies took to the mountains, hoping by their example to inspire great change.

Urban guerrilla warfare was first considered an adjunct to rural combat on the Cuban model. As Brazilian guerrilla leader Carlos Marighella put it:

> The urban guerrilla is not afraid of dismantling and destroying the present Brazilian economic, political, and social system, for his aim is to help the rural guerrilla and to collaborate in the creation of a totally new and revolutionary social and political structure, with the armed people in power.[2]

But after Cuba, most rural guerrilla organizations were defeated fairly easily or isolated in their mountain redoubts. Even in Venezuela, where urban violence was unleashed on a large scale in aid of a Castro-style rural struggle, their efforts proved fruitless; and when Che Guevara's Bolivian foco was mopped up in 1967, the Latin radicals faced essentially the same choice that European youths had confronted almost a century earlier, after the defeat of the Paris Commune, the insurrectionary workers' government that seized control of Paris in 1870. Either they could become part of a weak and endangered loyal opposition, or they could redefine political action in terms more congenial to nineteenth-century anarchists than to modern Marxists.

Before World War I erupted, anarchist and populist students based in European cities had assassinated scores of political leaders, soldiers, and policemen, often sacrificing their own lives in the process. But the masses were not inspired by their example to rebel. Shifting the foco to the city—the center of business and political power—inevitably entailed a return to practices associated with this old-style "heroic" terrorism. In the country, guerrillas could look and act like soldiers; in the cities, they might well be thought to be criminals or lunatics.

Still, in view of the powerful right-wing reaction to Castro's victory then sweeping the continent, many thought the risk worth taking. The 1964 coup by the Brazilian armed forces against the liberal Joao Goulart government heralded a continentwide movement to the right, culminating in the bloody overthrow of Chile's Popular Unity government in 1973.

To the incentive of hope was thus added that of desperation. Not only were rural guerrillas wiped out and half a dozen civilian governments toppled or endangered, but the economic boom that had drawn tens of thousands of new students into the secondary schools and universities ended in stagnation and decline. Political scientist Ernst Halperin is no doubt correct to link the development of urban guerrilla groups to the enormous increase in the Latin American student population during the 1950s and 1960s.[3] First, industrial expansion fueled the influx of middle-class (and some working-class) youths into the schools; then economic downturn lengthened the period of studies, increased the dropout rate, and unleashed a virtual army of idealistic, ambitious, action-oriented ex-students upon societies unable or unwilling to meet their needs. Only the Peronist guerrillas in Argentina had anything resembling a working-class base (and that, as it turned out, was tenuous). In general, as Halperin remarked:

> These movements express the despair of young members of the administrative class, radicalized and alienated from society by the deterioration of their prospects in countries of stagnant economy.[4]

As in Czarist Russia a century earlier, terrorism erupted when a new intelligentsia, dreaming of power and service, found itself unable to realize its goal: "The administration of profound and worthwhile social change instead of mere paper-pushing in a deteriorating welfare bureaucracy."[5]

The earliest, largest, and most ambitious and politically sophisticated urban guerrilla organizations thus arose in the industrialized "southern cone" nations, where the effects of economic downturn and political disappointment were most pronounced. The Uruguayan Tupamaros were first in the field, followed by less powerful movements in Brazil and Bolivia and a violent campaign by radical Argentine youths that shook that country to its core. Political differences separated each group from the others; in Argentina, for example, sizable Peronist, Trotskyist, and Guevarist organizations operated relatively independently, although occasionally they collaborated on large-scale operations like the famous 1972 jailbreak at Trelew Prison that freed members of all three groups.[6]

Nevertheless, it is their common characteristics that are most striking. Latin urban guerrilla groups tended to be large; although estimates are unreliable, the Tupamaros probably commanded the services of some three thousand activists, and the total number of Argentine guerrillas may have been as high as six thousand.[7] Virtually all of the larger groups followed a similar pattern of development. Beginning as heretical offshoots (or youth groups) of larger opposition parties, they attempted at first to avoid indiscriminate terrorism, to exploit their links with mass organizations, and to provoke a military overreaction, which they believed would increase dramatically their own strength. In fact, it was their initial success that was most dramatic. The Tupamaros' Robin Hood tactics generated sympathy among broad sectors of the Uruguayan population fed up with corruption, inflation, and economic domination by foreigners. Bolivian guerrillas established links with embattled workers in the tin mines. Their Argentine counterparts pulled off a series of dazzling kidnappings of executives of foreign companies, which permitted them to finance larger-scale operations against the police and the army. By the early 1970s, even some representatives of the Old Left, with its traditional aversion to small-group violence, were characterizing urban guerrilla activities as socially revolutionary, on the theory that the activists were linked to the masses through a new mass vanguard of workers, farmers, and students. This impression was strengthened by the failure of existing mass parties and trade unions to cope either with the economic crisis or with the threat of military takeover.

According to Belgian Marxist Ernest Mandel, for example, guerrilla attacks were helping to prepare the workers and poor peasants for an inevitable armed confrontation with the state. He wrote:

> Under the given circumstances, with the given social and economic instability in Latin America, the profound influence of the Cuban revolution on the vanguard of the mass movement, the decline of control of the traditional working class leaderships over that same vanguard, the explosive character of mass mobilizations which lead to rapid confrontations with the army, the emergence of the army as the mainstay of bourgeois power . . . and its relative strength as opposed to the extreme fragility of all political formations of the ruling classes, a long period of gradual rise of mass struggles under conditions of relative . . . bourgeois democracy is extremely unlikely . . . [and] a head-on collision between the mass movement and the army is unavoidable.[8]

As a result, Mandel, a leader of the Trotskyist Fourth International, approved the armed struggle tactics adopted by his admirers in the Argentine ERP—a position he later admitted had been mistaken. Interestingly, what misfired in this analysis was not Mandel's description of these circumstances, which might under some conditions have produced a revolutionary mass movement, but his assumption that initiating armed struggle was the best way to develop and lead such a movement. In reality, the guerrillas' initial military successes accelerated their political undoing. The logic of their position as an underground army and the savagery of state repression produced a rapid escalation of personal violence—a kind of gang war of increasing brutality—that isolated them from would-be constituents and exposed them to intense counterterror. In brief, it proved impossible for them to confront the police, the army, and right-wing vigilantes head-on while preparing the masses to resist a military coup.

Of all the Latin guerrilla groups, the Tupamaros and the ERP were probably the most determined to avoid the terrorist trap —isolation from the communities they hoped to influence—by combining selective violence against the regime with political agitation among middle-class professionals, workers, and the poor. Thus, both Uruguayan and Argentine guerrillas attempted initially to minimize personal violence by limiting their activities to the destruction of property, "expropriation" of banks, seizure of radio stations, and kidnapping for ransoms which were regularly paid. The Tupamaros distributed "liberated" food and money to the poor, established communication with liberals in the Uruguayan parliament, and published stolen documents showing the extent of government corruption. The ERP seized factories during labor disputes, held "revolutionary trials" of unpopular managers, and lectured the workers on the need for revolution. Nonetheless, all guerrilla groups found themselves drawn in stages into a bitter vendetta from which the masses stood aloof, especially when it became clear that those in power, who were supported by secret army organizations, were prepared to out-terrorize the terrorists.

In 1969, for example, the Tupamaros briefly "liberated" the town of Pando, capturing the police chief and deputy chief, with no fatalities on either side.[9] A number of their fighters who fell into a police trap afterward were gunned down while trying to surrender, while others were imprisoned and tortured. A few months later, their comrades kidnapped an American police advisor, Dan Mitrione, "tried" him, and, after some debate within the organization, killed him. This generated further right-wing terror, making nonviolent political work by the guerrillas virtually impossible. In 1971, attempting to break out of their isolation, the Tupamaros aligned themselves with a leftist parliamentary coalition—the Broad Front—that polled approximately 20 percent of the vote in national elections. In 1972, the army seized power, smashed Uruguay's political parties and trade unions, and liquidated the rest of the guerrillas.

A similar tragedy was played out in Argentina on an even larger scale. The Argentine guerrillas—in particular, the Peronist Montoneros—were less inhibited than were the Tupamaros about using assassination as a weapon, but, like the Tupamaros, generally avoided indiscriminate assaults on civilians. Targeting police stations, vulnerable army units, government officials, and representatives of U.S. and European companies, they set a furious pace:

> Between January 1969 and July 1971, fifty-three Argentine police were killed by guerrillas. In May 1970, former President [Pedro Eugenio] Aramburu was kidnapped and killed by the *Montoneros*. The ERP kidnapped a British consul and the FAP assassinated a former chief of police. Guerrillas raided banks, shot isolated soldiers, attacked police stations, seized radio stations, and raided armories.[10]

Guerrilla ruthlessness was more than matched, however, by the tactics of the military forces and the death squads of the Argentine Anti-Communist Alliance, a right-wing terrorist organization covertly supported by Argentine military leaders. Their strategy was, essentially, to liquidate the guerrillas by destroying their social environment: the new intelligentsia. Tens of thousands of suspected subversives were jailed and tortured, taken from their homes to be shot, or simply made to "disappear" as the Argentine Right saw its chance to settle old scores with a host of enemies, including trade union and farmer organizers, leftist professors, liberal politicians, troublesome journalists, priests, and students.[11]

In the eyes of the regime, what made the Argentine guerrillas particularly dangerous was their connection with mass working-class parties like those of the Peronist movement—organizations that condemned the guerrillas' violent practices but among whose members they could sometimes find support. In fact, even before the "dirty war" began, the guerrillas had failed to generate a mass uprising or even to convert a significant number of members of these organizations to the revolutionary cause. Like the Tupamaros, they discovered it was impossible to function simultaneously as urban guerrillas and organizers of a mass resistance movement.

Ironically, a popular uprising did occur in Chile, in defense of an elected regime. There, in 1973, some thirty thousand people lost their lives in an unsuccessful attempt to resist the overthrow of President Salvador Allende's populist government by the Right.[12] By contrast, in Bolivia and Argentina, where urban guerrilla activity was most intense, there was little resistance to military coups outside of the guerrilla camp itself. As Mandel had predicted, the generals did cast aside the mask of parliamentary procedure, unleashing a reign of terror that liquidated both the activists and those suspected of sympathizing with them. Rather than activating the masses, however, this excess of state violence silenced them. Rebels who were determined to act like soldiers and not like mere terrorists were drawn into open battles with the army and annihilated—a lesson not lost on their admirers in western Europe and the Middle East.

Urban guerrilla groups thus arose in Latin America out of a combination of hope and desperation: hope for profound and worthwhile social change, desperation born of political defeat and economic decline. Although European governments were generally far more stable than were their Latin counterparts, terrorism in western Europe and North America had a similar psychogenesis. Hope for radical change was aroused by the New Left's notable success in mobilizing mass opposition to traditional parties and policies throughout the West. Desperation followed the movement's sudden collapse. Again it was a new intelligentsia, created to serve the needs of public and private bureaucracies, that provided leadership in the period of mass upsurge. And again, when the upsurge abated, smaller groups generally drawn from the same social base supplied those urban guerrilla cadres committed to going it alone. To be sure, as Laqueur has observed, "The nationalist-separatist terrorist groups almost always consist of young people of lower social background than the socialist-revolutionary groups." Even so, he continues, "Inasmuch as the nationalist-separatist movements have a left-wing fringe, this again consists of intellectuals of middle-class background or white-collar workers."[13] Furthermore, when one looks at the leadership strata of even the more proletarian groups, like the PLO and the IRA, the predominance of students, teachers, poets, professionals, administrators, and other "brain workers" of various sorts is striking.

This new intelligentsia was a product of the twenty-year industrial boom centered in the United States that created the post–World War II consumer society. The main features of this new order were the domination of economic life by large corporations and the domination of political life by large state agencies. Wherever they looked during the 1950s and early 1960s, acute observers saw bureaucracies expanding. Corporations seeking to exploit their new preeminence in the world market set about recruiting and training the "new class" of technicians, managers, information specialists, and engineers, while governments vastly expanded their social services, regulatory functions, and armed forces. The apparently insatiable demand of private and public organizations for trained, white-collar personnel created an unparalleled growth in postsecondary educational institutions. In the United States, for example, the number of students attending colleges and graduate schools rose from 3.2 million in 1959–60 to 7.5 million in 1970.[14] Even before the economic expansion that propelled this growth began to taper off in the mid-1960s, however, signs of discontent were beginning to appear, especially among that sector of the new intelligentsia in social service occupations (teachers, welfare workers, civil servants, publicists, priests, and so forth). The war in Indochina, the black civil rights movement, and a series of increasingly severe economic recessions galvanized this discontent, but a rebellion of the new intellectuals was likely in any event. For two decades, children of the middle class and of aspiring workers had been trained in the arts of social management, imbued with the idea that socially useful work was more important than personal wealth, and led to believe that both useful work and material comfort were their due. Instead, they ran headlong into established power and the imperatives of profit—dull jobs in unresponsive bureaucracies, economic insecurity, persistent inequality, and war.

It was not the rebellion itself, but its scope and political potency, that was surprising. In the United States, the handful of students and ministers who had participated in sit-ins in the early 1960s soon found themselves in the vanguard of a broad-based, nonviolent civil rights struggle, while others became the nucleus of a potent movement of protest against conscription and the Vietnam War. Black nationalism—largely a response to the spontaneous ghetto riots of 1964–68—achieved a large following in the North under the leadership of militant intellectuals like Malcolm X and Black Panther party founders Huey Newton and Bobby Seale. Similar nationalistic movements supporting the rights of Hispanics, Native Americans, women, homosexuals, and students grew with equal rapidity, and French-speaking Canada experienced a wave of enthusiasm for Quebecois independence. In Europe as well as in North America, a new generation of radicalized, college-educated youths espoused pacifism, socialism, feminism, sexual freedom, and the nationalism of the oppressed. While the nationalist cause was revived in Northern Ireland by the young leaders of the Catholic Civil Rights Movement and in Spain by the Basque militants of the ETA, French and Italian students (more influenced by leftist ideas than most of their American counterparts) attempted to rally industrial workers and the unemployed to the New Left banner. The French students' occupation of the University of Paris in 1968 triggered a wave of wildcat industrial strikes that posed a serious threat to the government of President De Gaulle, forcing him to prepare the army for possible military intervention.[15] Months later, during Italy's "hot autumn," leaders of both the Christian Democratic and Communist parties pulled out all the stops in opposing a wave of student strikes, wildcat strikes, factory occupations, and stormy demonstrations centered in Rome and in the industrial North.[16]

It seemed to many otherwise sober commentators that some great social transformation was on the way.[17] Rebellious youths refused to play the political game according to accepted rules.

Almost unwittingly, they tapped rich veins of popular discontent which made establishment politicians take notice and worry. The New Left was not a party, but a movement or congeries of movements: a hodge-podge of groups led by charismatic figures who favored nonviolent "direct action"—strikes, demonstrations, occupations, civil disobedience—and disdained electoral and parliamentary maneuvering. Drawn from diverse and contradictory philosophical sources, its followers mingled elements of Marxism with group nationalism, utopian socialism, and religious enthusiasm to create a new amalgam owing more to Mohandas Gandhi and Sigmund Freud than to Marx. New Left philosophy reflected the interests and moods of the new intelligentsia—ambitious, idealistic, passionately antibureaucratic, and intensely self-involved.

Much like rebellious Russian students a century earlier, the members of the New Left believed that the awakening they were experiencing had the potential to awaken society—to transform it from the bottom up. Somehow (perhaps through a general strike or through massive civil disobedience) the masses in the industrial nations would liberate themselves from economic exploitation, political domination, and sexual repression. Once liberated, they would proceed to create a new-model society. Neither monopoly capitalist nor Soviet socialist, this new society would be a postcapitalist utopia dedicated to individual self-realization. The activists' high expectations were nurtured by the fact that large groups were being set in motion by the actions of smaller groups of enthusiasts. If sit-ins could generate mass civil disobedience and major changes in the law, if a few thousand radical students could trigger a nationwide antiwar movement, if the urban ghettos were already racked by spontaneous rioting, then surely a mass movement was abuilding. What might it not do when fully developed? These apocalyptic expectations were shattered in two short years (1968–70) by a combination of state violence and political reform. Confronted by police power on the one hand and established working-class organizations' opposition to radical change on the other, the loosely organized, ideologically amorphous New Left disintegrated.

The movement's fall was, if anything, more dramatic than its rise. In the United States, assassinations eliminated its most popular and potent leaders: Malcolm X, Martin Luther King, Jr., and Robert Kennedy. FBI director J. Edgar Hoover sanctioned an official program to "penetrate and disrupt" seditious organizations, federal and state police authorities conducted a virtual shooting war against the Black Panther party, and volatile demonstrations (such as the mass protest at the Democratic convention of 1968 in Chicago) were brutally dispersed.[18] At the same time, Congress passed a series of historic civil rights bills and social welfare programs, and Richard Nixon was elected president on a platform that promised to revive détente with the Soviet Union and end the war in Indochina.

The movement to liberate Quebec was dealt with in much the same manner by the Canadian government, which meted out punishment to militants of the Quebec Liberation Front (FLQ) and increased cultural autonomy to the French-speaking population. Similarly, in Europe, with the full cooperation of the Socialist and Communist parties, the De Gaulle regime suppressed the student-led uprising of May 1968, while the Italian government survived its "hot autumn" by drawing Communists and Christian Democrats into closer collaboration. (This was the "Historic Compromise" in which the Christian Democratic Party agreed to share power with the Italian Communists, while the Communist party agreed to renounce any revolutionary aims.) Shortly thereafter, Protestant resistance and British intervention put an end to the civil rights movement in Northern Ireland; moderate Socialists assumed power in Britain and Germany; and men of affairs continued to conduct their nations' affairs much as they had in the past, although they now faced a new problem—economic downturn.

The response of European youths to this debacle was prefigured by the fate of the leading American student organization, Students for a Democratic Society (SDS). At its 1969 convention, the SDS split into three components—one departing to rejoin the Democratic party, another enlisting in the Old Left under the Maoist banner, and a third, the smallest, forming the Weather Underground, which conducted a guerrilla war of a peculiarly bloodless sort against U.S. government and business institutions.[19] (A fourth faction slipped quietly out of activist politics and into the youth counterculture.) In similar fashion, most members of the New Left in Europe found their way back to one of the traditional opposition parties or into the nonviolent extraparliamentary opposition. A small minority—minuscule in most countries when compared with Latin American guerrilla groups—graduated from occupying universities and leafletting factory workers to bombing military installations, hijacking airplanes, and kidnapping public figures. Their collective names are well known, and a great many are still in use: Red Army Fraction, Red Brigade, Direct Action (France), ETA, IRA Provisionals, PFLP, Ustache (Yugoslavia), Black Order (Italy). The urban guerrillas' ideas and tactics are important, and will be considered shortly. It is already clear, however, that similar causes in Latin America and western Europe produced similar effects.

Except where it has been proletarianized to some extent by association with purely nationalist movements, terrorism remains the violence of the intelligentsia. Moreover, it is the violence of a new intelligentsia, one that has severed its ties with both the upper classes (masters of the corporate and state bureaucracies) and the lower classes, which the terrorists hope eventually to activate by setting a heroic example and by "intensifying calamities."[20] Historical analysis suggests that this breaking of connections is first a social event, then an ideological response to social change. In Europe, as in Latin America, a great wave of industrial growth drew large numbers of new workers into the cities, forced rapid expansion of the state apparatus, and greatly increased the demand for social-management workers and professionals. In both locales (but particularly in Latin America and southern Europe), this surge of expansion ended quite suddenly and was replaced by economic stagnation and instability. As a result, the following conditions were apparent in both hemispheres:

1. Multiplication of the number of marginally-employed or unemployed city workers. Job competition intensifies divisions between newer (unorganized) and older (unionized) workers, and between racial and ethnic groups. Increase in crime and low-level social disorder. Decline in labor solidarity and militancy.

2. Shakeout of undercapitalized or overextended businesses. Increased turnover of small enterprises and further capital concentration in large corporations. Search by business for new markets and investment opportunities out of the older industrialized areas and in other countries. Increased pressure on government to cut expenditures for social services, assist business recapitalization, and strengthen repression of disorderly groups.

3. Dry-up of intermediary social-management jobs. Expansion of the repressive bureaucracies, especially the police, court system, and armed forces. Young intellectuals are compelled to choose between working exclusively for the repressive state or attempting, in some manner, to work for the people. The intelligentsia's social coherence is shattered.

Under these circumstances, some intellectuals sought jobs with big business or accepted employment by the state; others became involved in insecure petty-bourgeois occupations or bohemian lifestyles. Still others, refusing to surrender their revolutionary ideals and ambitions, attempted to place their talents at the service of the fragmented, increasingly impoverished working class.

Of course, this did not make the latter group terrorists, for if there had been a political movement offering any reasonable hope of uniting and empowering the have-nots, it would have drawn them strongly into its orbit. Militant mass movements are an *antidote* to terrorism, because, among other reasons, they enable politicized intellectuals to use their skills as communicators and administrators without forcing them to choose between words and action. If no such movement exists, however, radicals determined to keep faith with lower-class constituents confront a painful choice. They can devote their lives to political organizing and teaching in the hope that somehow, some-day, their words will generate mass action. They can substitute dramatic but nonviolent acts for words, expecting that the masses will sooner or later respond to their moral example or "witness." Or they can act on the theory that educating the masses will be achieved only by armed struggle.[21] These teachers by violent example are the terrorists.

This scenario of the intelligentsia being sprung loose for violent action by social change has been reenacted many times since the Russian terrorists of the 1870s first astounded the world with their suicidal boldness. Prior to the advent of extended terrorist campaigns in Brazil, Uruguay, Argentina, Italy, and West Germany, each of these nations experienced a burst of economic development followed by a period of stagnation; a large increase in the urban population, many of whom were left stranded in the city when the economic tide rushed out; the disappearance of reform-oriented social-management jobs; and an increase in state repression. In each case, the more militant working-class political parties and trade unions were either conservatized from within or suppressed. And in each case, the exploitation of pariah groups and classes (Latin American Indians, European migrant "guest workers," American blacks and rural migrants) intensified. The result was a crisis of the intelligentsia. Interestingly, in the industrialized nations, those most affected by the crisis were not necessarily the intellectuals of the Left, with their ties to the trade unions and working-class political parties, but those associated with more individualistic and spiritualized occupations or causes—for example, religious activists, academicians, artists, and community organizers. Given a precipitating event—frequently an official outrage against some pariah group—ambitious idealists without a creative ruling class to follow or a rebellious lower class to lead have often taken upon themselves the burden of representative action.

Perhaps the clearest example of this dynamic at work is pro-

vided by the rise of Italy's Red Brigade, the largest of the more
ideological European groups. Italy was probably more altered
by the economic boom of the 1950s than was any other European nation; the subsequent economic slowdown, which struck
in the mid-1960s, therefore had more dramatic effects in that
country. Industrial expansion had caused two great migrations:
workers moved from the impoverished South to the industrial
North in search of manufacturing jobs, and youth of all classes
invaded the schools and universities in search of social-management careers. By the end of the decade, however, unemployment was soaring even in the North, and the Italian universities
were graduating thousands of ambitious, idealistic youths with
no prospects for jobs suited to their skills and interests.

Moreover, the economic crisis accentuated the unevenness of
development that had been an unpublicized characteristic of
Italian (and Latin American) industrialization. The South remained poor despite the economic boom of the 1950s; unemployment and suffering in cities like Naples increased during
the 1960s; and land prices remained too high to accommodate
a major movement of workers back to the farm. More dramatically, in Turin, Genoa, and Milan, where Communist city governments represented the forces of law and order, unemployed
workers and street youths squatted in abandoned apartment
houses, defying the authorities to evict them. The economic
slowdown further undermined Italy's inefficient public order
and social-service systems, a development that tempted activists to retaliate by creating their own version of vigilante
justice.

Still, this need not have led to large-scale terrorism had there
been a credible alternative to going it alone. But in the mid-
1970s, when young militants looked for an established political
party or national coalition to influence or to join, all they found
was the Historic Compromise. The largest Communist party in
the West, having declared itself a party of moderate reform, was
preparing to join forces with the conservative ruling party, the
Christian Democrats![22] Radical intellectuals in search of allies
thus found them only among the small organizations of the

Italian extraparliamentary Left, some of which became fronts for urban guerrilla activity.

It is worth emphasizing that the breaking of connections that precipitates terrorist action is not complete until the search for a militant mass organization proves fruitless. Where there is no political party able to both command substantial support and attract the radical intelligentsia—where the mass organizations are not militant and the militants are not influential—the stage is set for a terrorist response to economic and political crises.

Contrast the Italian situation, for example, with that of France, which experienced comparatively little indigenous terrorism during the 1970s. In France, as in Italy, a large Communist party turned away from professing revolution and toward Eurocommunist reformism. But during the late 1970s, the French Communist Party (PCF) contracted an alliance with the Socialist Party and other groups on the Left rather than with the traditional conservative parties. Moreover, it proposed a program of extensive reform calling for nationalization of key industries and a shifting of tax burdens onto the shoulders of the business community. Although hardly a Leninist-style revolutionary party, the PCF and its allied labor and professional organizations functioned at least temporarily as credible opposition to the Gaullist government, drawing ambitious student activists and young workers, if not into the Party itself, then into one of the many nonterrorist organizations on its periphery.[23] Much the same may be said of England, where the Labour party opened itself up to an influx of young militants, and of the United States, where elements of the New Left participated in the "capture" of the 1972 Democratic party convention by the forces of Senator George McGovern. In Germany, by contrast, the phlegmatic Social Democrats did not offer much of an alternative to traditional Christian Democratic policies, and the Communist party was illegal. The strength of the German economy prevented a severe downturn (and the social disorder that might have accompanied it) and kept the number of German terrorists in the hundreds rather than in the thousands. Nevertheless, for radical youths interested in significant social change, there was little apparent alternative to "direct action" until the mid-1980s, when the Social Democrats veered to the left and the Green party replaced the Free Democrats as Germany's third party.

This evidence suggests that societies with a high potential for terrorism are those in which social classes and the strata within those classes are pulling apart or dis-integrating. An older class structure and the rules that helped sustain it is disorganized by rapid, uneven social change, while a new structure promising new opportunities for collective action has not yet emerged. Antonio Gramsci, the Italian Marxist leader who died in one of Benito Mussolini's prisons, described the situation in a nutshell:

> The crisis consists precisely in the fact that the old is dying and the new cannot be born; in this interregnum a great variety of morbid symptoms appears.[24]

In Italy during the 1970s, an ever-widening gap separated the big industrialists tied into the Common Market from the small businesspeople injured by runaway inflation, and an even wider chasm separated the business classes from the mass of industrial and farm workers struggling to maintain their living standards with little hope of rising out of the proletariat. Furthermore, "horizontal" dis-integration separated migrant and nonmigrant workers, northerners from southerners, older people from younger, and practicing Catholics from nonpractitioners. Support for terrorism among elements of the intelligentsia reflected severe dis-integration of the petty bourgeoisie, a situation with parallels in Latin America during the 1960s and Czarist Russia before World War I. At such times, intellectuals have divided into violently opposed groups on the basis of their choice either to serve the state or to attack it. Again, the key factor is not simply the presence of a radical intelligentsia, but its predicament in a society ripped apart by growing divisions between and within classes. It is this dis-integration that makes formation of a mass militant opposition difficult, and that creates within each class a certain constituency for terrorism.

If this approach to the causes of terrorism has some validity, we should be able to use it negatively as well as positively—that is, to show that where the intelligentsia has *not* been sprung loose for independent action, terrorism does not become endemic. In the United States, for example, what most requires explanation is the relative absence of indigenous terrorism during the past two decades, despite the presence of radicalized youth, oppressed minorities, and any number of inviting bureaucratic targets. Why has there been relatively little terrorism on these shores? It is common among scholars to insist rather dogmatically that terrorism is more likely to occur in democratic than in totalitarian societies. But if this were true, why is domestic small-group violence so rare in democracy's homeland? The most common response—that the United States has an "open society" that permits peaceful redress of grievances—is clearly insufficient. For one thing, the grievances of large American groups remained unremedied, in many cases as a result of deliberate government or business policy. For another, western Europe, which is rife with terrorism, is more open to political dissent and social experimentation than the United States. Moreover, the open society theory contradicts the thesis that terrorism thrives best under democratic skies. A better answer will be found in the social history and the present condition of the American intelligentsia.

The American New Left, for example, a movement primarily of radical intellectuals, grew most rapidly during the 1960s and early 1970s, when federal and state bureaucracies also were expanding rapidly. The postwar economic boom ended more slowly in the United States than in Europe or Latin America, permitting certain painful adjustments (like migration of labor to the South and West) to occur. Serious economic problems did not surface in an obvious way until the 1973–74 "oil crisis." Even then, unemployment remained well below European levels until the end of the decade. Under these circumstances, young intellectuals were not prevented, on the whole, from fulfilling the social-management roles they had trained for. During the late 1970s, potential recruits who might otherwise have turned the Weather Underground or the Black Panther party into a Red Brigade were studying in university human services departments, using Ford Foundation funds to survey conditions in the urban ghettos, or working for government social welfare agencies. Meaningful reform did not seem a forlorn hope in the post-Nixon era—the era of affirmative action and environmental protection, government-supported medical care for the elderly, and legal services for the poor.

Furthermore, those few Americans who embarked on the path of "direct action" found that outside the intelligentsia they were without the minimum basis of political support necessary to mount sustained campaigns of violence. This was not the case in Italy, where the Red Brigade embedded itself in communities of young factory workers; in Germany, where the Red Army Fraction found sanctuary among the despised foreign workers; or in Northern Ireland, Spain, and the Middle East, where nationalist terrorists were supplied and succored by their conationalists. But in the United States, the Symbionese Liberation Army was betrayed to the police by residents of the Oakland, California, ghetto in which the terrorists had hoped to vanish. And the Weather Underground found itself virtually without support among the youth who had been characterized as America's only revolutionary class by Underground leaders. Most of its members surfaced voluntarily, in despair, while a handful formed a short, violent alliance with members of the Black Liberation Army, itself a remnant of the black nationalist movement that had been pulverized by police violence years before.[25]

More generally, we can say that the American intelligentsia lacked the relative social coherence of its European counterparts and that, as a result, its violence-prone elements found themselves utterly without an infrastructure after the New Left collapsed. The European student movements were also defeated in the late 1960s. But they remained student movements, organized on a national basis, with a certain potential for exploitation by urban guerrilla groups. Moreover, publishers, professors, journalists, lawyers, scientists, and even some

business-people, small but not insignificant in number, remained committed to either the far Left or far Right cause, and
a few of these (to be sure, a minority of the minority) provided
European terrorists with a type of support not available to any
American group. Thus, there was in the United States little
internal basis for the reproduction of Left terrorism. Once the
Weather Underground was put out of action, no Bernadine
Dohrn Brigade appeared to pick up the torch relinquished by
the Underground leader. Even the killing of Black Panther leaders Fred Hampton and Mark Clark in Chicago by Cook County
sheriff's police officers did not generate the new cycle of violence many had expected. Terrorism in the United States was
reproduced only among groups with small but coherent political bases founded on ethnicity: Puerto Rican nationalists,
Cuban counterrevolutionaries, and rural white racists.

Comparing the modern history of Europe's urban guerrillas
with that of American terrorist organizations, we can see that
the frequency and intensity of terrorist acts have little to do
with the distinction between democracy and totalitarianism,
and a great deal to do with the traditions and social conditions
of the native intelligentsia. Of course, industrial societies have
no choice but to create and recreate the intelligentsia; few have
undertaken to liquidate this group as a class, as Stalin did in his
way and the Argentine generals did in theirs. Whether young
intellectuals will be driven by hope and desperation to undertake independent military adventures depends upon numerous
factors, the most important of which are the extent to which the
intelligentsia is integrated into the society, the availability of
social-management careers, apparent opportunities for meaningful political change, and the presence or absence of local
constituencies for terrorism both inside the intelligentsia and
out. Compared with these internal causes of terrorism, the external causes so colorfully publicized by Red network and state
sponsorship theorists seem relatively insignificant.

PART III

THE VARIETIES OF MODERN TERRORISM

Chapter 6

Revolutionary Terrorism: The Anarcho-Communists

CONSIDERING the brevity of the average terrorist career, western European terrorism is now in its fifth or sixth generation since 1968. This remarkable fact has generated a few somewhat tentative attempts at explanation, of which the most prevalent is the idea that democratic regimes are too lenient, too punctilious about individual rights, to be efficient at stamping out violent dissent. Now, if this means that no other Western government has opted thus far for the Argentine solution—a no-holds-barred "dirty war" against the entire intelligentsia—this notion is obviously true. The salient fact, however, is that no European or North American government has felt compelled to choose between unleashing a full-scale counterterrorism campaign and submitting to radical destabilization.

A reign of counterterror is precisely what many urban guerrillas had hoped to provoke. That they failed is attributable not so much to liberal restraint as to their own inability to spread rebellion far beyond a narrow circle of alienated intellectuals and oppressed workers. As a result of their political weakness, terrorists could be singled out for very harsh treatment (indeed, for assassination) without rending the entire fabric of legality. Democratic norms *were* suspended when it came to dealing with suspected terrorists, be they the American Black Panther party, the German RAF, or the IRA.[1] The guerrillas' inability to overcome their isolation made it possible for Western governments to treat them very harshly without generalizing intense repression to the entire intelligentsia or even to the entire far Left.

The continuation of low-level terrorism in the industrialized nations therefore remains essentially unexplained—a gap in understanding that is not filled by references to liberal weakness, Soviet plots, or the Italian national character. As will be discussed later in this chapter, radical nationalist groups like the IRA Provisionals and the Palestinian PFLP survived by adapting their ideas and tactics to the requirements of mainstream nationalism. What is harder to explain is the persistent violence directed by anarcho-communist groups like the RAF and the Red Brigade against their own governments in the industrialized West. Although they have collaborated on occasion with nationalists, the immediate goals of the anarcho-communists are much more ambitious than, say, reunifying Ireland, establishing Basque autonomy, or creating a Palestinian state. They aim at nothing less than the destruction of the capitalist system in its Western homeland and the construction of a new system run from the bottom up by the working class.[2] At the same time, however, they lack most of the advantages that have permitted nationalist organizations to thrive: broad-based coalitions, wealthy sponsors, intense social disorder, and a popular cause.

How, then, have they survived? In part, the answer depends upon what is meant by survival. Virtually all of the original leaders and a good many of the cadres of the important Red terrorist groups of the 1970s (RAF, June 2d Movement, Red Brigade, Primea Linea, Angry Brigade, Weather Underground, and others) were eliminated either through capture and imprisonment, murder, suicide, or voluntary dropouts. In the early 1980s, a series of effective blows against the larger, more elaborately organized groups weakened them quite seriously. Military defeat intensified pressure along political fault lines, and groups like the RAF and the Red Brigade splintered badly.[3] The surprise was that the splinters lived on. Attacks continued in the form of somewhat simpler operations by smaller groups that were less vulnerable to police penetration. Moreover, not only did these groups survive, they multiplied: new formations, presumably composed of recruits, continued to announce their presence with bombs, kidnappings, assassinations, and so-called expropriations. Elements of the Red Brigade and the RAF —no doubt containing few survivors of the pre-1978 period— have focused their more recent attacks on North Atlantic Treaty Organization (NATO) bases and American military personnel.[4] Newer organizations include the West German Revolutionary Cells (RZ), which killed Minister of Finance Hans Herbert Karry of Hesse, West Germany, in 1981; France's Direct Action; the United Freedom Front and May 19 Movement, which have claimed responsibility for some fifteen bombings in the United States since 1982; Belgium's Fighting Communist Cells; and any number of small organizations in Italy, which still experiences from five hundred to one thousand incidents of terrorism each year.[5] Europe and the United States are also experiencing a resurgence of far-Right violence, a phenomenon often ignored by terror network theorists in the West. Active groups include the American KKK, the Aryan Brotherhood, the Order, and assorted other neo-Nazi organizations; Germany's German Action Group and Hoffmann Military Sports Group; and Italy's Black Order, perpetrator of the devastating attack on the Bologna railroad station that killed eighty-six persons in August 1980.[6]

It is possible to view this decentralization of terrorism as an indication that Western governments have won the war of the 1970s against indigenous rebels. Anarcho-communist violence has receded from the high-water mark of 1977–78, when the RAF killed West Germany's leading industrialist, its most influential banker, and its chief prosecutor, and blew up the German Embassy in Stockholm; and when the Red Brigade abducted and then executed Aldo Moro, former Italian premier and principal architect of the Historic Compromise between Christian Democrats and Communists. For a time, the Italian government, caught between escalating violence by Red and Black terrorists, seemed headed for possible disintegration. The terrorist organizations disintegrated more rapidly, however—a process accelerated in 1981, when the kidnapping of an American general, James Dozier, resulted in the arrest of hundreds of Red Brigadists and generated further splits within that organization. At present, no European regime feels itself seriously threatened by terrorist violence, but so long as attacks continue, the internal war cannot be said to have been won. The long-term consequences of persisting disorder are unpredictable, and terrorism in the West is nothing if not persistent.

We return, then, to the principal questions: why, after the death or capture of virtually every important anarcho-communist leader of the 1970s do new recruits persist in following the fatal path of Meinhoff and Curcio? Why are they unable to recognize, as Laqueur says, that for powerful capitalist states this sort of violence is no more than "a minor irritation . . . a nuisance"?[7] What sort of people are these, and what do they hope to accomplish by such outrageous sacrifices?

No doubt there are many reasons for what seems to be a crazy persistence, including the desire to avenge fallen comrades and a thirst for historical notoriety, not to mention other desires and neuroses both banal and bizarre. But reducing the urban guerrilla's motivation to some personal interest or psychological complex obscures an essential point: terrorists are people possessed (as Dostoyevsky put it) by ideas.[8] Since many of these ideas are shared by nonterrorists, it may be helpful to imagine them as concentric circles or rings, with the outer rings representing those ideas most widely held and the innermost ring those peculiar to terrorist thinking (see figure). We can understand terrorist ideology in context by describing these rings from the outside in.

Outer Ring.   Many urban guerrillas are possessed by the vision of a political and social order radically different than the present system, infinitely more desirable, and obtainable in the relatively near future. This is not what makes them terrorists, but it is certainly one key to understanding who they are.

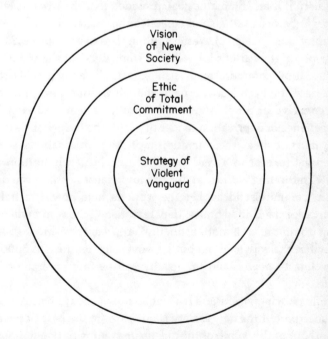

Vision
of New
Society

Ethic
of Total
Commitment

Strategy of
Violent
Vanguard

Terrorist Ideas in Context

Anarcho-communists, for example, share with the rest of the far Left the vision of a classless, stateless world society that has eliminated poverty, inequality, and war—a place in which industrial abundance is managed directly by the workers in their own interest. There are numerous versions of this good society, but all spring from a common appreciation of the scandalous contradiction between potential abundance and actual scarcity, not only worldwide but also in the wealthier nations themselves. Numerous schools (Marxist, anarchist, syndicalist, Christian Socialist, and others) agree that the next breakthrough in human evolution depends upon the working class obtaining control of the mightiest industrial machine on earth. To unleash the West's productive potential and manage it in accordance with classical communist political values (radical egalitarianism, cooperation, planning, self-management, internationalism, and direct democracy) is the goal. According to the far Left, it is an obtainable goal, provided that the workers take control before capitalism incinerates the planet.

How is the powerful Western ruling class to be displaced? On this point, the various schools part company. But the vision of rich-nation communism persists, especially among declassed Western intellectuals who have enough technical imagination to conceive of alternatives to the profit system, and enough experience of deprivation to identify with the have-not classes. For most of them, the communism of the poorer nations is not a model (except in a very partial sense), but an indication of how continuing world scarcity and imperialist hostility can deform communist ideas. Let the workers take power in Italy, France, or the United States, they reason, and the world will see that communism is not antithetical to prosperity and democracy but the way to attain both. Conversely, let the rich minority cling to power, and the results will be fascism and world war.

The glowing vision of a realizable utopia always has its dark counterpart: if the new society is not born (to use Marx's metaphor) out of the womb of the old, its unavailing birth pangs will also kill the mother. What distinguishes many urban guerrillas (and certain segments of the nonterrorist ultra Left) from others on the far Left is their insistence that the nightmare has already arrived—that the advanced capitalist nations are already fascist or that world war three is even now under way.[9] Two groups are most likely to accept this grim, despairing version of modern history: those exposed to the brutality inflicted on Third World peoples by the Western democracies, and those impressed by the continuity between German, Italian, or Japanese fascism and rule by postwar industrial elites. Even if their views were accurate, of course, this would not necessarily justify resorting to small-group violence. Nevertheless, it is worth noting that for some intellectuals, the dark vision of the future has overtaken utopia. They believe that fascism is here and that they are the Resistance.

Middle Ring.   One may be a social visionary without dedicating one's entire life to "the cause." Like many clergy and religious enthusiasts, members of the armed forces, and political activists, terrorists have embraced an *ethic of total commitment* that requires that they live systematically, in accordance with ideological duty. Not for them the luxury of a private life separated from a job or career; members of groups requiring total commitment generally substitute the life of the group for that of the family. As for the customary gap between theory and practice —words and deeds—their lives are devoted to eradicating that distinction in action. When Nechayev called his terrorist handbook *"Catechism* of the Revolutionist," he was recognizing (and reflecting) the correspondence between the orders of the church and the terrorist brotherhood. Similarly, when Marighella wrote that "the urban guerrilla's reason for existence . . . is to shoot," he was acknowledging membership not in any conventional army, but in a military order.[10] Politically, the idea of a conspiratorial association demanding total commitment dates back to the era of the French Revolution, when François Babeuf's largely theoretical secret society, the Conspiracy of Equals, became a model for real groups like the Italian Carbonari and the Russian Decembrists.[11] One may therefore conceive of the terrorist as a totally committed activist whose calling combines aspects of the religious, military, and political orders—a person attempting to live a radically integrated life through violent politics.

None of this description is new; Ch'en, Andre Malraux's archetypical terrorist (see chapter 1, pp. 11–13), is far more a warrior-priest than a politician. He is one of those young intellectuals who finds the great separations of modern life—between public and private life, individual interest and group purpose, sacred principles and profane practices—intolerable, and who attempts to unify them through personal action.[12] Fanatical he may be, but this sort of fanaticism is more widely shared than many of us realize, especially among young adults of religious background. Among the West German and Italian urban guerrillas, the children of ministers and other religiously committed individuals have been more prominent than have the children of Communists.[13] A common bond is the essentially religious notion that in order to bring the desired future into existence, one must live it immediately. Almost always this means organizing or joining a small group whose social constitution prefigures the world to come and whose very existence is a protest against the accepted moral order. Thus, when Father Daniel Berrigan, a practitioner of nonviolent resistance to war, pleaded with the Weather Underground to give up violence, he did so as an inhabitant of the same generic territory: the future-in-the-present. Although a Christian pacifist, he shared the perspective that one can *will* the future society into existence (or at least that one should try), as well as the key belief that exemplary small-group action has the capacity to awaken the wills of others.[14] Nevertheless, his pleas went unheeded by those who considered violence a duty and nonviolent resistance a utopian deception. While borrowing some of the strategic assumptions of radical Christianity, the urban guerrillas served another god. Their path was not the priest's but the warrior's.

Inner Ring.   Central to most terrorist thinking is a strategy of *violent vanguardism* that sees acts of exemplary violence as a lever that can move society in some desired direction. In its most optimistic, revolutionary form, this strategy assumes that some

target group is ready to rebel, and attempts to trigger that rebellion through acts that are designed to be imitated. In its more
pessimistic—and common—form, the assumption is that while
the violence will not be widely imitated, it will generate a series
of events that have the potential to provoke mass rebellion. The
optimistic, "subjective" version resembles radical Christianity
in that its immediate aim is to activate the wills of others: that
is, to make converts. The more pessimistic, "objective" version
resembles behavioral science rather than religion. By manipulating events, it aims to create an environment in which a mass
uprising is conceivable.

Europe's anarcho-communist guerrillas have combined these
perspectives to some extent, but among the modern groups, the
objective form tends to predominate. Accepting their small
numbers and political weakness, they seek to inject violence
into the political system in such a way as to destabilize it over
the long run, by weakening the hold of established institutions
over their members. The kidnapping and execution of Aldo
Moro by the Red Brigade, for example, was a deliberate attack
on the Italian political center. It was launched to embarrass both
Communists and Christian Democrats, embroil them in personal controversy, and make their collaboration more difficult
—all for the sake of promoting long-term political polarization
in Italy.

Particularly in view of the common stereotype of terrorism
as mindless violence, it is worth emphasizing the rationality, at
least in a short-term sense, of certain terrorist acts. Moro did
praise his captors' seriousness and dedication, and he did beg
his own party's leaders for his life. The Christian Democrats
split bitterly over this issue, the Communist party was forced
to take a hard-line position against negotiations, and the government appeared, by turns, to be indecisive, vengeful, and
inept. (Most Italians, while strongly disapproving of the Red
Brigade, understood their message when the car containing
Moro's body was deposited in a spot exactly equidistant from
both Communist party and Christian Democratic headquarters.) If the aim of the Moro kidnapping was to create a revolu-

tionary situation in Italy, as some analysts have maintained, it obviously failed. But the evidence suggests that the guerrillas' immediate purposes were more concrete and foreseeable, and that even dissenting Brigadists considered the operation a great success.[15]

Were they justified in thinking so? This depends upon how one assesses the central principle of anarcho-communist strategy: the conviction that protracted armed struggle between terrorists and state authorities has the capacity to polarize Western societies—to destroy their political center—thereby unleashing a mass struggle that the Left will win. (For ultranationalist or fascist organizations, substitute "the Right will win.") It is useful to examine this principle seriously rather than writing it off as demented or fantastic. If one believes, for example, that Italy and other Western nations are vulnerable to radical polarization, the Red Brigade's apparent defeat following the kidnapping of General Dozier was merely a battle lost, not a war. And to the extent that the Italian political center appears to have weakened, it may not be a lost battle. To be sure, the Brigade failed to accomplish its ultimate goal: to provoke a violent right-wing reaction that would either destroy the Communist party or force it to lead a workers' revolution. On the other hand, it did manage to gain some support among workers in Italy's industrial North—in particular, among southerners stranded in the cities after the economy went flat—who were disenchanted with both Communists and Christian Democrats. Similarly, the Brigade's German counterparts, although smaller in number and more isolated, have apparently had some success in securing sanctuary among "guest workers" from Turkey and other poor countries.[16] Those who follow the terrorist road today believe that with the political center visibly decaying, their existing bases can be expanded. What seems now to Western regimes a minor irritation can in time become a true internal war.

Anarcho-communist strategy derives originally from nineteenth-century theorists, who argued that dramatic violent attacks had three principal functions: to inspire emulation, to provoke repressive violence, and finally, to generate a mass uprising. These functions were thought to be related elements of a cycle: overreaction by the state would inspire new waves of terrorism, new waves promote overreaction, and so forth, until the political center collapsed. The collapse of the center would tear the blindfold from the eyes of the workers and the poor, and would cause them to recognize the futility of compromise, the impotence of liberal hope, and the need to join the armed struggle (see discussion in chapter 10). Brazilian guerrilla chief Marighella, ambushed and killed by police in 1969, put forth the thesis clearly in his "Minimanual of the Urban Guerrilla." When terrorism reaches a certain level, he explained,

> The government has no alternative except to intensify repression. The police networks, house searches, arrests of innocent people and of suspects, closing off of streets, make life in the city unbearable. . . . The political situation in the country is transformed into a military situation in which the "gorillas" appear more and more to be the ones responsible for errors and violence, while the problems in the lives of the people become truly catastrophic . . . watching the revolutionaries, the people now understand that it is a farce to vote in elections which have as their sole objective guaranteeing the continuation of the military dictatorship and covering up its crimes.[17]

Marighella wrote this about an existing military dictatorship —the Brazilian junta that had overthrown the liberal government of President Goulart. By extension, however, terrorism could be used to force the militarists to take power from a corrupt, inefficient centrist regime. Thus, many Red Brigadists hoped that sufficient chaos would provoke a seizure of power by the Italian army and bring on open conflict between forces of the Left and Right. Similarly, German supporters of the RAF were not entirely displeased when the authorities in Bonn constructed a special courthouse, jailed defense lawyers, and devised new rules of criminal procedure to try captured leaders of the Baader-Meinhoff gang.[18] Exactly one century before Marighella met his death, Nechayev had written:

> Our society will employ all its power and all its resources in order
> to promote an intensification and an increase in those calamities and
> evils which must finally exhaust the patience of the people and drive
> it to a popular uprising.[19]

In the modern version as well, it is thought that the proletariat
as a whole, which is considered to be either brainwashed or
asleep, can be awakened only by extreme measures—by being
caught in the crossfire between the state and the extremists. In
a sense, it matters little whether workers initially approve or
disapprove of the terrorists' acts, so long as they are shocked
into the realization that the social peace engineered by the
center is a facade, and that the facade is breakable. The assumption common to both the old terrorism and the new is that
polarization favors the oppressed. Violence and countervio-
lence will break the psychological fetters bonding the lower
classes to their social superiors. The workers will rally to the
Left when the Right resorts to naked force.

It is hardly astonishing to rediscover in the new terrorism so
many themes associated with anarchist and populist movements of the last century. Intellectuals effectively isolated from
the bulk of the working class tend to make similar assumptions.
They assume, for example, that the principal obstacles to revolution are bad ideas—ideas that reinforce what Franz Fanon
called "the native's sense of childish inferiority"[20] and keep the
working class docile. By the same token, students, young
professionals, and intellectuals without social status (according
to Nechayev, "that section of educated youth which has sprung
from the people and has felt the full extent of the pain suffered
by the people")[21] are considered the vanguard: the only group
capable of perceiving the reality of class domination behind the
masks of consumerism and fake democracy.[22] Their natural
allies (at first) are social outcasts, especially the unemployed
and rootless; persecuted ethnic groups or nationalities; and particularly oppressed ("superexploited") communities of workers. In time, however, the proletariat as a whole will be awakened to reality by the tactics of confrontation and the strategy

of polarization. In this scenario, the hero is the intellectual who identifies so completely with the outcast as to become one of them—a selfless fighter who despises reform, opposes all bureaucratic systems (including centralized state socialism), and believes that the working class, once awakened, will improvise new forms of self-management and democracy. The villain is of course the ruling class, particularly those agents of the status quo who trick the people into believing that they are agents of progress and change.

Virtually all of these related ideas were revived during the 1960s by the New Left. So long as that movement had a mass following, they were perfectly consistent with student sit-ins, peaceful demonstrations, symbolic acts of civil disobedience, and other forms of nonviolent protest. When its following disintegrated, however, they proved to be equally consistent with urban guerrilla warfare, particularly after the ultimate goal —mass uprising—had been redefined. The New Left's failure to secure substantial working-class support, which led directly to the defeats of 1968–70, was its real turning point. Certain veterans of the student revolt emerged from the experience convinced that while radical reform or social revolution was still on the historical agenda, workers in the advanced industrial states could never be brought to liberate themselves through nonviolent protest, parliamentary politics, *or* formation of a mass revolutionary party. "What we need," said Daniel Cohn-Bendit, "is not an organization with a capital O, but a host of insurrectional cells, be they ideological groups, study groups—we can even use street gangs."[23]

The new armed-struggle groupings may have drawn spiritual inspiration from Marx and Mao Tse-tung and learned military techniques from Irish or Palestinian commandos, but their chief theoretical guides were thinkers like Herbert Marcuse, Franz Fanon, Abraham Guillen, and Antonio Negri—opponents of orthodox Marxism and apostles of a new awakening. The great problem addressed by each of these thinkers was the pacification of the Western working class in the period following World War II. Marcuse put it most dramatically. Under the pressures of modern consumerism, he argued, Western workers had developed a second nature—a set of false needs that could be satisfied only by maintaining the existing capitalist system intact. Therefore, these workers ceased to be a revolutionary class in the sense understood by earlier Marxists.[24]

Marx and Lenin had assumed a fairly close connection between the reality of class oppression and the development of revolutionary class-consciousness by workers. True, the intellectuals had a vital role to play in assisting this development; without a vanguard party, Lenin asserted, it might never occur. But the chief obstacles to a mass awakening (traditional deference, fear, gullibility, and resignation) would be battered down, in effect, by history itself. The workers did not have to be lectured on the effects of war and depression, inequality and need. They needed merely to learn that these effects had a cause, and to understand that, with proper organization and leadership, it was within their power to remove that cause. This view, Marcuse declared, did not reckon with a fully developed capitalist system's power to cloud people's minds by manipulating both public institutions and private desires. The workers equated socialism with Stalinism and monopoly capitalism with free enterprise. Identifying themselves primarily as consumers rather than producers, they had lost consciousness of their collective role in production and their potential to become a ruling class. In popular language: they had been effectively brainwashed, and could no longer be considered a primary source of rebellion against this system. Hope for qualitative change therefore rested with outsiders—either the oppressed masses of the Third World or internal groups excluded from the prevailing consensus (in particular, racial or national minorities and radical youths).

To this rather bleak analysis, the doctrines of Fanon added hope, for Fanon (a psychoanalyst and a bitter opponent of colonialism) emphasized the capacity of political violence to liberate its practitioners from psychological manipulation. Colonial oppression, he taught, rests for the most part on the native's feelings of guilt and inferiority, which are a result of suppressed rage against the colonial "parent" that is turned inward against oneself and one's own people. Transforming the rage into violent action—literally, killing the parent—is both a declaration of independence and an affirmation of the community of natives.[25] This idea spoke directly to European youths, especially those whose parents (and the political systems they had constructed) had been implicated in fascism or in the slaughter of colonized peoples. Moreover, if participation in anticolonial terrorism à la the Battle of Algiers could tear the native out of traditionalistic slumber, could it not also free the European worker from the hypnosis of consumerism?

Fanon had restricted his remarks to the colonized world, but as Marcuse implied, the Western worker was as "underdeveloped," politically speaking, as any Algerian peasant—perhaps more so, for while dominated classes in the Third World at least know they are dominated, in the West, domination comes disguised as technological and administrative rationality.[26] Violent action liberates the practitioner, but it also has the capacity to awaken the sleeper, to galvanize the uncommitted, to interfere with the smooth flow of managed news and to pierce the veil of administrative rationality. Thus, the first act of the German group that was to become the Red Army Fraction was to set fire to a department store; in Italy, the anarchocommunists' initial targets (in addition to openly fascist groups) were bureaucrats and judges—real executors of the law and symbols of faceless impersonality.

What is the difference between this new terrorism and the old? Surely it is not, as some impassioned critics claim, that modern terrorists are more ruthless, more fanatical, or more subject to external manipulation than were terrorists of the old school. The chief differences are attributable to the passage of time, not to alterations in character. Modern anarcho-communists are influenced politically by heterodox neo-Marxists like Marcuse and Fanon, and socially by the fact that, as a group, their own origins are considerably more proletarian than were those of nineteenth-century students. The polarization they hope to generate is, in theory, based on class; they look to the working class with the same combination of expectant longing and desperate frustration that the Russian Narodniki felt for the peasantry. The fact that European workers have already been organized by Communist and Socialist parties also makes a difference. While attacking them politically, modern terrorists frequently act as if they believed that existing workers' parties (especially the Communist parties) could be *reformed*—that is, forced to act on the basis of their old-time revolutionary slogans. The original Red Brigade, in particular, nurtured the hope that its war against the government would trigger a revolt of the Communist party's rank and file against that party's tepid Euro-communism. By provoking the government and the military forces to commit anti-popular excesses, they hoped to make the Communists fight.

When this plan did not succeed, anarchism in the urban guerrilla movement, which pictured revolution as a great mass explosion, tended to give way to Guevarism, which assumed that in time, small armed nuclei themselves could become a Red army. If revolution could spread slowly through the population like an "oil patch" while the regime's power slowly decayed, mass intervention might be delayed (as it had been in Cuba) until the final, decisive battle.[27] This notion, which substitutes a protracted series of attacks and counterattacks for a big bang theory, saves the hypothesis of terrorist-engendered revolution by redefining the role of the terrorist fighter. Rather than acting as the fuse that detonates a mass uprising and burns itself up in the process, the terrorist fighter becomes a long-term combatant in a war of attrition—someone whose duty is to fight and survive until other units appear and until links between them can be established. To those who accept this redefinition, the workers' failure to react strongly to the Moro execution or to the Red Army Fraction's orgy of killing and suicide proves nothing. Nor does the authorities' success in disrupting large guerrilla organizations and rounding up their leaders necessarily give them reason to despair. On the contrary, if the work of the decapitated organizations is continued even on a localized, spontaneous basis by new recruits, one can view this as evidence that the revolution is spreading—or at least that it cannot be stamped out.

To most observers this seems little more than a fanatical delusion. Rebellion is *not* spreading rapidly throughout the intelligentsia and into the working class. Repression is *not* intensifying so as to antagonize bystanders and polarize Western societies. Terrorism, as Laqueur says, has become low-level violence: a "nuisance," rather than a threat to the social order. The trouble with this formulation, however, is that it underestimates the social and political changes that give terrorists reason to believe that their actions are not in vain. To relegate European terrorism to the status of historical irrelevance or nuisance is to assume that Western regimes are fundamentally stable and that the only political choices realistically available and acceptable to the public are those offered by the present governing party (or coalition) and its parliamentary opposition. But what if this apparent stability is merely concealing deepening social divisions and increasingly bitter political disagreements? Behind the facade of reasonable compromise and polite debate, how stable are the capitalist democracies really? These issues are beyond the scope of this book; let it suffice to say that one need not be a mad dreamer to perceive sources of serious instability in the advanced industrial nations, particularly in those whose share of the world market is declining. Tendencies toward Right/Left polarization are increasingly evident not only in Italy, where the Historic Compromise has now been buried, but virtually across the board.

Item: In recent years, the British Labour party has moved significantly to the left; the Conservative party of Prime Minister Thatcher has moved to the right; and the centrist Social Democratic Alliance has gained little ground. Since 1983, Great Britain has been wracked by the most passionate and violent wave of industrial disputes since the 1920s, and remains unable to solve either Northern Ireland's troubles or its own racial problem. With unemployment in 1986 at a fifty-year high, the fastest growing political groups in England were the Labour party's left wing and the fascist National Front.

Item:　In the mid-1980s, Premier François Mitterand's moderate Socialist government in France came under intense attack from both erstwhile Communist allies and traditional Gaullist opponents. In 1984, French steelworkers in the Red Belt of industrial suburbs around Paris burned down the Communist party headquarters in Longwy to protest the government's austerity policies. That same year, in elections to the European Parliament representing the Common Market countries, startling gains were made by the neofascist, anti-immigrant National Front. In 1985, the French Communist and Socialist parties disbanded their Left Union; and in 1986, an electoral victory by Jacques Chirac's conservative alliance dramatically increased the strength of the far Right in the French legislature. During the past two years, French society has experienced the most serious outbreak of terrorism since World War II.

Item:　The year 1983 saw the end of West Germany's bipartisan foreign policy, as mass demonstrations against the emplacement of U.S. missiles in Germany drove the Social Democratic Party toward a neopacifist, neutralist position. In 1984, while Christian Democrats maintained power, German metalworkers led the most bitter strike in the history of postwar Germany, and a new wild card in German politics—the Green party—dramatically increased its strength in local and national elections. Observers in the mid-1980s noted a resurgence of German nationalism, expressed on the extreme Right by an increase in the number and size of neofascist groups. Meanwhile, ultra-Left groups launched a series of armed attacks against NATO installations and German weapons manufacturers. These attacks were apparently coordinated to some extent with similar actions by anarcho-communist groups in France, Belgium, and Portugal.[28]

Indeed, fairly serious polarizing trends are present not only in most western European nations, but even in the United States. Here, the process is at an earlier stage of development, but the essential preconditions for it are present; with the social distance between classes and races increasing, American politics are clearly being ideologized.[29] Since the late 1970s, this development has taken place primarily from the top down. The dominant center-Right party has moved strongly to the right; the loyal center-Left opposition has shifted to the left; and the fastest-growing, most energetic, most intense organizations have appeared on the left fringe of the Democratic party and on the right fringe of the Republican. By far the most serious polarizing force to appear on the American political scene in recent years is the religious Right. In 1986, television evangelist Pat Robertson entered several presidential primary elections, while a host of Christian fundamentalist candidates declared their intention to run for lesser offices.

Conventional political analysis minimizes this Right/Left polarization on the grounds that the Reagan presidency has produced a new conservative consensus that will serve the same stabilizing function as did the previous New Deal consensus. But this analysis is faulty on several counts. What made liberal government relatively stable was its ability to pacify workers, farmers, small-businesspeople, ethnic minorities, and the poor, by making them the beneficiaries of public programs and by controlling their grass-roots organizations. Conservatives in power are now dismantling these programs on the theory that the resultant economic benefits will render them obsolete. At the same time, they have attempted to bypass traditional working-class organizations by appealing to their constituents on the basis of noneconomic values—for example, patriotism, religious sentiment, traditional morality, and the dream of individual wealth.

Even if successful, the conservatives' method of building a mass political base produces a consensus very unlike that of the New Deal—it is far thinner in terms of organization and much more dependent on a popular president. Moreover, the infusion of passionate moralism into local politics is profoundly polarizing. While small-scale terrorism against abortion clinics erupted in response to the extreme Right's Right to Life campaign, a far more violent struggle was waged by the Order, an overtly fascist organization whose leaders were convicted in 1985–86 of charges ranging from murder and assault to conspiracy to overthrow the government.[30] Similarly, nationalist militancy in foreign policy—such as the support of far-Right guerrilla groups in nearby nations—has a spillover effect domestically. Omega 7 is more feared in the Cuban-American community than it is in Cuba![31] Most important, the conservative coalition's frank bias toward big business, unless combatted by effective and militant lower-class political organizations, leaves weaker, less prosperous groups without a means of effective self-expression. We need to remember that increased terrorism is predictable when the working class and the poor lack organizational champions, and when young intellectuals are deprived of opportunities for useful public employment.

Terrorism is the product of social dislocation. It is a *symptom* of political instability—a sign of the partiality of a false consensus. It is quite another thing to claim, as anarcho-communists do, that terrorism is a *cause* of instability and a mighty force for polarization in the industrial nations. In order to become more than a mere nuisance, the several hundred armed fighters now following the lead of Direct Action or the Red Brigade must become several thousand, with a base of political support extending into the hundreds of thousands. Nationalist fighters have frequently reached these numbers; Red guerrillas have very seldom. Now, this sort of guerrilla expansion is highly unlikely to occur, but it is not out of the question, assuming that demobilization of the working class and the poor continues and that broad sectors of the intelligentsia see no other opportunities for leadership. But even if this should occur, and terrorism were to become a destabilizing force, who would benefit? The urban guerrillas' faith (based on their belief in mass spontaneity and self-organization) is that with the political center destroyed, the workers would naturally turn left. All of the available evidence, however, suggests that when urban guerrilla attacks do not mobilize the working class, the ultimate beneficiaries of terrorist-engendered polarization are the forces of the Right (see chapter 7).

Of course, this is exactly what Trotsky meant when he insisted that terrorism does not organize the workers for action, it reduces them to the role of mere spectators who will soon be clamoring for a return to law and order (see chapter 11). During the 1970s, this critique was vindicated at a tragic price in Latin America, while in Italy (where Red Brigadists and their allies have at times numbered in the thousands), a less acute polarization has driven the Communist party to the right without unleashing any compensatory mass organization on the Left. Trotsky's remarks are also echoed in an interesting way by recent commentators like Brian Jenkins, who has described anarcho-communist terrorism as "political theater."[32] Beginning with the assumption that Western workers are manipulated through the mass media by the purveyors of false consciousness, many urban guerrillas view themselves as a *countermedium*—the producers of violent "anticommercials" designed to shock the workers out of their consumerist stupor. But updating the definition does not change reality: an audience is still an audience. It may be moved by exemplary action, but it is rarely, if ever, organized to act collectively. In revolution, it has been said, the masses themselves ascend the stage of history. If "political theater" has generally proved more useful to the forces of order than to those of change, this is because terrorism, in the final analysis, keeps the spectators in their seats.

Terrorist action has its own logic, which frequently sets at naught the goals of its practitioners. The most serious error made by the Red guerrillas has been to ignore the effects of protracted small-group struggle on their own politics. What happens to groups with leftist sympathies when the goal of the massive workers' uprising is replaced by a new vision of slowly spreading guerrilla war? When attempts to create a Red army take precedence over all other forms of organization and struggle? As we will see in the following chapters, under the pressures generated by protracted warfare there is a powerful tendency for urban guerrillas to veer right, away from socially revolutionary politics and toward traditional nationalism.

Chapter 7

The

Left-Nationalists:

New Tactics in

the Old Cause

AT FIRST GLANCE, there seems to be little difference between the terrorism of the Red Brigade or Red Army Fraction and that of left-nationalist groups like the IRA Provisionals, the PLO, or the Basque ETA. For one thing, these organizations sometimes supply each other with training facilities and logistical aid, and

occasionally (although rarely) they collaborate on specific operations.[1] For another, they speak a similar leftist language: "The
struggle against Israel is first of all a class struggle," declares the
platform of the PFLP.[2] Perhaps most important, they share
similar strategic and tactical perspectives; for example, they
agree that "indoctrination of the masses will not precede the
staging of the armed struggle but will be achieved by it."[3] To
be sure, the logic of terrorist action creates profound similarities
between ideologically diverse groups (see chapter 11). Even so,
it is useful to begin with an appreciation of the important
differences between these major schools of political violence.

The most significant difference is situational. We live in an
age of intense nationalism, a period when it is easier to mobilize
support for national liberation (or expansion) than for any other
cause. Clearly, to make oneself an alien in one's own country
by attacking its government and traditional institutions is not
the same as joining with fellow nationals to attack some alien
oppressor. In the former case, the guerrillas are compelled to go
it alone, hoping through provocative violence to create the conditions for a social upheaval. In the latter, some upheaval has
already occurred; the guerrillas are generally able to attach
themselves as an extreme (ultra) faction to an organized movement already committed to fighting for national independence.
The anarcho-communists have no organized allies; indeed, the
purpose of their activities is to create them from scratch. The
ultranationalists almost always have allies, although their relationship with parent organizations like the original IRA and
umbrella organizations like the PLO is often stormy. The purpose of ultranationalist activities is to influence the more moderate nationalist groups, to appeal over their heads to their mass
constituencies, and ultimately, to replace them as leaders of the
national struggle. Frequently, this competition gets out of control and a mini–civil war erupts within the nationalist ranks.
The expulsion of Arafat's guerrilla group Al Fatah from Lebanon by Syrian-backed elements of the PLO has many prece-
dents.[4] But even when engaged in fratricidal struggle, ultrana-

tionalist groups usually enjoy an advantage denied the anarcho-communists: the masses they want to lead have already been set in motion.

Thus, in Northern Ireland, in the Basque region of Spain, and in the Middle East, armed coalitions fighting for national independence had already established a certain legitimacy among their people before the ultranationalist groups appeared. During the late 1960s and the 1970s, the intellectuals gravitated toward nominally leftist organizations like the IRA Provisionals, the Basque ETA-V, and the Palestinian PFLP. These "ultras" charged their parent organizations with ineffectiveness, careerist appetites, and softness toward the enemy. Vowing to continue the violent struggle at all costs, they counterposed their own hardness and scorn for "respectable opinion" to the more conventional, compromising nationalism of their movements' official wings. Leaders like George Habash of the PFLP frequently expressed themselves using Marxist language, and one PFLP operation in particular—the 1975 kidnapping of the OPEC oil ministers in Vienna—was apparently aimed at the Arab ruling class, which was viewed as a collaborator with Israel and the United States.[5] Nevertheless, the ultras' commitment to class struggle remained, for the most part, entirely theoretical. In practice, their leftist leanings were overwhelmed by passionate nationalism and by coalition politics based on the principle of national unity.

For the left-nationalists, as for their competitors, the primary business at hand was to rid national territory of foreign rule by making it too difficult and costly to govern. Almost always, this meant subordinating differences within the oppressed nation to the common interest in combating the national enemy. Almost always, it implied strict nonfraternization with that enemy's working class. To participate with other conational groups in the independence struggle—much less lead them—the ultras found it necessary to put their revolutionary ideas and practices on the shelf. Theory yielded to apparent practicality (for example, the need to raise funds from friendly businesspeople and governments), and social revolution was postponed to a theoretical second stage of struggle which was scheduled to begin after national independence was achieved. For the time being —which meant for the indefinite future—the Struggle *was* the Revolution.

The conservatizing effect of this postponement appears first in the practice of nationalist groups, then in their ideology. Arafat's wing of the PLO, for example, has found it increasingly difficult to maintain even a nominally socialist posture while courting Arab-American businesspeople, Kuwaiti officials, and Jordan's King Hussein. Habash's PFLP has moved from fire-eating class struggle rhetoric to a marriage of convenience with Syria's Hafez Assad. (Assad is called a radical in the West because he hates Israel and accepts Soviet military aid, when in fact, his socialism is of the most moderate kind imaginable, with two-thirds of the Syrian labor force employed in private enterprise.)[6] Similarly, the IRA Provisionals' Marxist professions seem increasingly irrelevant to the drawn-out communal war in Ulster, and leftist elements within the Basque ETA umbrella have lost ground steadily as the first stage of their struggle is prolonged.

During the 1970s, left-nationalist groups brought off a number of spectacular operations, including the kidnapping of Canadian officials James Cross and Pierre Laporte by the Québecois FLQ, the assassination of Spanish Prime Minister Carrerro Blanco by elements of the ETA, and the hijacking of the OPEC oil ministers by an international team organized by the PFLP.[7] But they were also capable of acts of apparently senseless, indiscriminate violence like the Lod Airport massacre, the IRA Provisionals' bombing of English pubs, and attacks on athletes, school buses, and other civilian targets. The murder of Leon Klinghoffer, an American Jew, by PLF cadres aboard the cruise ship *Achille Lauro* and the bombing of the Rome and Vienna airports by members of the Palestine Council continued this cruel tradition into the 1980s. I call these acts "apparently" senseless because to outsiders they seem unrelated to any foreseeable objective and almost random in their choice of targets. But it is essential to understand that attacking unarmed civilians makes perfect sense to nationalists at war, whether they are terrorists or the soldiers of a recognized state.

As French philosopher Raymond Aron has stated, we now live in "the age of total war,"[8] a period in which the intimidation of civilian populations by bombing cities, using terrifying weapons, and destroying the enemy's economic infrastructure is accepted practice. Therefore, the charge that terrorist attacks à la Lod Airport are acts of irrational barbarism rests on the unstated premise that because terrorists are not really the army of a nation at war, they are not entitled to use the forms of terror appropriate to established nations at war. The point emerges more clearly if one tries to distinguish the bombing of London, Dresden, or Hiroshima during World War II from the massacre of civilian tourists at Lod Airport. The Lod Airport attack was one of a series of attempts by the PFLP (using Japanese Red Army personnel) to isolate Israel by attacking its tourist trade and its transportation links with the rest of the world. Although brutal and horrifying, the attack was more limited in purpose, more selective, and less cruel than the nuclear holocaust at Hiroshima. But while most Americans would probably defend the Hiroshima and Nagasaki bombings as legitimate acts of national self-defense, the Palestinians are not recognized in the West as a nation entitled to claim and defend territory by force of arms. As a result, they are not accorded the moral privilege that virtually all recognized nations claim when they terrorize civilians in time of war.

Surely, it must be possible to tell the difference between legitimate nationalism and terrorism. There is little doubt that President Harry Truman, who ordered the atomic bombing of Japan, functioned during the closing years of World War II as the authorized representative of the American nation. Moreover, the destruction of Hiroshima and Nagasaki was rationally related to the nation's goal of winning the war quickly, while the Lod Airport massacre accomplished nothing for the Palestinian people. In fact, a critic might add, the PFLP has a weaker claim to represent the Palestinian people than does the PLO, which is formally recognized by a number of states.

But none of these distinctions is tenable. In the first place, if the Palestinians, the Northern Irish Catholics, or the Basques do not have a valid claim to nationhood, then even an organization supported by 95 percent of their people can be defined as terrorist when it resorts to violence. Repeated declarations by Western governments that the PLO is a terrorist organization are based not on polls of Palestinian opinion, but on an implicit denial of the right of *any* Palestinian organization to wage armed struggle. Second, even if one accepts the validity of Palestinian national claims, it is not clear that the wing of the PLO now under Arafat's leadership is the sole legitimate representative of that people. (Certainly the Syrian-supported groups that helped drive Arafat from Lebanon do not think so.) Nationalist organizations tend generally to be larger and more amorphous than anarcho-communist groups. Frequently (as in the PLO's case), they take the form of umbrella coalitions that embrace various ideological subgroups and that, as a whole, claim the right to speak for an entire nation or ethnic population. But continued defeat deprives the larger, relatively more moderate groups of legitimacy vis-à-vis the coalition's extremists, and makes it difficult to say who—the moderates, the extremists, or forces entirely outside the umbrella—speaks for the more passive sectors of the population.

One of the paradoxes of nationalist politics is that, so long as an organization fails to win its struggle for national liberation, its claim to be the legitimate national representative will always remain in doubt. Groups like the PFLP or the Shiite Hezbollah in Lebanon therefore function as violent pressure groups within the nationalist coalition. Their historic function (as Begin, former leader of the anti-British terrorist group Irgun, so well understood) has been to force the moderates to either fight or yield the leadership. The PFLP's notorious activities of the 1970s were designed as much to drain support from Arafat's Al Fatah as to do immediate damage to Israel. Furthermore, it appears that they succeeded, to an extent, in forcing Al Fatah to adopt the more militant armed struggle posture that ultimately drew the Israelis into Lebanon. The IRA Provisionals' activities had a somewhat similar impact on the IRA's Official wing, just as the 1985 hijacking of TWA flight 847 by Shiite extremists propelled the relatively moderate leader of the Amal militia, Nabih Berri, into confrontation with the United States. This being the case, how can one accord legitimacy to Amal, Al Fatah, or the Official IRA, but deny it to Hezbollah, the PFLP, or the IRA Provisionals?

From a nationalist perspective, it is the *struggle* that is either legitimate or illegitimate. If illegitimate, all groups that resort to violence are considered terrorist, no matter how large their numbers or how broad their popular base of support. If legitimate, all who strike a telling blow for the cause may be considered popular representatives, no matter how small their numbers or how limited their ideological appeal.

What this tells us is that, from the perspective of nationalism, it is impossible to distinguish patriots from terrorists on objective grounds. Attacks on civilians are not distinctively modern, and they provide little basis for distinguishing the good terrorists from the bad. Historical evidence suggests that those deemed freedom fighters or patriots are no less prone to terrorizing enemy civilians, when such tactics seem necessary, than are those considered terrorists. Begin's much-repeated claim that the Irgun eschewed attacks on Arab civilians is clearly inaccurate. His organization did massacre civilians when necessary, but was spared the necessity of doing so more frequently by its enemies' weakness and the strength of the official Jewish army, the Haganah.[9] Indeed, even the question of who *is* an "innocent civilian" is a vexed one from a nationalist perspective. Lebanese Shiite attacks against American civilians were designed to demonstrate that U.S. taxpayers financing Israel's war in Lebanon were responsible for killing innocents in that unhappy land.[10] In essence, pursuing nationalist goals by whatever means are necessary means killing innocent civilians. Nationalism *is* indiscriminate—and in fact, potentially genocidal—because the only distinction it recognizes in the heat of battle is the separation between "our" people and "theirs."

The designation of a religious, racial, or national group as an enemy people is the unmistakable sign that purportedly leftist nationalists have unloaded their ideological baggage and are on the way to becoming pure (conventional) nationalists. Moreover, it is the tie that binds them to the far Right, making it possible, for example, for the PFLP to train neo-Nazis at its Lebanese bases.[11] At one time, guerrilla groups that took their Marxism seriously, like Nayef Hawatameh's Popular Democratic Front for the Liberation of Palestine (PDF), avoided attacks on enemy civilians on the theory that class struggle, not simply nationalism, was their cause.[12] Nevertheless, by 1974 the PDF had been stymied by the failure of other methods of combat and was losing ground politically to the less inhibited PFLP. In that year, PDF guerrillas mounted an attack on the Israeli village of Ma'alot, seizing the schoolhouse and, after an attack by the Israeli army, killing twenty-one hostages, all schoolchildren. This action signified the practical conversion of Hawatameh's organization from Marxism to conventional nationalism. Class distinctions are clearly as irrelevant to Palestinians who attack school buses and airports as they are to Catholic and Protestant militants who bomb each other's pubs in Northern Ireland; Druses and Christians who destroy each other's villages in Lebanon; or Hindus, Sikhs, and Moslems who slaughter each other in India.

Now, it is fundamental to Marxism that communal warfare is not social revolution. Lenin made it clear that while Marxists should fight for the liberation of oppressed nationalities, their primary task is to overthrow capitalist rule in both the colonized and the advanced nations, and to build socialist states. For them, there is no such thing as an "enemy people." Lenin wrote:

The Socialists of the oppressed nations must particularly fight for and maintain complete, absolute unity (also organizational) between the workers of the oppressed nation and the workers of the oppressing nation. Without such unity it will be impossible to maintain an independent proletarian policy and class solidarity with the

proletariat of other countries in the face of all the subterfuge, treach-
ery, and trickery of the bourgeoisie; for the bourgeoisie of the oppressed nations always converts the slogan of national liberation
into a means for deceiving the workers.[13]

Again and again, the originator of the Marxist theory of imperialism warned against "the attempt to paint the bourgeois-
democratic liberation trends in the backward countries in communist colors," demanding that the fight for national
self-determination be consistently "subordinated" to the struggle for social revolution.[14] (Interestingly, he singled out "the
need to combat Pan-Islamism and similar trends which strive to
combine the liberation movement against European and American imperialism with an attempt to strengthen the positions of
the khans, landlords, mullahs, etc.") According to Lenin, Communists should support national liberation movements "only
when they are genuinely revolutionary."[15]

Clearly, attacks on civilians defined as enemy simply because
they belong to a particular national, racial, or ethnic group have
as little to do with social revolution as did the Nazis' slaughter
of people belonging to what Nazis deemed inferior races.
Nevertheless, by portraying their particular national or ethnic
struggle as part of a worldwide class conflict, ultranationalist
groups continue to attract young intellectuals with an inclina-
tion toward social radicalism. It is important to see how this is
done. How does one convince a student like Kozo Okamoto of
the Japanese Red Army that, in killing tourists and Israelis at
Lod Airport, he is a Marxist advancing the cause of world
revolution? The proof generally goes something like this: as
Lenin taught, capitalism is now in its most advanced and destructive stage. This is the era of imperialism, in which finance
capital wielded by the great industrial powers dominates the
world market. This force divides the world into oppressor and
oppressed nations, a cleavage that duplicates on a global scale
the distinction within each nation between the bourgeoisie and
proletariat. Class conflict in the oppressor states, however, is

mitigated or even eliminated by imperialist superprofits. Corrupted by creature comforts, the workers in these nations collaborate with their rulers in exploiting the peoples of the Third World. At the same time, class conflict in the oppressed nations is mitigated or even eliminated by common victimization. The bourgeoisie of these countries (including oil magnates, landlords, and priests) may act in an "objectively" revolutionary manner by resisting imperialist domination.

Hence, the major premise of Marxist doctrine—that the owning and working classes of every nation are two irreconcilably opposed forces headed for ultimate collision—disappears. Class conflict *within* nations is replaced by war *between* oppressed and oppressor states; to be an uncompromising Third World nationalist is therefore to be a social revolutionist. Assuming that Israel, a client of the United States, is an oppressor nation, Okamoto arrives at the conclusion that killing Israelis and their visitors on orders of the PFLP advances the cause of world revolution.[16]

Why do Okamoto and his comrades not remain in Japan and liberate the Japanese from capitalist rule? Because the action is elsewhere, where the masses are awakening to the need for armed struggle. Implicitly, they accept the pessimistic conclusion, which is shared by conservative thinkers and New Left ideologues alike, that working people in the advanced industrial nations have become hopelessly conservative. Except for persecuted minorities and declassed intellectuals, Western workers are written off as captives of the consumer culture—as labor aristocrats who can be counted on to side with the forces of order in any struggle for serious social change. This is not a variant of communism that transposes class struggle to the world stage; it is the demolition of Marxism. For if the business class and the business state can solve their problems in the industrial centers—if they can avoid major wars and economic crises, turn an entire population of working people into a prosperous labor aristocracy, and permit these same workers to exercise democratic rights—there is nothing to stop them from doing the same thing, in time, on a world scale. In 1917, Lenin insisted, on the contrary, that imperialism was not a panacea for the bourgeoisie in the advanced countries, it was a poison. The creation of a privileged labor aristocracy is a temporary phenomenon:

> The receipt of high monopoly profits by the capitalists in one of the numerous branches of industry, in one of numerous countries, etc., makes it possible for them to corrupt certain sections of the working class, *and for a time* a fairly considerable minority, and win them to the side of the bourgeoisie of a given industry or nation against all others.[17]

But the overall tendency of imperialism is to intensify those inequalities between industrial states that are a primary cause of war, and those between classes that are the primary cause of revolution.

Unlike the ultranationalists who invoke his name, Lenin insisted that imperialism ends by impoverishing workers in the so-called rich nations. Because capitalists cannot stop competing for control of the world market, their nations' fortunes rapidly wax and wane. Those occupying a position as dominant as, say, that of the United States during the 1950s may appear to have overcome their internal contradictions by enriching their workers at the rest of the world's expense. The period of respite, however, is short-lived, for while the cost of maintaining and extending the empire grows, new competitors arise and old industrial plants decay. "On the whole," said Lenin,

> capitalism is growing far more rapidly than before. But this growth is not only becoming more and more uneven in general; *its unevenness also manifests itself in the decay of the countries which are richest in capital (such as England).* [18]

As a result, there is no basis on which to create a permanent labor aristocracy; problems that workers in the advanced countries had thought forever solved reappear in virulent form as deindustrialization occurs. Empirically, seeing what has become

of British, French, and North American labor in the basic industries, this seems fairly persuasive. But, as a modern commentator reminds us, Lenin's definition of the labor aristocracy as a
temporary minority of the workers is "not an empirical estimate
but a basic sociological proposition."

> The New Left/Third Worldist notion that the proletariat in the
> imperialist centers is a labor aristocracy in relation to the impover-
> ished colonial masses denies that the European and North American
> working class is centrally defined by its *exploitation* at the hands of
> "its" bourgeoisie. It is methodologically similar to the argument of
> apologists for apartheid in South Africa that black workers in that
> country are better off than those in the rest of Africa.[19]

The rich nation/poor nation dichotomy, pushed to the point
of eliminating serious class conflict in the rich nations, is not
Marxist in any sense of the word, but populist. (It was Bakunin,
not Marx, who prophesied a war of the poor nations against the
rich.) The hostility of left-nationalist groups to class struggle,
as opposed to communal warfare, is most clearly demonstrated
when, in practice, they collaborate actively with their bourgeoi-
sies in attacking the workers and farmers of some alleged
enemy nation. Saudi money helps finance the PLO, Syrian
money the PFLP, and North American money the IRA. What
sort of socialism do such sponsors think they are helping to
create? For their own reasons, the Soviets also support a variety
of self-proclaimed national liberation organizations, knowing
full well that such movements are not socially revolutionary
and even intervening on occasion to keep these organizations
from going too far in the direction of class struggle.[20] Ever since
Joseph Stalin made Chiang Kai-shek a member of the Comin-
tern, the official justification for this sort of thing has been the
two-stage theory: the oppressed nations must experience a nationalist revolution before they can hope to have a social one.[21]
The real justification nowadays is simpler. The Soviet Union,
like the United States, supports violent movements that it believes will further its own national interests. And, like the

United States, its expectations in this regard are frequently disappointed.

From the nineteenth century to the present, ultranationalist terrorism has primarily been a response of the intelligentsia to imperialism, which is viewed both as personal insult and as despoiler of the national honor. It is not difficult to understand the rage and humiliation experienced by educated youths who are compelled to witness the daily effects of foreign domination on their nations and their national cultures. Nor is it hard to appreciate the sources of the fanaticism that impels some of them to mount near-suicidal attacks against superior forces. Recall that John Wilkes Booth shot Abraham Lincoln not to save the defeated South but to satisfy its honor. How fanatical might you or I become if our family home were bulldozed by command of some foreign occupation authority, or if our national language and customs became those of a despised ethnic group? How angry might we be when those who resisted the process of denationalization disappeared into military prisons? And how ashamed might we feel, not just because of defeat and occupation, but because we had been offered—and perhaps tempted by—the opportunity to collaborate with the occupier? Among the victims of imperialism, particularly the intellectuals, anger fuses with a passionate desire to cleanse the nation (and oneself) of shameful foreign influence. It is no exaggeration to suggest that the craving for national and personal redemption is the psychological taproot of nationalist terrorism.

Whatever the terrorist's ideological preference, the logic of the two-stage struggle is deeply conservative. Eventually, this logic bends ideology to its purpose; in time, left-nationalists making war in small groups against an alien authority tend to become centrist or even right-wing nationalists. This does not mean, however, that they become impotent. On the contrary, discarding socially revolutionary goals and demands frequently gains them powerful allies, rich sponsors, and an established position in the nationalist coalition (that is, the government-to-be). At a certain point, they may even cease to be terrorists, in the sense that we use the word; from practitioners of small-group violence, some nationalists have become the leaders of mass struggles. This gives others hope, with the result that although none of the nationalist groups currently active in Europe, the Middle East, or central Asia has come close to "liberating" its territory, virtually all have survived into the mid-1980s. (Note also that the only terrorist groups in the United States to have shown any staying power over the past decade are organizations of Puerto Rican and Cuban nationalists—the FALN and Omega 7.)[22] The price of this survival is the gradual abandonment of the Red for the Black. It is acceptance of one's nation, rather than one's class, as the primary unit of politics.

So powerful is the practical appeal of nationalist politics that even the anarcho-communists, who have sworn to make war on their own ruling classes, are strongly affected by it. The Red Brigade's shift from kidnapping businesspeople and kneecapping prosecutorial officials to attacking NATO bases and U.S. military personnel has now been followed by the RAF, Direct Action, the Fighting Communist Cells, and other Red terrorist groups from Portugal to Greece. Clearly, this shift is not total; U.S. bases have always been acceptable targets, and local magnates are still fair game. But more and more frequently, even the local objects of terrorist attention are defense ministry officials, weapons manufacturers, and other symbols of collaboration with the Americans.[23] What factors are producing this new wave of anti-American, anti-NATO attacks? At first, bombing U.S. officers' clubs and expropriating the contents of NATO arsenals seemed merely a part of the anarcho-communists' general program. In the early 1980s, however, their increasing tendency to strike foreign targets appeared to be linked to their domestic organizational weakness (for example, the capture of their original leaders). More recently, U.S. Defense Department officials have characterized the attacks as "a frustrated reaction to the decline of mass protest and civil disobedience once directed against NATO's missile deployment plans."[24] Each of these explanations contains a measure of truth, but each is also missing something: the gravitational pull of nationalism.

Early in 1985, a nightclub in Greece frequented by American military personnel was blown up. It was immediately assumed that leftist guerrillas were responsible, but the neofascist National Front took credit for the attack. One week after the nightclub incident, an American military base in West Germany was bombed—not by the RAF, but by one of the numerous neo-Nazi groups now proliferating in that country.[25] This indicates that American installations in Europe (and other symbols of foreign domination) have been targeted for attack by far-Right terrorists as well as by purported leftists, and for obvious reasons: a wave of nationalism is sweeping the continent, creating both an audience for antiforeign political theater and sources of new urban guerrilla recruits. Consider the protest movement triggered by the emplacement of American missiles in the NATO nations—a movement not nearly as intense as that of the 1960s, but one that appealed to elements of all classes, particularly the middle-class intelligentsia. On the one hand, it revived the dream of an independent European confederation, nuclear-free and neutralist, and capable of challenging both of the current superpowers for world economic supremacy. On the other hand, this movement tapped a hotter, more particularistic and traditional vein of nationalism which runs just below the surface of polite Euronationalism. In West Germany, for example, the Green party (now the Federal Republic's third largest parliamentary party) is considered leftist because it favors nuclear disarmament and usually votes with the Social Democrats; but the Greens also advocate German reunification and cultural renewal, "post-parliamentary politics," and a cult of nature, complete with athletic clubs and organized hikes in the Bavarian Alps.[26] Meanwhile, the overt nationalists of the far Right are flourishing as they have not done since the 1930s. In France, the xenophobic, racist National Front took 10 percent of the vote in the 1986 national elections—another indication of how the political wind is blowing in western Europe.

When anarcho-communist guerrillas attack NATO bases in preference to, say, local business offices, they do so knowing that to a great many of their fellow nationals, NATO means foreign troops on foreign soil, just as the Atlantic Alliance and the Common Market mean domination of native economies by foreign capital. To the French, NATO means the Germans; to the Belgians, it means the French; and to everyone, it means the Americans, whose forty-year "occupation" of Europe is as displeasing to rightist nationalists as to leftists. Furthermore, whatever their professed political orientations, those who attack NATO children's schools or tourist facilities frequented by foreign civilians exhibit the Lod Airport mentality that rejects all class distinctions in favor of an implicitly racist nationalism. At the present writing, Lod-style attacks on foreign tourists have not yet been mounted by European terrorists, and one hopes that they will not be attempted. Nevertheless, in the near future they seem likely to occur. Bit by bit, the Red guerrillas' accommodation to nationalism is erasing distinctions between them and the xenophobic Right. And the far Right, as we shall soon see, is the most effective practitioner of nationalist terrorism.

Chapter 8

Far-Right Terrorism in the 1980s

THE FIRST nationalist terrorists to play a recognizably modern role were the Spanish guerrillas who rose up in the early 1800s in the name of the Spanish monarchy to combat the imperialism of Napoleon.[1] Ever since, imperialism, the nationalism-in-practice of great powers, has generated terrorism, the nationalism-in-practice of the weak. Naturally, those representing established nations refuse to recognize any kinship between themselves and the "bandits," "criminals," and "revolutionaries" attempting to bomb and hijack their way to respectable statehood; but despite all denials, the kinship exists. It was

Menachem Begin, a rightist nationalist, who remarked that "a fighting underground is a veritable state in miniature: a state at war."[2] And it remains true that, ideological aims aside, the nationalist guerrillas' practical model is the wartime national state—the ethnic nation in arms.

Clearly, there are certain similarities in practice between terrorists at opposite ends of the ideological spectrum—for example, anarcho-communists and neofascists. Their reasons for preferring violent action to words are analogous; their targets are in some cases identical; on occasion they have trained together; and as previously noted, terrorists with leftist sympathies tend to shift more or less unconsciously to the right during the course of a long, violent campaign. The impression of similarity is further strengthened when ideologically opposed groups attempt to manipulate each other, especially when they take credit for the same attack. Thus, the French European Nationalist Fascists (FNE) claimed responsibility for the 1980 bombing of a Paris synagogue, although many believe the act was perpetrated by Palestinian ultras.[3] Similarly, debate still rages over whether the would-be papal assassin, Ahmet Ali Agça, acted at the behest of his own neofascist group, the Turkish Grey Wolves, or on orders of the Bulgarian Communists.[4] Given this confusion—not to mention the strangeness of all terrorism from a moderate perspective—it is not surprising that many observers consider far Right and far Left terrorists to be brothers under the skin. Viewed from the center, all extremes seem more or less identical; but we would be making a serious mistake if we took this illusion literally.

How do Red and Black terrorists differ? To begin with, they ordinarily occupy fundamentally different positions in relation to state power. Both may work to overthrow the established regime and the legal institutions that legitimize it, but rightist guerrillas often have allies or sponsors where the leftists do not: in the police, armed forces, and state security agencies, as well as among ultraconservative businesspeople and landowners. These connections are most obvious in cases of rightist vigilantism, where urban guerrilla groups are closely related to or merged with secret organizations in the armed forces, and are covertly supported by the wealthy backers of large political parties.

The most recent examples of this sort of organization, the death squads of El Salvador and Guatemala, follow the same path trodden earlier by Argentina's Anti-Communist Alliance, the Greek rightist terrorists of the 1960s, and by the Algerian Secret Army Organization (OAS), the secret army of the French *colons*.[5] Typically, such groups specialize in assassination. Their most intense violence is aimed at liberal politicians (or soft conservatives), labor and farm organizers, leftist intellectuals and priests, Communists, Jews, foreigners, and others deemed to be alien influences or enemies of the traditional nation. Typically, too, their membership is drawn from the lower classes (in particular, from the ranks of the lumpenproletariat), while their leaders tend to be of the upper or upper-middle class.[6] Students are not absent from such movements, but rightist vigilantism is decidedly not the violence of the intelligentsia; in fact, intellectuals are frequently its favorite target!

This type of violence is really a form of *state* terrorism, since the vigilantes represent either an authoritarian regime in power or dissident elements within the ruling class and the armed forces. This helps to explain their peculiar destructiveness: since they aim to destroy mass organizations like labor unions and peasant associations, the vigilantes of the far Right kill large numbers of "traitors," using torture and similar methods designed to discourage others from following their lead. Furthermore, while leftist guerrillas usually aim their fire at office-holders, soldiers, police, industrialists, and collaborators within their own ranks, the rightists target social groups based on racial, ethnic, or religious identity. Finally, the far-Right fighters are frequently protected by the state's internal security forces if, indeed, they are not members of those forces. As a result, they may not be required to take desperate risks. Their vigilante activities may thus become a sort of part-time job, lasting a good deal longer than most terrorist careers of the Left.[7]

Admittedly, at this point we are comparing apples and oranges: the activities of vigilantes with access to state power are one thing, and those of terrorist outsiders are another. Nevertheless, even when one turns from Central American death squads to neofascist groups in the industrialized nations, certain key differentiations persist. This is primarily because far-Right terrorists are seldom complete outsiders even in the most democratic capitalist states. In Italy, for example, where neofascist groups have been proliferating since the mid-1970s, organizations like the Black Order and the Armed Revolutionary Nucleus (NAR) have been convincingly linked to the Italian Social Movement (MSI)—a large neofascist party with a number of powerful backers.[8] The Red groups, in contrast, have not been assisted by any party of comparable size or strength—and certainly not by the Italian Communist party, perhaps their most implacable enemy. Similarly, the terrorists of the European Right have generally been treated far more gently by internal security forces than have those of the Left. According to journalist Thomas Sheehan, for example,

In 1976 and again in 1978, judges in Rome, Turin, and Milan fell over each other in their haste to absolve 196 neo-fascists of crimes ranging from murdering a policeman to "reconstituting Fascism." . . . When it comes to fascist terrorism, Italian authorities seem to be a bit blind in the right eye.[9]

Sheehan also estimates that approximately one-third of the members of FNE, the French fascist group, are police officers.[10] In the United States, the overlap between the KKK and local police forces is a matter of public record, not only in the South but in cities like Chicago and Los Angeles, while occasional intimate cooperation between the Klan and the FBI (as well as between Omega 7 and the CIA) is equally well documented.[11] Of course, the extent to which far-Right terrorists in the West enjoy state protection should not be exaggerated. In the United States, for example, the FBI has undertaken a serious campaign against members of the Aryan Brotherhood and the

Order, organizations of the rural white lumpenproletariat dedicated to assassinating blacks and Jews.[12] Still, to assume an identity of extremes, with government acting as a neutral policeman, obscures that fact that right-wing extremism sometimes proves very useful to those in power, while left-wing extremism usually does not. Ever since the czar's secret police created the Black Hundreds to stir up anti-Jewish pogroms, this usefulness has been based in part on the Black terrorists' ability to focus mass anger on minority group scapegoats, and in part on their willingness to undertake covert action on behalf of the state. (Recall that the team of covert operatives used by President Nixon's campaign organization to burglarize the Democrats' Watergate office included several right-wing Cubans who originally had been recruited by the CIA to attack Cuba.[13]) Particularly because the far Right's influence is strongest on the level of local law-enforcement agencies, the result is a disparity of treatment as between Black and Red terrorists. Consider the 1979 slaying of five members and associates of the Communist Workers party by the KKK and neo-Nazis at an anti-Klan rally in Greensboro, North Carolina.[14] It is difficult to imagine that if their roles had been reversed, the communists would have been acquitted, as the fascists were, of both murder and conspiracy to violate their victims' civil rights.

It is in Europe that the impression of Red-Black similarity is strongest. There, neofascist groups attract a greater number of students and intellectuals than they do in the United States (although not nearly so many as do the anarcho-communists). The French, German, and Italian fascists have professorial as well as military leaders. They detest "bourgeois commercialism," they aim to destroy the liberal state, and they want to drive Americans out of Europe. All of these goals are shared by the left-terrorists, as revealed most dramatically early in 1985, when attacks on American military installations in Germany were mounted independently by anarcho-communist and neo-Nazi groups. But as a general rule, it is the choice of targets that most clearly distinguishes right-wing from left-wing urban guerrillas. In Italy, these have included antifascist rallies, union meetings, theaters, express trains, city halls, and railroad stations—all crowded with people at the time of the attack.[15] In Germany, neo-Nazis bombed the Munich Oktoberfest and several shelters housing foreign guest workers, while their French counterparts attacked synagogues, foreign workers' camps, and places frequented by North African immigrants. Considering this evidence, terrorism expert Bruce Hoffman concludes:

> Left-wing terrorist tactics are like those of sharpshooters who carefully pick specific victims, while right-wing tactics are more like those of bombing aircraft, which aim at larger numbers of people but still are not quite indiscriminate in their targets. Both sides seek targets that are lucrative from their point of view—left-wing terrorists kill a Moro or a Schleyer, while right-wing terrorists bomb a synagogue or a train station. The difference is that the right-wing terrorist incidents result in larger numbers of victims.[16]

In one sense, Hoffman's comparison seems accurate enough, although exaggerated. Leftist terrorists who bomb department stores, as a group called Action Christian Klar (Klar being an imprisoned RAF leader) did in Dortmund, West Germany, in March, 1985, can hardly be termed "sharpshooters!"[17] But, unlike modern neofascists and old-time anarchists who hurled bombs into bourgeois cafés, the anarcho-communists usually avoid attacking massed groups of civilians. This is not because they are necessarily more scrupulous than the far-Right terrorists, but because they want to provoke a fight between the masses and the state, while the far Right wants the masses to attack "alien elements" in their midst. Neofascist violence is certainly not indiscriminate; its targets are carefully chosen. But since they are so often chosen on the basis of race, religion, nationality, or ideology, the targets are quite frequently enemy communities or mass groups. The Black Order's devastating attack on the Bologna railroad terminal was aimed not only at Bologna's Communist government but at its Communist voters. Mass targeting is typical of rightist nationalist terrorism, but it is also typical of all terrorists who wage an essentially communal war, whether their political labels read Left, Right, or Center.

Nationalist terrorism can be highly effective when an entire community defining itself on the basis of race, religion, or nationality is aroused to rectify and avenge past wrongs. While right-nationalist guerrillas remain on the fringes of European politics, they have moved onto center stage in the Middle East and Asia, where religious fundamentalism expresses widely-felt longings for national redemption and national power, self-purification and revenge. Sunni Moslem zealots, operating under the loosely-structured umbrella of the Moslem Brotherhood, have attacked the Grand Mosque in Mecca, assassinated Prime Minister Anwar al-Sadat of Egypt, waged communal war in Lebanon, and threatened numerous Arab governments deemed secular and corrupt.[18] The Lebanese Hezbollah and smaller Shiite factions using the name Islamic Jihad blew up the U.S. Marine base at Beirut Airport and the American and French embassies in Lebanon and Kuwait, and hijacked a TWA airliner, holding the passengers hostage for the release of coreligionists imprisoned in Israel.[19] Sikh extremists, retaliating for an army assault on their Punjab headquarters, killed Indian Prime Minister Indira Gandhi and blew an Air India passenger plane out of the sky, causing more than three hundred deaths.[20] Western governments reacted to these events with baffled rage, as if the phenomenon were mysterious and unprecedented. Criticism from what might be called the "anthropological school" portrayed the terrorists (especially the Shiites) as weird fanatics intoxicated by alien passions for martyrdom and destruction. ("Barbaric" and "uncivilized" were President Reagan's favorite adjectives in the weeks following the 1985 hijacking of TWA flight 847.) Yet the structure of this violence was not at all unfamiliar.

Fundamentalist terrorism is, to begin with, fundamentally nationalist. In some cases, this is obvious: the Sikh militants aim to convert India's Punjab into an independent Sikh nation, just as the ultraorthodox Gush Emunim movement in Israel hopes to annex that nation's occupied territories. In other cases, however, the violent movement seems more religious than political and more international than nationalist. Indeed, some Western observers would like to replace the Red network theory of terrorism, which is obviously inapplicable to most fundamentalist violence, with an Iranian, Syrian, or Libyan network theory.[21] But the evidence strongly suggests that Shiite terrorism, like that of the Moslem Brotherhood, is unusually decentralized. Not only is there little Iranian control over the activities of, say, the Islamic Jihad in Lebanon, there is virtually no Lebanese control. The relationship of the Hezbollah organization to Nabih Berri's Amal militia seems roughly analogous to the relationship of the IRA Provisionals to the Official IRA, while the Islamic Jihad stands in the shoes, so to speak, of the Irish Liberation Army. Fundamentalist terrorism is organized in the Moslem world on a national basis, with volatile extremist groups standing on the fringes of nationalist coalitions, just as they do in the West.

Of course, each fundamentalist group wants its native country to be governed by sacred law. As the history of Roman Catholicism demonstrates, however, a transnational religious ideology can be perfectly consistent with the most intense right-wing nationalism. Not only do assorted Islamic fundamentalists differ from nation to nation about the proper definition of Islamic law, they generally refuse to challenge either the existing structure of nation-states or the dominant economic interests in any state, so long as these are native. In Iran, businesspeople no longer have martinis with their lunches; this corrupt Western practice has been forbidden. But they still have business lunches, as business is excepted from the category of corrupt Western practice. In Lebanon, Shiite fighters die with the name of Allah on their lips and visions of the Heavenly Garden in their minds (in some cases, no doubt), but what they are fighting for is the liberation of Lebanon from foreign occupation and Shiite hegemony in a reborn nation. Similarly, the Moslem Brotherhood in Egypt assassinated Sadat—an act deemed just and inevitable by Khaddafi of Libya—to avenge his

Camp David "betrayal." But the Egyptian fundamentalists' patriotic goal—a pure, powerful Egypt that is dominant in the Arab world—puts them on a collision course with Khaddafi.

It is not so much false as superficial to describe fundamentalist fighters as motivated by a mad desire for martyrdom, by slavish obedience to religious leaders, or by a barbaric lust for revenge. They *are* religious fanatics, but religious ideology is the medium by which they express political convictions, including their hatred of Western domination, their dreams of national redemption, and their social conservatism. (Similarly, the Orthodox far Right in Israel claims biblical authority for a policy of establishing all-Jewish settlements on the West Bank, while other parties justify the same policy on secular grounds.) Furthermore, this description of fundamentalists is essentially racist, since it assumes that "civilized" Westerners, when aroused, do not seek martyrdom, follow orders blindly, or lust for revenge. In the United States, military martyrs are given the Congressional Medal of Honor posthumously, provided that their martyrdom was glorious enough. And anyone who thinks that following orders and taking one's just revenge are not Western virtues should take the time to view a representative sample of Hollywood war movies produced between 1942 and 1945, or the more recent productions of actor Sylvester Stallone.

Even the absorption of politics into religion is not as alien to Western traditions as some commentators would have us think. In seventeenth-century England, theology fused with politics to produce the great upheaval known as the English Revolution.[22] But it is true that English Puritanism was socially revolutionary, pitting the middle classes against the landed aristocracy and the established church, while Moslem fundamentalism is clearly reactionary, representing the interests of local *mullahs*, landowners, and businesspeople against those of foreign business, poor peasants, and urban workers.[23] Attempting to base a modern political system on sixth-century Islamic law may be quixotic, but it is not socially neutral, as liberals and leftists have discovered to their sorrow in Iran. What fundamentalist leaders offer their lower-class followers is the ideal of membership in a nation that is politically independent, morally pure, socially orderly, and feared by others—a nation like a family in which each member knows his or her place, and in which traditional relationships of domination and subservience are maintained under the paternal guidance of the priesthood.[24]

This conservative collectivism is analogous to what Europeans of the 1930s called "clerical fascism": a form of far-Right nationalism that has great attraction for both the very rich and the very poor in unevenly developed nations long dominated by foreigners. Its leading representative in the West today is Aleksandr Solzhenitsyn, who dreams of a Russian counterrevolution led by fundamentalists of the Orthodox Church in the name of traditional authority and the "Russian spirit."[25] It is typical of this philosophy to link ultraorthodoxy in religion with ethnic nationalism in politics—an unhealthy brew, particularly for nonbelievers, members of ethnic minorities, and women. Again, the notion that such ideas are un-Western flies in the face of historical experience. Clerical fascism was a powerful movement in eastern Europe and the Baltic states during the inter-world war period, and its exponents (their cause advanced by terrorism) wielded power briefly in both Poland and Hungary.[26] Of course, it was not until the Iranian Revolution that a postwar government fell under the control of militant fundamentalists; far-Right nationalism is now a more powerful force in the Arab world than it is in Europe.

Interestingly, both Western conservatives (including the current American government) and Arab commentators tend to downplay or ignore the right-wing political character of Moslem fundamentalism. For the Americans, Shiite terrorism represents a competing nationalism—and an anti-Christian one at that!—that threatens American interests in the Arab world. Following Israel's 1982 invasion of Lebanon, a host of pundits and politicians branded all acts of armed resistance to the Israeli occupation terrorist, thus ignoring the (potentially mortal) distinction between left-leaning Shiites like Nabih Berri and his challengers on the Right. Arab commentators, approaching the problem from a secular nationalist perspective, make a similar, although opposite mistake. For them, fundamentalist terrorism is simply part of a legitimate movement of national liberation. Thus, Hisham Melhem, a Lebanese journalist, writes:

> That the struggle against Israeli occupation in southern Lebanon has among its dimensions a religious one is not surprising, nor should this be disturbing if viewed in its historical context. History clearly shows that when a colonized or occupied society fights for independence and freedom, it uses in its struggle every resource in its national culture.[27]

On the one hand, Melhem accurately recognizes that Shiite attacks on Israeli occupation troops were part of a mass movement of resistance, not acts of isolated terrorism. He is also correct in noting that major components of the Lebanese resistance "are unequivocally committed to [a] nationalist agenda, not to the establishment of an Islamic utopia."[28] On the other hand, he makes exactly the same assumption about the fundamentalists that the Iranian left-nationalists of the Mujhadeen movement made about the Ayatollah Khomeini before he began executing them. That is, Melhem considers them mere nationalists who are ultimately capable of being reasoned with or controlled by the moderates.

The seriousness of this error is underscored by Melhem's critique of contrasting Western attitudes toward "political Islam" in Lebanon and in Afghanistan:

> Because Islamic mobilization in Afghanistan is seen by the West as essentially anti-communist and serves Western strategic interests, political Islam in that context is much lauded and supported materially and politically. However, when political groups draw on Islamic concepts and heritage to defend their beleaguered societies against Israeli occupation, as is the case in Lebanon, political Islam in that context is much maligned, and reduced in one fell swoop to political atavism, irrationalism and backwardness.[29]

What confusion! For while it is certainly true that American policy toward national liberation movements is inconsistent, short-sighted, and crudely imperialist, it is no libel to call the Afghan fundamentalists atavistic, irrational, or backward. What else would one call a movement whose feudalist platform includes destroying secular schools, undoing land reform, restoring the "bride price," and returning women to the veil?[30] It is essential to take ideology more seriously than this, and to understand that far-Right nationalists may often be as reactionary as they seem.

I argued earlier that the leftism of leftist terrorists is consistently undermined by the exigencies of nationalist struggle, with the result that, over time, they tend to drift politically to the Right. I conclude this discussion by noting that no such contradiction troubles the guerrillas of the far Right. They begin where other terrorists frequently end: embracing elitist violence in the name of a frankly elitist cause. One of the advantages enjoyed by rightist nationalist fighters in their competition with opponents in the movement is the relative consistency of their theory with their practice. (Another, of course, is their access to private wealth.) Protracted armed struggle that bypasses the masses, then traumatizes them, and finally induces them to accept an order-restoring savior is a rational, albeit somewhat uncertain and difficult, strategy for the ultranationalist elite. The Right would prefer, if possible, to arouse the masses as an ethnic or religious nation (or both) to attack aliens and nonbelievers, community against community, each led by its traditional chiefs.

Terrorism is *not* an effective method of mobilizing the lower classes to make social revolution. If the have-nots are passive, terrorism will not activate them; and if they are aroused, as Lenin said, that is the time to organize a revolution rather than an assassination (see chapter 12). But terrorism *can* be an effective method of inflaming communal strife—of pushing races, religious groups, or nations toward war. Examples of this dynamic are legion. The assassination of socialist leader Jean Jaurès by French right-nationalists removed a major obstacle to the mobilization of French workers for World War I, while a more massive campaign by Japanese right-terrorists prepared that nation for military rule and the next world war.[31] In Palestine, the Irgun and Lehi (Stern Gang) organizations helped provoke communal struggle by blowing up British headquarters at the King David Hotel in Jerusalem and by assassinating United Nations mediator Count Folke Bernadotte, while extremists in the Palestinian camp were liquidating compromisers like the Jordanian leader Prince Abdullah.[32] Hindu and Moslem provocateurs attacked each other's communities to sabotage Mohandas Gandhi's plan for a united India, and a Hindu fundamentalist (it could as well have been a Moslem) ended the Mahatma's life.[33]

Of course, small-group violence does not create a sense of hostile nationhood any more than it generates class-consciousness. It merely accelerates an existing motion. The true source of this motion, I think, is the imperialist nation-state, which produces nationalist terrorism by way of both opposition and imitation. A world dominated by such states stands perpetually poised on the brink of communal war. The inhabitants of well-established nations are prepared to slaughter enemy nationals on command; world war is communal war writ large. Ethnic and religious communities in the weaker nations are prepared to slaughter each other to achieve national hegemony or separation. Communal war is world war in miniature. Fanon observed that colonized natives do not merely want to kill the colonizer; they want to *be* the colonizer.[34] Of the colonizers, one might say: they dare not look the terrorist in the face for fear of recognizing in his disfigurement their own image.

PART IV

TERRORISM
AND SOCIAL
REVOLUTION

Chapter 9

Rival Prophets:

Bakunin and Marx

IN 1872, Karl Marx and his supporters in the first International Workingmen's Association expelled the anarchist leader, Mikhail Bakunin, from the International. The major charge against Bakunin was that he had created a "secret society" within the organization—and so he had, for Bakunin could no more live without conspiracy than Marx could live without debate. An aristocrat by birth, Bakunin employed his considerable skills as an anarchist theorist, philosopher of national liberation, and plotter of insurrections to challenge the communists for control of the European workers' movement. In the work of Bakunin and, even more, in that of his young colleague Sergey Nechayev, we discover the prototype of modern terrorism—a rationale and mindset that are clearly recognizable more than a century later. And in the great controversy between Marx and the anarchists—a debate which, in some respects, continues still—lies the origin of Marxism's quarrel with the philosophy of the bomb.

Bakunin has rightly been called "the prophet of primitive rebellion, of the conspiratorial revolutionary party, of terrorist amoralism, of guerrilla insurrectionism, of revolutionary dictatorship, and of the emergence of a new ruling class that would impose its will on the people and rob them of their freedom."[1] The anarchist firebrand disdained the lengthy debates and limited mutual-aid activities of the first International. For him, the disputes between rival schools represented in that organization were a poor substitute for "action"—that is, organizing rebellions. Actually, Bakunin was less a terrorist in the modern sense of the word than an old-style insurrectionist. He hoped to seize power quickly with a group of elite conspirators, and unleash a mass revolt against property and authority from the base provided by such a *coup d'état.*[2] His method was to turn up in a city or rural district during a period of civil disorder and work with rebels of various persuasions to convert spontaneous rioting into this sort of revolution. From Vienna and Warsaw to Naples and Lyons he plied his insurrectionary trade, spending a great deal of time in prison as a result. Critics noted that Bakunin's revolutionary fervor never flagged, his plotting never ceased, and his rebellions never succeeded. An absurd figure in some respects, he nonetheless incarnated a new type of political personality equally hostile to the values and institutions of capitalism and to those of scientific socialism—the revolutionary mystic, soon to become a revolutionary terrorist.

In the second quarter of the nineteenth century, one did not need to be a mystic to believe in revolution; expectations of an imminent social upheaval were widely shared. The industrial revolution had destabilized European society to the extent that few governments on the Continent felt themselves truly secure. With new groups clamoring for recognition and older elites resisting displacement, the potential for civil violence was very high. Although Europe's conservative monarchs managed to avoid major wars, internal revolt flared virtually everywhere, and a gifted agitator could place himself without much difficulty at the head of an urban riot or rural uprising. To Bakunin, every local rebellion, whether led by disgruntled aristocrats, liberal businesspeople, urban artisans, or peasants, was part of a growing wave of antistate violence that promised to liberate humanity from its three great curses: government, property, and religion.[3] Since the state seemed to him the primary source of oppression, the destabilization of government at every level was to be welcomed and promoted. Bakunin and his comrades dreamed of a great uprising of the masses—defined as the urban poor in the West and the peasants of eastern and southern Europe—that would destroy the state system and immediately usher in a new age of voluntary cooperation and freedom. In his apocalyptic vision, violence was to sweep away the old order like an irresistible flood, leaving the common folk, for the first time, in control of their own destiny.

Immediately recognizable in this revolutionary anarchism are certain themes that later became associated with terrorism. Rather than looking to the workers of the industrial nations as the chief engine of radical change, the anarchists put their faith in the most downtrodden and outcast sectors of the population: the peasants and the criminal element. ("We shall ally ourselves," wrote Nechayev, "with the world of the intrepid brigands, who are the only true revolutionaries in Russia."[4]) These anarchists were more at home in the "savage" East than in the "civilized" West, and more successful as organizers in Spain and Italy than in Germany or France. Moreover, in their eyes the distinction between political and military activity was insubstantial. Violence, they thought, does not merely open the road to the good society by creating a more democratic state; it *produces* the good society directly by annihilating the state. The line between destruction and creation thus grew faint, for the "all-destroying popular revolution" simultaneously destroys and liberates. Thus, "the urge to destroy is also the creative urge."[5] This connotation of revolution implies that existing oppressive institutions (the state, the church, the banks) are not deeply rooted in society—that they are foreign bodies that can be swept away by violence, leaving healthy, natural social structures (the peasant commune, the urban cooperative) standing. Applied to nations dominated by foreign interests, the concept appears again and again as a justification for nationalist terrorism, which promises to generate immediate justice by ridding the nation of some foreign excrescence.[6]

In Bakunin's thinking, we can trace a transition from insurrectionism, with its emphasis on mass violence, to terrorism, which is the violence of small groups attempting to "represent" the masses. At first, the anarchist's emphasis on the mass uprising seemed to exclude terrorism as a revolutionary strategy:

> Revolutions are not made arbitrarily, nor by individuals, nor even by the most powerful associations. Independently of all will and conspiracy, they are always brought on by the force of circumstance. One can foresee them, sometimes feel them approaching, but never accelerate their explosion.[7]

On the other hand, he saw no inconsistency in proposing the creation of "a powerful but always invisible revolutionary association which will prepare and direct the revolution."[8] According to a friendly witness, Bakunin's basic plan was

> . . . to organize a conspiracy composed of determined men, ready to sacrifice themselves and who would all gather at a given moment; then, at an appointed place, with arms in their hands, they would carry out a revolt. They were to attack the Town Hall first, and next pass to the "liquidation" of the existing regime, that is to say, the confiscation of properties, factories, etc.[9]

After this, the revolutionary association would disband in order to permit self-rule by the people. The promise of abdication was necessary to resolve the contradiction between the conspiracy's elitism—its willingness to act for the masses—and its goal of stateless democracy. This contradiction, in turn, reflected the great social distance separating aristocratic or middle-class radicals like Bakunin from the masses they hoped to liberate.

So long as revolution appeared imminent, terrorism played a minor part in anarchist strategy. The role of the conspiracy, in

Bakunin's thinking, was merely to trigger the great uprising that would sweep all distinctions away; and if the uprising were not far off—if the masses were not sound asleep, but only dozing momentarily—there was no need to contemplate an extended campaign of small-group violence. It was with the *downturn* in revolutionary expectations after 1860 that the sense of separation from the mass clientele became most acute and that terrorist philosophy, in the modern sense, was born. The young Russian populist Nechayev (with whom Bakunin had an onagain, off-again relationship) was among the first to advocate conspiratorial violence as a method of arousing and educating the masses rather than as a direct route to the seizure of power. He offered the classical justification for heroic terrorism: attacks on the state would provoke intense, indiscriminate state repression; repression would deprive the government of legitimacy and radicalize the masses. Terrorism, in other words, was the lever that revolutionary intellectuals could use to move the enormous weight of a passive people.

Nechayev's manifesto, "Catechism of the Revolutionist," thus reflects a pessimism at odds with earlier anarchist expectations, as well as with Marx's enduring faith in the revolutionary potential of the workers. At the same time, it bespeaks a highly developed, if not megalomanic, sense of control over events. If Minister A is assassinated, Minister B will order his troops to attack popular demonstrations, thus radicalizing at least some of their participants. These will attack Minister C, provoking more intense counterattacks and widening the circle of combatants in this internal war. It is clear that to Nechayev, the enemy is not just the ruling class or even the state itself, but tradition's iron grip on the mind of the people. The function of terrorism, therefore, is not to provoke an immediate seizure of state power, but to make a popular uprising possible by demystifying authority. Declares Nechayev:

> Our society has only one aim . . . the total emancipation and happiness of the people, that is, the common laborers. But, convinced that their emancipation and the achievement of this happiness can be

realized only by means of an all-destroying popular revolution, our society will employ all its power and all its resources in order to promote an intensification and an increase in those calamities and evils which must finally exhaust the patience of the people and drive it to a popular uprising.[10]

There is no room here for nonviolent politics; reform is the enemy rather than the ally of revolution. The masses are not to be spoken to, taught, organized, led to the picket lines, or even led to the barricades—they are to be *awakened* by involving them in calamity (that is, by forcing the state to attack them). This requires an organization based on the principle of the closed cell, rigidly controlled from the top, and dedicated solely to destruction. "We have lost all faith in words," says Nechayev. "For us the word is of significance only when the deed is sensed behind it and follows immediately upon it." What does he mean by "deed"?

Real manifestations [are] only a series of actions which destroy something absolutely: a person, a thing, or an attitude which is an obstacle to the liberation of the people.[11]

In practice, this means that the revolutionist must sever all ties with "the civil order and the entire cultured world, with all its laws, proprieties, social conventions and its ethical rules."[12] In particular, the revolutionist must be prepared to assassinate ministers and generals; to rob and, if necessary, kill the rich; to destroy property; to blackmail influential persons; and to compromise or otherwise eliminate pseudorevolutionaries. To the obvious objection that such actions may frighten and antagonize large sectors of the population, Nechayev believes the worse, the better. He therefore opposed the assassination of the czar, preferring to leave him alive as a symbol and a target for popular wrath (a piece of advice not accepted by the young terrorists who blew up Czar Alexander II in 1881).[13]

By associating himself with Nechayev in the late 1860s, Bakunin played into Marx's and Engels's hands. Nechayev's murder of a disciple he considered disloyal (his only terrorist act!) gave the socialist leaders further ammunition in their campaign to discredit Bakunin and expel his followers from the International. In the end, Marx moved the organization's headquarters to New York, effectively killing it in order to prevent the anarchists from using it to further their own purposes.[14] There was no doubt a personal side to this dispute. Marx considered Bakunin an ignorant demagogue, and probably envied his ability to inspire followers with fanatical devotion. Bakunin branded Marx a dictatorial pedant, and very likely envied his analytical power. Each man considered the other a serious threat to the incipient workers' movement. Much more was involved, however, than just a clash of personalities. Beyond conflicting egos, their disagreement reflected a conflict of philosophies that persists even today.

Bakunin was an enthusiast, a romantic intoxicated with the power of the will, a sufferer who identified with all sufferers, an artist who believed in sudden transformations: from effete aristocrat to revolutionary bandit, obsequious peasant to guerrilla warrior, brutal past to shining future. He conceived of revolution as an enormous explosion of lower-class violence produced by bringing together two extremes. The secret society, composed of upper-class conspirators like himself, was to be the spark; and the most downtrodden layers of the population—dispossessed peasants, criminals, and workers fresh from the farm—was to be the tinder. One is always conscious, with Bakunin, of the vast social distance separating this gentrified agitator from his clients at the bottom of the social heap. To overcome this distance, Nechayev said, it was necessary for wealthy radicals to become exiles from the cultured world. More important, it was essential to stop simply thinking and talking—the normal occupation of privileged intellectuals—and start acting.

Violent action plays a critical role in terrorist philosophy because it is seen as the primary method of bridging the gap between leaders and followers, the alienated intellectuals and the oppressed masses. The intellectual who robs a bank or assassinates a government official becomes an outlaw, severing his or her ties with the upper classes and joining his fate to that of the outcasts. He or she ceases to be a mere critic and spectator, a person dominated by words and ideas. Terrorism promises a release from that bondage to abstraction which alienates the thinker from the society of (unthinking) doers. Its principal allure, which frequently outweighs the hope of inflicting serious damage on the state, is the opportunity to stop playing a revolutionary Hamlet and to join the real world of toilers and sufferers—or better yet, to *lead* the oppressed by setting an example of passionate, principled activism.

Intellectuals who conceive of themselves as minds in search of bodies generally imagine the masses to be bodies in search of minds. Violence is essential to mass struggle, they believe, because it enables the oppressed to repudiate the traditional role of silent sufferer and become the makers rather than the objects of history. For Bakunin and his political heirs, therefore, revolutionary violence is not simply an ugly necessity, an instrument the lower classes must use to conquer state power; it is a liberating force, creative in direct proportion to its destructiveness, through which divided individuals and societies may become whole.[15]

The anarchists dreamed of igniting the blaze that would level all distinctions and annihilate the centralized, bureaucratic state; if it failed to materialize quickly, individual heroes and martyrs would keep the flame alight until the people awakened. Their revolution was essentially terrorism writ large. Marx rejected terrorism because he conceived of a different sort of revolution entirely—not a spontaneous, all-destroying wave of underclass violence, but an organized uprising of the urban proletariat. Proletarian revolution, he insisted, had nothing to do with the anarchist fantasy of universal destruction and redemption. The workers of the industrialized nations were not backward, passive creatures lost in dreams of tradition, awed by power, and requiring awakening by terrorists. They were a modern class, awakened continuously and ruthlessly by life in the modern city, by their role in production, and (ironically) by the political weakness of their masters.

The bourgeoisie finds itself involved in a constant battle. At first with the aristocracy; later on, with those portions of the bourgeoisie itself whose interests have become antagonistic to the progress of industry; at all times, with the bourgeoisie of foreign countries. In all these battles it sees itself compelled to appeal to the proletariat, to ask for its help, and thus to drag it into the political arena. The bourgeoisie itself, therefore, supplies the proletariat with its own elements of political and general education.[16]

Politically, that is, business is caught in a vise: it cannot seize and maintain power without opening up politics to mass participation, but politically mobilized workers continually threaten to overstep the bounds of bourgeois legality and to challenge the business class for control of the state. Therefore, while for Bakunin the revolution is an all-destroying explosion of the underclasses, for Marx it is the "old mole"—a series of increasingly serious confrontations between organized workers and owners culminating in the seizure of state power by the proletariat.[17]

This revolution, Marx believes, will be violent because ruling classes do not ordinarily surrender power peacefully; but political violence does not have the same magical properties for Marxists as it does for anarchists. The workers' revolution is not a direct route to utopia. It does not annihilate all authority, but leaves standing an industrial society led by the working class and a state under working-class control. Marx insists that the workers' initial task is not to destroy the apparatus of government but to master it. Industrial abundance equitably distributed, not revolutionary violence per se, will cause coercive institutions to "wither away."[18] Thus, he branded Bakunin's notion of a Slavic peasant revolution "schoolboy's asininity," explaining that,

A radical social revolution is tied to certain historical conditions of economic development; these are its prerequisites. It is therefore only possible where, with capitalist production, the industrial proletariat occupies at least a significant position among the mass of the people.[19]

The operative word here is "radical." Many groups are oppressed; many are revolutionary in a subjective sense; but a revolution that merely communizes poverty is not really radical. Only the proletariat—an oppressed class wedded to industrial expansion—can eliminate material scarcity and inaugurate a new age of human development.

It is this confidence in the working class—in its revolutionary will and capacity for self-government—that most sharply distinguishes Marx's social vision from that of the anarchists and terrorists. To him, the industrial proletariat was not an inert body; it was a thinking mass, capable of being enlightened by words and of pursuing a common program. Furthermore, there was little reason to doubt the combativity of Western workers. From the beginning of the Industrial Revolution until the Commune of Paris was established in 1871, they proved, if anything, all too ready to rebel. It seemed clear, therefore, that what they needed most was not terrorist inspiration or instigation, but models of correct program and effective organization. Marx advised his followers to work openly with others, where possible; to organize trade unions and political associations; and to campaign for specific reforms like universal suffrage and the ten-hour work day. Nonviolent campaigns that increased the political weight of the working class, intensified class-consciousness, and strengthened the workers' ability to act collectively, would accelerate the revolutionary process, not retard it. Even in nations without parliamentary institutions, Marx insisted that Communists should collaborate with ultraliberals (in European parlance, the "radical petty bourgeoisie") to overthrow the old order and set the stage for a workers' revolution.[20]

How would such a revolution take place? Unlike Bakunin and Nechayev, Marx and Engels never published a handbook (no less a catechism) of revolutionary strategy. This was because a conspiratorial elite—the audience for virtually all revolutionary handbooks from Nechayev's onward—played no role in their conception of revolution. To begin with, the leader-follower gap was not a problem that concerned them. With the workers awakening to their own interests under the hammer blows of economic crisis and war, and the intelligentsia driven by these same forces into the ranks of the proletariat, the social gap tended naturally to disappear.[21] The function of revolutionary intellectuals, therefore, was to advise and help organize the workers, not to act for them. Class war, Marx believed, would be open warfare, fought from beginning to end by massed forces rather than by any vanguard of intellectuals claiming to represent the people. In Germany, for example, he advocated the formation of workers' militias which would fight with the bourgeois democrats to overthrow the monarchy but would then "put themselves at the command not of the state authority but of the revolutionary community councils which the workers will have managed to get adopted."[22] These councils would be centralized afterward under the leadership of a revolutionary party capable of pushing the democratic struggle through to socialism—a movement Marx called "The Revolution in Permanence."[23]

This famous strategic formula avoided Bakunin's contradiction between the conspiratorial elite and the mass movement. In fact, it reversed the process envisaged by the anarchists. According to Marx, a mass uprising initiated by the workers themselves would eventually bring a revolutionary party to power, rather than vice versa. The precedent of the great French Revolution weighed strongly on the imaginations of those who believed that it was the Western proletariat's destiny to complete the democratic movement begun in 1789. Marx's conception of revolutionary community councils was democratic to the core, as well as being prophetic of the workers' councils formed during the Commune of Paris and the Russian revolutions of 1905 and 1917. But its usefulness was limited primarily to revolutionary situations that began, as did the French Revolution, with a joint struggle of the bourgeois liberals, workers, and peasants against a reactionary regime. In this situation, workers' councils emerging more or less spontaneously during the first phase of violence—the link between proletariat and party—would be protected in infancy by divisions within the bourgeois camp. In effect, Marx's strategy saved the democratic character of the revolution by postponing the wedding between proletariat and party until a later stage of the struggle, until after the masses had taken up arms and primitive institutions of workers' democracy (the councils) had already appeared.

In the same year in which he called for the formation of workers' militias in Germany, Marx polemicized bitterly against those within his own organization, the Communist League, who wished "to pre-empt the developing revolutionary process, to drive it artificially to crisis, to create a revolution *ex nihilo,* to make a revolution without the conditions of revolution."

> For them, the only necessary condition for a revolution is an adequate organization of their conspiracy. They are the alchemists of the revolution, and they share all the woolly-mindedness, follies, and *idées fixes* of the former alchemists. They throw themselves on discoveries which should work revolutionary wonders: incendiary bombs, hell-machines of magical impact, *emeutes* which ought to be the more wonder-making and sudden the less they have any rational ground. Always busy and preoccupied with such absurd planning and conniving, they see no other end than the next toppling-over of the existing government. Hence their deepest disdain for the more theoretical enlightenment of the workers about their class interests. . . .[24]

This is the classic Marxist polemic against terrorism—indeed, against all forms of violence that attempt to eliminate objective obstacles to social revolution through the exercise of revolutionary will. Still, it is not to be understood abstractly as an attack on "the Jacobin legacy" of mass revolutionary terrors,[25] or as a statement of opposition either to conspiracy in general or to violence. Marx writes with the conviction that revolutions will take place in the West during his own lifetime. He assumes a rising tempo of class struggle, and does not deal directly with questions relevant to more quiescent periods when the workers' movement is weak and mass expectations are low.

This is one reason why Marxists and terrorists often seem to be arguing past one another: terrorist movements generally appear at times and in places where, for one reason or another, militant mass workers' organizations do not exist. Given the absence of such organizations, most Marxists would agree that the primary task is to build them, not to engage in armed forays against the state. But some literalists interpret the master's opposition to terrorism as excluding virtually all workers' organizational activities that are not overt, peaceful, and legal—a position that in fact substitutes the goal of reform for that of revolution. (Thus, German Social Democrat Karl Kautsky condemned the Bolsheviks as "terrorists" for leading a violent revolution in Russia.[26]) Other Marxists have leaned so far in the opposite direction as to exonerate urban guerrilla bands from the charge of terrorism, even though their activities may be indistinguishable from the "absurd planning and conniving" pilloried by Marx.

It is in fact impossible to extrapolate from Marx's or Engels's teachings a position on conspiratorial organizations and political violence that would be applicable at all times and in all places. The best we can do is note that Marx opposed both terrorism and reformism at a time when premature attacks against the state seemed the greater danger to the workers' movement. He believed that the business class had no choice but to create and enlarge the industrial proletariat. It had no choice but to promise workers prosperity, dignity, and self-determination. And finally, it had no choice but to renege on these promises. Marx did not worry much about the workers' fighting spirit; capitalism could be counted upon to generate new causes for rebellion in the form of economic crises, wars, and increased exploitation. What did concern him was the political maturing of the working class—the ability of working people to perceive their collective interests and pursue them effectively, to build a new society as well as destroy the old—in short, their capacity to *rule*. In this respect, a successful reform campaign like the fight for the ten-hour work day might prove to be as revolutionary, in the final analysis, as any act of violence. The formation of the first International Workingmen's Association in 1864 reflected this understanding.

This is not to say, however, that the Communist leaders preferred reformism to terrorism. On the contrary, they despised those who denied the need for a workers' revolution, and found the terrorism of the Russian Narodniki more admirable than the liberals' habit of begging the czar for limited reforms.[27] Moreover, in 1871, Marx brought upon himself the charge of terrorism by coming to the defense of the Commune of Paris after that insurrectionary regime's execution of hostages, including the archbishop of Paris, in retaliation for the shooting of prisoners by the official government at Versailles.

Nowadays, the Commune of Paris is not much on people's minds, but it was one of the great turning points in Western political history. With Louis Bonaparte's army in the field being mauled by the Prussians, the workers and small traders of Paris seized their quarter of the city, proclaimed the end of France's second empire, and inaugurated a workers' republic. For eight months, the Red flag flew over the Hotel de Ville, but in the end, the Commune was drowned in blood by the French government. Not since the massacres of the religious wars had Europe seen such a holocaust; estimates of the number of workers killed by General Marie MacMahon's troops run from twenty to eighty thousand![28] Marx vehemently defended the Commune on the grounds that it was the authentic representative of the French proletariat, a radically democratic government intended "to serve as a model to all the great industrial centers of France."[29] There was no question here of supporting small-group violence in order to awaken the slumbering masses; in 1871, the workers and shopkeepers of Paris were quite awake. The Commune was their creation. In the war of words that followed its fall, Marx's critics accused him of going over to the side of the terrorists—of advocating antistate violence in the name of an unrealizable utopia. But while Bakunin considered the Commune "the negation of the state," Marx recognized it as a workers' state in embryo.[30] The principal lesson of the episode, in his view, was that "the working class cannot simply lay hold of the ready made state machinery, and wield it for its own purposes."[31] In order to succeed, a workers' revolution must smash the military and political institutions of the bourgeois state and replace them with new institutions of workers' democracy.

The violence of the Commune *was* similar to terrorism in one sense: the Paris uprising was intended to *trigger* popular uprisings in other cities and in the countryside; it was not part of a coordinated national struggle. (Sympathetic revolts did take place in Lyons and Marseilles but were smashed, while the military blockade in Paris prevented the communards from communicating with the rural provinces.) With the advantage of historical hindsight, we would have to consider the rebellion premature, as Marx himself did in a letter written ten years after the fact.[32] However, since there was no disputing the *mass* character of the Commune (". . . the first revolution in which the working class was openly acknowledged as the only class capable of social initiative, even by the great bulk of the Paris middle class."[33]), the question of small-group violence was never raised. Those who considered the Commune of Paris terrorist were really objecting to revolutionary violence per se—a position considered by Marx to be hypocritical and reactionary.

In a sense, the Paris upheaval had confirmed Marx's critique of terrorism. The young proletariat was a revolutionary class which had no need for terrorist incitement, and certainly no need to be caught in the crossfire between some militant vanguard and the state. On the other hand, the Commune's terrible defeat threw other aspects of the analysis into serious doubt. In the French Revolution, the masses had triumphed essentially through strength of numbers. Even in 1850, when Marx denounced terrorism and called for workers' militias instead, one could still envisage a great mass of insurgents armed with sticks and stones, one-shot rifles, and a few artillery pieces, defeating most of the armies of Europe. It was the American Civil War of the 1860s that first revealed the impact of the Industrial

Revolution on warfare; and in May 1871, when the French army bombarded Paris with long-range artillery while guardsmen armed with repeating rifles and Maxim guns mowed down insurgents and their families, the lesson was made brutally clear. The proletariat could not win such battles without leadership and planning, without allies, and without somehow neutralizing the awesome power of a modern army.

Equally revealing was the fact that both the big guns used to shell the capital and the army used to subdue it were returned to the French for that purpose by their Prussian conquerors. While insurgent Paris was cut off from other urban centers and from the countryside, bourgeois governments cooperated across national boundaries to suppress the threat to property! The workers had arisen alone, not together with the liberal bourgeoisie and farmers, and they had done so at a time and in a place in which they did not yet constitute a majority. Their military weakness thus reflected weaknesses both of political organization and of theory. (Marx noted, for example, that for all their radicalism, the communards had not dared seize the Bank of France, much less march on Versailles.[34]) The experience of the Commune of Paris therefore suggested that social revolution could not succeed without strong political organization on a national, if not an international, scale.

In this sense, the events of 1870–71 vindicated Bakunin. It was clear that revolutionary workers could not take power without smashing the institutions of bourgeois government, particularly the armed forces. However democratic it might be, the Western bourgeoisie would not stand by idly while its very existence as a class was being threatened. If radical revolution were still on the agenda in the industrial nations, it would need much more than strikes, riots, or even the formation of workers' militias. It would require a powerfully led, centralized, unified organization—a party capable of conducting war as well as organizing trade unions—in short, some sort of semiclandestine conspiracy. Whatever else it might have been, the first International was obviously not such an organization; recognizing its impotence, Marx and Engels buried it without regret. On the other hand, terrorist adventures of the kind contemplated by Nechayev—and soon to be undertaken by the Russian Peoples' Will organization—now seemed even more irrelevant to the revolutionary cause. The strong states created by Western capitalism would obviously find it easier to deal with small-group violence than with massive, spontaneous urban uprisings. The violence of a few hundred militant intellectuals could never achieve what the communards had failed to accomplish.

Thus, with the West on the verge of a great upsurge of industrial expansion and social unrest, both Communists and anarchists found themselves, for the time being, without a workable strategy for revolution. In opposing Bakunin's conspiratorial plotting, Marx had clearly pointed out the difference between a social revolution and a mere *coup d'état*. Terrorism might kill a despot, or perhaps even force a ruling clique from power, but only mass violence could overthrow a social class. How such violence could be organized, however, given the power of modern armies and the willingness of capitalist states to use them, Marx did not say.

It seemed, therefore, that mass revolutions could not be successful, while conspiracies, although potentially successful in their own terms, could not be social revolutions. The expulsion of Bakunin from the International and the demise of that organization one year after the fall of the Commune of Paris dramatized contradictions that were to sunder the European labor movement in the coming decades: mass action versus elite conspiracy; agrarian East versus industrial West; nonviolent politics versus "direct action." While continuing to preach the gospel of social revolution, the followers of Marx moved steadily toward the politics of reform, and the heirs of Bakunin toward terrorism.

Chapter 10

The Logic of

Terrorist Action

COMMON SENSE in the conservative West divides the political universe into violent and nonviolent spheres. We associate terrorism with revolution and social disorder, not with politics as usual. Yet, the first wave of serious terrorism struck Europe not during a period of disorder but at a time somewhat like the present, when revolutionary movements were weak or nonexistent, governments were conservative but politically flexible, and most opposition groups were committed to seeking peaceful reform.

This was the late Victorian era—a period of unparalleled industrial expansion and concentration. In this "Gilded Age," successful entrepreneurs became barons of industry while workers struggled to organize; all who could joined in the scramble for wealth, and those who could not emigrated or starved.[1] Internationally, save for colonial wars, the world was at peace. National energies were directed inward, toward industrial development and political reform. While Western capital poured into overseas investments, leaders like William Gladstone, Otto von Bismarck, and Czar Alexander II combined the militant defense of economic privilege with a new liberalism in political affairs. Serfdom was abolished in the East, and suffrage extended to male workers in the West. New political parties contended in parliaments and trade unions became mass organizations almost overnight. But the heyday of bread-and-butter reform was also the incubator of terrorism. Wherever the pace of political change suddenly slackened after having raised expectations of great social transformation; or where industrial expansion victimized some groups after having benefited others, the seeds of violence were sown.

In the late nineteenth century, as now, what set the stage for extended terrorist campaigns was the pacification of the working class. Western industrialists needed strong, stable governments to maintain order at home and defend their ubiquitous interests abroad. The profits of the "second industrial revolution" and the worldwide expansion of capitalist enterprise made it possible to conclude what was, in effect, a new social contract with organized labor. If the workers' movement would function as a loyal opposition, accepting the norms of bourgeois legality and foregoing claims to represent other have-nots, business would negotiate with union representatives in the factories and socialist deputies in parliament. Labor leaders willing to adapt their revolutionary heritage to the limits of reformist practice could deliver tangible benefits to constituents and nurture hopes of achieving a peaceful revolution at the ballot box.[2] Even in Germany, where Marxists prided themselves on their militant orthodoxy, this new deal proved irresistible; but its acceptance transformed the terms of classical Marxism from within. The state was no longer considered to be a mere weapon of the bourgeoisie, but a more or less neutral arena in which workers could compete peacefully for power. Class struggle now meant campaigns for higher wages, parliamentary seats, and legislation favorable to worker interests. Internationalism became an abstraction, for acceptance of one's nation as the primary unit of politics was the essence of the new consensus. In short, the working class in each industrialized nation was led step by step to consider itself one interest group among others rather than a class capable of representing all of society.[3]

In the West, a minority of intellectuals resisted this trend, arguing that evolutionary socialism was an impossibility and insisting that the new social compact was bound to end in economic collapse and war. Especially vocal were young anarchists and nationalists, who sought to represent those excluded from the benefits of industrialism or victimized by it. They hoped for an eventual awakening of the people but were determined to carry on class war with or without the active participation of their clients. Acting alone or as members of small combat groups, they nevertheless managed in a few years to assassinate dozens of high state officials, including the presidents of France and the United States, the kings of Italy and Portugal, the prime minister of Spain, and the empress of Austria.[4] In Russia and in the East, where a working class was just being formed and where autocratic oppression alienated even the aristocrats, terrorism was more widespread. The first wave of Russian terror—in a sense, the first modern terrorist campaign—was generated by the populist youths of the People's Will organization, the Narodniki, who killed Czar Alexander II, among other notables.[5] In a second wave, terrorists associated with the Combat Organization of the Socialist-Revolutionary party eliminated interior ministers Dmitry Sipyagin and Vyacheslav von Plehve, Grand Duke Sergey Romanoff, and Premier Pyotr Stolypin, as well as robbing banks, destroying property, and generally terrorizing the Russian bureaucracy.[6] (Significantly, this activity generated the most ruthless right-wing counterterror seen up to that time— the activities of the notorious Black Hundreds.) Meanwhile, from the late 1880s forward, nationalist avengers representing diverse political ideologies liquidated enemies from Ireland to India. They were particularly active in the Balkans, where the assassination of the Austrian archduke by a Young Bosnia zealot unwittingly triggered World War I.

To understand a terrorist movement, we must always consider both the activists *and* their clientele.[7] From the late 1870's until the outbreak of World War I, the activists tended to be students, intellectuals, and declassed professionals—young people of middle-class or even aristocratic origin. ("In this respect," Laqueur writes, "Russian terrorism resembled the composition of [modern] terrorist groups in Latin America in which the sons and daughters of the middle and upper-middle class have traditionally predominated."[8]) This intelligentsia grew at an enormous rate in the 1860s and 1870s, far outrunning the capacity of most societies to provide suitable jobs for educated, idealistic young people bent on social service. Virtually all of the terrorists began as reformers, hoping to better their clients' lot as well as their own through peaceful politics. In Russia, for example, the People's Will was the successor to the nonviolent Go To The People campaign.[9] The turn to violence generally coincided with a shattering of expectations caused by economic slowdown and the failure of major reform campaigns.[10] Thus, the terrorists' clients tended to be groups ignored or abandoned by reform politicians; victims of industrial progress like the Russian peasantry, whose cause was embraced by the People's Will; the impoverished and subjugated Irish, charges of the Fenian movement (a secret revolutionary society, organized circa 1858); numerous other oppressed nationalities, each with its terrorist champion; and the destitute—landless peasants, marginally employed workers, and criminals—who were the particular concern of the anarchists. Would-be leaders without a mass following found some support among groups without effective leaders. But they did not require much support to conduct campaigns of theatrical violence against state officials and the rich.

Despite their relative isolation, the young terrorists considered themselves the only true revolutionaries in a period of reformist corruption. Even their enemies agreed that these impassioned bomb-throwers were the very antithesis of the pragmatic labor leaders, parliamentary liberals, and agrarian pacifists who were the principal opposition figures of the era.

Nevertheless, their dramatic and terrifying actions were usually far more radical than their ideas. More often than not, the good society of terrorist dreams turned out to be a rather tame combination of liberal democracy and preindustrial utopia. The Narodniki envisaged a decentralized democracy that would restore the peasant commune—the *mir*—to its ancient position of preeminence. Many anarchists shared this vision, adding to it the notion of an industrial plant managed by free, autonomous trade unions. And the nationalists wanted little more for their people than self-determination—freedom from foreign domination. Moreover, all of the schools of terrorism shared a sense that the masses, now either beaten or bought, could not act for themselves—that they required representation by an armed minority. The apparent incapability of workers and peasants to accomplish their own salvation led anarchists, populists, and nationalists alike to propose structurally similar two-stage theories of revolution.

In the first stage, terrorism, the activist intellectuals were to act for the masses—on their behalf but without their participation. They would sow terror among the clique in power, which would expose its weakness, provoke brutal overreaction, and inspire mass support for radical change. Later, in a more vaguely-defined second stage, the masses would act for themselves. The clear tendency of this doctrine was to turn the mass revolution into a next-world utopia; in practice, if the masses did not immediately arise, the armed fighters tended to consider their own struggle to be the revolution. Nikolai Morozov, a Narodniki sympathizer, put forth this substitutionist thesis clearly:

All that the terroristic struggle really needs is a small number of people and large material means.
This presents really a new form of struggle.
It replaces by a series of individual political assassination, which always hit their target, the massive revolutionary movements, where people often rise against each other because of misunderstanding and where a nation kills off its own children, while the enemy of the people watches from a secure shelter and sees to it that the people of the organization are destroyed. The move-

ment punishes only those who are really responsible for the evil deed. Because of this *the terroristic revolution is the only just form of a revolution.* [11]

Morozov and his comrades advocate terrorism not as an *incitement* to mass revolution but as a method of *bypassing* the corrupted or intimidated masses. They prefer small-group violence to a popular uprising for two reasons: it keeps oppositional activity under the control of the "better elements" of society, and it punishes only the evildoers in office. Terrorism thus represents legitimate revenge. Morozov's views seem radical because he advocates violence, but his politics are essentially those of the reform-minded aristocrats and liberal petty bourgeoisie. Revolution, in this view, is not a war in which one social class attempts to overthrow another; it is a surgical operation to remove parasitic public officials. Its purpose is not to create a workers' and farmers' government, but to eliminate obstacles to the spontaneous self-expression of the nation.

This commitment to tyrannicide betokens acceptance of a Great Man theory of history, but in negative form:

> Brutal force and despotism are always concentrated either in a few or more often in one ruling person (Bismarck, Napoleon) and stop with his failure or death. Such people should be destroyed in the very beginning of their career, be they chosen by the army or plebiscite.[12]

Bad Great Men were the problem. The solution was good Great Men and Women—selfless revolutionary terrorists who dared to assume personal responsibility for their violent deeds. Like many of their modern successors, the founders of European terrorism emphasized the need to demystify power by demonstrating that a single determined individual—a "nobody"—could lay low the mightiest prince or general. The terrorists' job was to generate disorder so as to create an area of liberty in which the masses might overcome long-conditioned deference, fear, and immobility. Thus, according to Morozov, the social revolution would take place only *after* the People's Will had succeeded in "destroy[ing] oppression by consecutive political assassinations." This second-stage revolution, a peaceful transformation, could then be led by the revolutionary terrorists themselves.[13]

More than a century after Czar Alexander II's assassination, we still find Narodism suggestive (and not just because one of those executed for a later attempted regicide was Lenin's elder brother). To begin with, it illustrates terrorism's role as the "dark twin" of reformism. As reform socialists abandoned the goal of overthrowing the business state, they too adopted a two-stage theory of political action: first, organize the workers as a pressure group, a bargainer operating within the boundaries fixed to protect the interests of great property. Later, use the legally acquired power to collectivize property and transform political institutions from within. Eduard Bernstein, who coined the phrase "evolutionary socialism," pointed out that in practice, stage two tended to be indefinitely postponed and stage one indefinitely extended.[14] Reformism (as Bernstein perceived it) converts means into ends; but this is precisely what terrorism does when it abandons faith in the imminence of popular revolution and substitutes the terroristic revolution for a mass mobilization. Nechayev was the first to announce postponement of the revolution until the masses had been awakened by an intensification of calamities. The Narodniki and Western anarchists, who practiced what he only preached, went a step further: acting as the People's Will, they would eliminate the obstacles to social revolution. But if these obstacles were not deeply rooted in society—if they could be personified, as Mozorov thought they could, by Bad Men—then removing them would be much more than a prelude to revolution. It would be an essential part of the revolution, perhaps even the only violent part.

At this point, terrorism and reformism virtually merge. For if a small minority of armed fighters can cripple despotism and liberate the people, the second stage of national liberation (supervised by ex-terrorists in power) may well be gradual and nonviolent. The terrorist revolution thus becomes a sort of violent election that replaces one slate of representatives with another pledged to a platform of peaceful social transformation. Especially where the terrorist struggle is protracted, activists come to believe that their own activities represent the violent phase of the social revolution, with a long period of peaceful evolution scheduled to begin immediately afterward. The result of *this* conversion of means into ends is what might be called the depolitization of terrorist action. With mass action both postponed and tamed, social revolution becomes a remote goal —an article of faith rather than a realistic political objective. What is real is the immediate struggle, which aims to remove or intimidate public officials, create a climate of disorder, force the government to overreact, and create heroes and martyrs. But ironically, all of these aims are politically neutral. Even if secured, they leave open the questions of who will take advantage of the existing regime's weakness to create a new order, and what that order will look like. The terrorists' fixation on stage one violence leaves stage two blank—an invitation, really, for the nation's "natural" leaders to come forth and govern once the regime's monopoly of force has been broken.

The conservative implications of this doctrine are well illustrated by the career of one terrorist, Gerasim Tarnovski, also known as Romanenko. Originally a Narodnik, Romanenko later became the leader of the Black Hundreds, the most powerful right-wing terrorist organization in Russia. While still a youthful radical, he pointed out that the speechless masses were unable to act for themselves and required representation by intellectuals:

This intelligentsia is thus obliged, yes obliged, to bear political freedom in Russia upon its own shoulders, using terror as its means.[15]

First, this militant elite would create a revolution by assassinating the bureaucrats in power and establishing a republic. Then, "imbued with the need for political freedom," the masses would obtain "full social liberation." How this liberation was to be accomplished Romanenko did not say, but he clearly

excluded the possibility of mass violence, arguing that "terrorist revolution" was "more reasonable, humanitarian, and conse-
quently more ethical in the methods which it uses than mass
revolution."[16] How humane, how enlightened, how . . . Christian was Romanenko to spare the masses the horrors of civil war
by substituting his own sacrifice for theirs! But this pseudoradi-
cal paternalism was clearly the obverse of the orthodox paternalism that soon claimed his loyalty. Indeed, even when writing
as a Narodnik, Romanenko's description of the enemy had
disturbing overtones:

> From the point of view of a healthy social morality, the removal of
> those individuals who bring down a whole nation to the level of a
> herd in order to exploit and humiliate it is a duty prescribed by the
> laws of natural justice.[17]

These words could have been uttered as easily by the later
Tarnovski-Romanenko, organizer of anti-Jewish massacres in
the Ukraine, or by Kern and Fischer, the right-wing nationalists
who assassinated German Foreign Minister Walter Rathenau in
1922, as by any radical!

Ideologically, terrorists have waved every flag; still, the structural congruence between Left and Right philosophies of terrorism is striking. The anarchists wished to smash the state apparatus in order to permit society to function naturally, which in
their view meant cooperatively, without private property.
Populists and liberal democrats wanted to smash it in order to
establish institutions protecting natural rights, which to them
meant free competition in economics and free elections in politics. And conservative nationalists advocated smashing it so
that the natural, or organic, nation, or the race, could exercise
its right to self-rule. Whatever their political affiliations, most
terrorists considered their acts a method of clearing away obstacles to the spontaneous self-expression of the masses. Irrespec-
tive of other differences, all terrorist schools counterposed the
negative tasks of the violent few in stage one to the positive
tasks reserved for the many in stage two. This structural

similarity has as its root a social reality: isolation of the intelligentsia, and immobility or fragmentation of the mass base. Left, Right, or Center, terrorist philosophies reflect and, to a great extent, accept the fact that large social groups are unable or unwilling to resist authority en masse.

The emergence of revolutionary terrorism generally signifies that a section of the intelligentsia, now cut loose from its normal social moorings, is determined to resist authority even if this means acting alone. What emboldens these relatively isolated militants to undertake terrorist careers? Very often it is the perception that the state apparatus is equally isolated—that the government, as one Narodnik leader put it, is "a *camarilla* [court cabal], a small and isolated faction, which represents only its own interests, and is not supported by any class of society."[18] This conception has two important implications. First, it suggests that behind the differences of opinion between rebels and authorities lies a certain equivalence. The militants and their enemies in power are in the same business, so to speak. They are generally drawn from similar social strata. They accept, at least for the time being, the same gulf between leaders and led. They both seek to monopolize violence in the interests of the passive masses, and the militants' task requires them to engage in practices similar to those employed by state terrorists, including infiltration, provocation, intimidation by example, and the execution of spies. This does not mean that terrorists and their foes are identical, although it is frequently difficult to tell who is working for whom. (In at least one case—that of the incredible Yevno Azev—the chief of an effective terrorist organization was also a top government spy.[19]) But it does imply that there is a logic to terrorist action capable of overpowering inconsistent ideological commitments.

If state officials are no better able than terrorists to mobilize mass support, the stage may be set for an extended gang war in which conspiracies in power and out battle for military supremacy, while the masses await the outcome. When the rebels win such a struggle, however, they do so not as representatives of a class but of the whole nation. The corollary of Marx's proposition that the government is "a committee for managing the common affairs of the whole bourgeoisie" is proletarian revolution.[20] Only a class can overthrow a class. The corollary of the Narodnik proposition that the government "is not supported by any class of society" is terrorist revolution: a violent campaign by a relatively small vanguard of fighters aimed at liberating all classes from political oppression. In practice, this doctrine leads toward national unity, not social revolution. Assuming that terrorists can sometimes undermine a regime's ability to maintain order, the groups most likely to profit from a period of instability, insecurity, and confusion are those capable of reconciling differences and restoring order: not the revolutionary Left, but the moderate Center or the ultranationalist Right.

The current of European terrorism generated in nineteenth-century Russia flowed well into the twentieth century not because such violence proved useful to social revolutionaries, but because it served the far more modest purposes of liberal or right-wing nationalism. Nationalist terrorism began in Europe with Spanish resistance to Napoleonic domination—a movement that was loyal to the deposed king. From that point onward, imperialism continually generated terrorist opposition of the most varied character. Liberals attacked the British in Ireland and Hindu fundamentalists in India. Pan-Slavic reactionaries challenged the Turkish sultan, and the most far-reaching terrorist act of modern times—the assassination of the Austrian archduke at Sarajevo—was the work of a liberal Bosnian youth seeking to free the Balkans from Hapsburg domination. Furthermore, the moderates have been equally prominent in more recent nationalist movements. During World War II, the only serious assassination attempt against Hitler was executed by conservative *Wermacht* officers, while after the war, effective terrorist campaigns were waged by right-wing nationalists in Palestine and tribal nationalists (Mau Mau) in Kenya.

The usefulness of this sort of campaign to diverse nationalist movements is not difficult to understand. For one thing, it provides a basis for unity among all opponents of the state. Where national liberation is a second-stage goal, leftists may believe that first-stage violence will open the path to socialism, while rightists imagine that disorder will spawn a state dominated by the upper classes, and liberals dream of a constitutional republic. Nevertheless, the usual implications of the two-stage struggle are clearly conservative, for if social revolution is *not* incited —that is, if the struggle is essentially between rival elites—then the balance of social forces existing outside of the narrow arena of armed conflict is likely to determine the future of the state. Nationalist terrorism can be effective precisely because it generates multiclass support for the depoliticized goal: freedom for the nation (see discussion in chapter 12). Furthermore, limiting the aims of terrorism to destruction—for example, using small-group violence to make a particular piece of territory ungovernable by an occupying power—is a more modest and realistic goal than simultaneously attempting to oust the foreigner and restructure one's society. Again, however, this limitation plays into the hands of conservative nationalists, whose goals are to expel the foreign oppressor while concentrating power in the hands of a local ruling class.

It seems, then, that the logic of terrorist action is not friendly to what Marx called "radical social revolution." Situationally, terrorist movements have been created, and to a large extent defined, by the absence of mass revolutionary fervor and organization. When mass demobilization is accepted as a fact, violent activists are led to substitute their own struggle for the ever-receding mass uprising. The result, as we have seen, is the progressive depolitization of the movement: a separation of first-stage means from second-stage ends that suits the purposes of reformers interested in political change, not social change. To Lenin and his comrades in the Russian Social-Democratic Labor party, the connection between terrorism and reform was of critical importance. By keeping Marx's critique of small-group violence while adapting certain terrorist principles to the needs of the mass struggle, the Bolsheviks hoped to find a revolutionary alternative to both.

Chapter 11

Terrorism and

Communism

IN 1902, a pamphlet by exiled Russian Socialist Vladimir Ilyich Lenin exploded among the European intelligentsia with far more force than any terrorist bomb. In imitation of an earlier essay much beloved by the Narodniki, it was called, *What Is to Be Done? Burning Questions of Our Movement.* [1]

When Lenin's pamphlet first appeared in Russia, opposition movements were still weak and disorganized, but a political awakening was clearly underway. Capitalist development, largely financed by western European interests, had significantly altered the Russian social landscape, and dissatisfaction with czarist rule was building toward the spontaneous popular outbursts of 1905. Among those dedicated to the violent overthrow of czarism, two approaches predominated. On one side were the terrorists of the Socialist Revolutionary party's redoubtable Combat Organization—lineal descendants of the Narodniki, but far better organized and armed. On the other

side were the collateral relatives of the western European reform socialists—Social Democratic labor organizers known in
Russia as the Economists. The Socialist Revolutionaries (SR's),
a party with considerable support in the countryside, combined
a revival of populist-style terrorism with attempts to influence
the growing industrial proletariat. Their Combat Organization,
dispatched to wreak havoc among the czarist bureaucrats, succeeded in assassinating a number of high-ranking officials and
(to an extent difficult to measure) in damaging the regime's
morale and efficiency. The SR's believed that when the state
apparatus had been sufficiently weakened by terrorist attacks,
workers and peasants would complete the job, convene a constituent assembly, and establish socialism. The Economists, on
the other hand, placed primary emphasis on organizing illegal
trade unions and agitating among the factory workers. They too
believed that their work was preparing the masses for an inevitable anticzarist uprising.

Lenin split the Russian labor movement—and eventually the
workers' movement worldwide—by forming a centralized
party of professional revolutionaries and refusing to commit it
to either reformism or terrorism. In *What Is to Be Done?* he asks,
"What is there in common between Economism and Terrorism?" His answer represents an important addition to the
analysis of terrorism.

> The Economists and the modern terrorists have one common root,
> namely, *subservience to spontaneity.* . . . . the Economists bow to the
> spontaneity of "the labour movement pure and simple," while the
> terrorists bow to the spontaneity of the passionate indignation of
> the intellectuals, who lack the ability or opportunity to connect the
> revolutionary struggle and the working-class movement into an
> integral whole. It is difficult indeed for those who have lost their
> belief, or who have never believed that this is possible, to find some
> outlet for their indignation and revolutionary energy other than
> terror.[2]

The terrorists have lost their belief in the revolutionary potential of the workers; the reformists profess such a belief, but are

unable to construct a political party capable of mobilizing this potential and leading the working class to power. Hence, the Economists rely on bread-and-butter unionism and the terrorists rely on their own heroic example to trigger a spontaneous uprising. But socialist revolution requires that mass struggles be intersected, influenced, and finally, led by a centralized party dedicated to establishing a workers' state. Left to themselves, Lenin insists, trade unions can never transcend the status of bargainer, while terrorist heroics bypass the workers' movement altogether. In the first case, activists abdicate leadership responsibility; in the second, they attempt to lead without linking themselves to the proletariat. What the movement needs is leadership linked to the masses through a large number of politically aware workers—that is, a *nonterrorist* party of the revolutionary vanguard.[3]

Lenin's concept brought immediate charges of elitism from both the Right and the Left. The terrorists considered him a stodgy, authoritarian reformist—a talker, not an actor; while the Economists, as well as many western European socialists, accused him of being a conspirator, an anarchist in Marxist clothing—in short, a terrorist! The second criticism was more serious to Lenin, for he addressed himself more to the Socialists, his old comrades, than to the SR's, who he considered hopelessly isolated from the proletariat. His position was that only a centralized party could mobilize the workers for insurrection *and* prevent terrorist-style premature attacks against the government.

> Precisely at the present time, when no such organization yet exists, and when the revolutionary movement is rapidly and spontaneously growing, we already observe two opposite extremes (which, as is to be expected, "meet"). These are: utterly unsound Economism and the preaching of moderation, and the equally unsound "excitative terror."[4]

Lenin's critics shared a populist faith in the ability of the masses to organize themselves; they distrusted his Jacobin tendencies and feared a dictatorship of his party. To the Bolshevik leader, however, the mass awakening *which was already occurring* would bind the strong party to an active mass base. For him, it was not a question of distrusting the people more than the Economists or terrorists did, but of trusting them enough to believe that, properly organized and led, they could overcome the limitations inherent in spontaneous action and proceed to establish a new social order. For this reason, he rejected the opposition of democracy to centralism, counterposing the "toy" democracy of his critics to the "real" democracy of a class in harmony with its leadership.[5] This conception of real democracy underlies his subsequent attacks on terrorism published in the revolutionary journal *Iskra* in 1902, a few months after the publication of *What Is to Be Done?* Here, Lenin emphasized the separation of the terrorists from the working class, clearly implying that their acts were not representative of the proletariat:

> In their naivete, the Socialist Revolutionaries do not realize that their predilection for terrorism is causally most intimately linked with the fact that, from the very outset, they have always kept, and still keep aloof from the working class movement.[6]

This judgment was not entirely fair. Although the SR's main base of support was in the countryside rather than in the cities, they did attempt to influence the workers' movement, and certain SR-controlled unions played an important role in the revolutions of 1917–18.[7] It would have been correct, however, to say that the Socialist Revolutionary party was two organizations rather than one, and that it never succeeded in coordinating the work of the Combat Organization with that of its labor and peasant associations. Even within their own party, the terrorist intellectuals remained essentially isolated. The major point, however, is that Lenin's commitment to real democracy excluded the idea of representative violence. The task of the revolutionary elite was to prepare the way for workers' insurrection, but the revolution itself—the violent overthrow of the state—

could not be accomplished by any elite. Violence is representative of the masses only when it is mass violence. Thus, Lenin
insisted that SR terrorism was "not connected in any way with
work among the masses, for the masses, or together with the
masses." Moreover, he maintained that,

> The organization of terroristic acts by the party distracts our very
> scanty organizational forces from their difficult and by no means
> completed task of organizing a revolutionary *workers'* party. . . .
> [*I*]*n practice* the terrorism of the Socialist Revolutionaries is nothing
> else than *single combat,* a method that has been wholly condemned by
> the experience of history.[8]

The themes sounded here have become familiar to subsequent generations of Marxists. First, terrorism is a distraction
from the main task of organizing a workers' party that can
command mass support. Second, it does *not* arouse the proletariat to do battle with property owners and the state. Contrary to the teachings of the SR's, political assassinations do
not automatically transfer strength from the state to the revolutionary forces. "Single combat" does not inspire workers to
participate in struggles against entrenched power. Rather, it
"has the immediate effect of simply creating a short-lived
sensation, while indirectly it even leads to apathy and passive
waiting for the next bout."[9] Third, since the state has a great
advantage over the terrorists in personnel, weaponry, and
military infrastructure, terrorism generally kills more revolutionaries than state officials.[10] It is simply not a strategy for
victory.

The same points were developed on a more general plane by
Lenin's comrade and the future commander of the Red Army,
Leon Trotsky. Trotsky saw with unusual clarity that terrorist
activity is designed to bypass mass struggle rather than ignite
it, and that it cannot, therefore, be representative of the working class. It is worth quoting at some length what have become
the classic statements of orthodox Marxist opposition to revolutionary terrorism. First, the tactical objection:

By its very essence, terrorist work demands such concentrated energy for "the great moment," such an over-estimation of the significance of individual heroism, and finally, such a "hermetic" conspiracy, that—if not logically, then psychologically—it totally excludes agitational and organizational work among the masses. . . . [T]errorism is far too "absolute" a form of struggle to be content with a limited and subordinate role in the party.[11]

Then, the strategic, ultimately philosophical objections:

The capitalist state does not base itself on government ministers and cannot be eliminated with them. The classes it serves will always find new people; the mechanism remains intact and continues to function.[12]

. . . If it is enough to arm oneself with a pistol in order to achieve one's goal, why the efforts of the class struggle? If a thimbleful of gunpowder and a little chunk of lead is enough to shoot the enemy through the neck, what need is there for a class organization? If it makes sense to terrify highly placed personages with the roar of explosions, where is the need for a party? Why meetings, mass agitation, and elections if one can so easily take aim at the ministerial bench from the gallery of parliament?

In our eyes, individual terror is inadmissible precisely because it *belittles the role of the masses in their own consciousness,* reconciles them to their powerlessness, and turns their eyes and hopes toward a great avenger and liberator who some day will come and accomplish his mission.[13]

Although beautifully stated, this is familiar ground. Trotsky added a new dimension to the analysis, however, by asking why this form of political activity was so common in Russia. Why in Russia and not, say, in England? And why in 1909 and not in 1809? Because terrorism is the creation of the radicalized intelligentsia, which, like the state itself, is a product of the peculiar conditions of Russian social and political development.

Before the very idea of destroying absolutism by mechanical means could acquire popularity, the state apparatus had to be seen as a purely external organ of coercion, having no roots in the social organization itself. And this is precisely how the Russian autocracy appeared to the revolutionary intelligentsia.[14]

This produces a second question: why did Russian students see the state as "a purely external organ of coercion" which could be destroyed by bombs and bullets? Basically, because of Russia's status as a developing nation—a client and victim of imperialism. Capitalism developed late in Russia, under the domination of the western European industrial powers. As a result, the native business class was weak, unable to lead a democratic revolution and bring absolutist government under business control. Instead, the czarist bureaucracy used European capital to arm itself with European military technology. "It thus grew into a 'self-sufficient' (in a relative sense, of course) organization, elevating itself above all classes of society," said Trotsky. Such a situation "could naturally give rise to the idea of blasting this extraneous superstructure into the air with dynamite."[15]

The same conditions forced the development of the Russian intelligentsia, creating a certain correspondence between the intellectuals—the would-be state—and the officials in power. Socially speaking, both were hothouse growths, lacking roots in native soil.

> In Russia the intelligentsia gained access to the ready-made cultural and political ideas of the West and had their thinking revolutionized before the economic development of the country had given birth to serious revolutionary classes from which they could get support.[16]

Like czarist bureaucrats, then, the terrorists were effectively isolated from their purported clients; and again like their enemy, they found themselves acting in a political vacuum, without these clients' participation or active support. In 1934, condemning the assassination of a prominent Stalinist official in Leningrad, Trotsky made this parallelism clear:

> Individual terrorism in this very essence is bureaucratism turned inside out. . . . Bureaucratism has no confidence in the masses, and endeavors to substitute itself for the masses. Terrorism behaves in the same manner. It wants to make the masses happy without their participation.[17]

The importance of this analysis is that for the first time attention is directed toward the social causes of terrorism, so that situations in which terrorist activity is likely to occur can be identified. Marx had indicted the anarchists for their failure to understand that capitalism, not the state, was the main enemy, and that the working class, not some revolutionary elite, was the main source of hope. Lenin had extended the indictment to include a new generation of terrorists (the SR's) and of socialists (the Economists) who shared a belief in the ability of the masses to overthrow the state spontaneously and without the aid of a revolutionary combat party. Trotsky now suggested that terrorism was to be expected in societies in which the state apparatus was relatively isolated from the middle classes, and the intelligentsia from the lower classes—societies in which political organization had, in a sense, outrun economic development, leaving both bureaucrats and intellectuals suspended over a void. Prerevolutionary Russia was a nation in which immense modern factories which were financed by foreign capital appeared almost overnight in cities without the most rudimentary urban services; in which a grain surplus marketed worldwide by foreigners was produced by peasants living under conditions of medieval squalor and superstition; in which businesspeople, liberal aristocrats, and intellectuals—indeed, virtually all literate classes—were considered potentially dangerous to public order and worthy to be spied on by the secret police. It is easy to understand how such a situation produced both a state apparatus and an intelligentsia that were cut off from local sources of mass support and tempted to war upon each other like rival gangs.

Why has small-group violence become such an important feature of the political landscape in the second half of the twentieth century? Trotsky's theory suggests that a precondition for sustained terrorist campaigns is the political isolation of the intelligentsia—or, put differently, the absence of a revolutionary party that is capable of linking these would-be leaders to a mass base. Recent history clearly bears out this inverse relationship between militant mass organization and terrorist activity. Recall, for example, that in modern Italy, the rise of the Red Brigade closely paralleled the Communist party's conversion into a party of moderate reform, and that in Argentina, Peronist collapse and Marxist conservatism isolated a generation of young activists from the workers they hoped to lead (see chapters 5 and 6).

What is the basis in society for such a political situation? In a word, forced development of both the intelligentsia and the state bureaucracy; underdevelopment of revolutionary classes. Iran under the late shah is a good example of this configuration, as is Russia under the last czar. In each case, uneven and chaotic industrial growth spawned new classes and social divisions, undermined the connections that had linked the intelligentsia with the state apparatus, and precipitated armed struggle between rival cliques.[18] Other examples of terrorism linked to the uneven development of backward societies come readily to mind; but the theory is capable of even broader application. If Lenin and Trotsky are correct, one would expect the violence of the intelligentsia to erupt even in more developed and autonomous nations, where this sector of the petty bourgeoisie is torn loose from its normal social moorings.

Ordinarily, ambitious, educated youths of middle-class background function as social intermediaries, representing the wealthy and powerful to their subjects and vice versa. During periods of relative social stability, they are absorbed into what we now call the "techno-structure" of technical and managerial occupations, with more politicized (or simply extroverted) young adults entering the social-management professions: education, government service, law, medicine, and communications. As a group, their normal political stance is reformist, reflecting their commitment to bourgeois values (for example, the pursuit of success) on the one hand and their exposure to lower-class problems and perspectives on the other.

But there may come a time when they can no longer hold continuity and change in balance. Then, from a moderating influence in politics, the intelligentsia may become an extremist force. We can hypothesize that where its ties to the ruling class are broken and those with lower classes maintained or reforged, "the young generation of the educated classes" (Lenin's expression) moves toward the Left. Where upper-class connections are maintained and those with workers or peasants dissolved, the intelligentsia moves to the Right. And where connections are attenuated or broken in *both* directions, the stage is set for responses to isolation that range from selling out and dropping out to terrorism.

To summarize: the leading Marxist thinkers opposed terrorism politically because it seemed useless, even counterproductive, to the struggle for a workers' revolution. Terrorism, they insisted, does not generate organized mass violence aimed at overthrowing the established order, it bypasses the workers, reducing them to passivity and disrupting the essential task of building a revolutionary party. If the masses are not the "tinder," ready to rebel at the drop of a well-placed bomb, they cannot be "ignited" by heroic violence and state repression. On the contrary, they become bystanders to a gang war between the radicalized intelligentsia and the police. If the masses *are* in a rebellious frame of mind, however, terrorism is a dangerous distraction from the task of converting spontaneous individual anger into organized, collective force. Lenin observed that terrorist and reformist thinking are structurally similar; terrorism is the violence of the isolated intelligentsia. Trotsky explained this similarity (and the sympathy of liberals for some types of terrorism) by suggesting that terrorist violence is likely to become a political tradition in semi-industrialized societies that develop under foreign economic domination. Pushing the analysis a step further, we see that elements of the intelligentsia may be sprung loose even in more advanced industrial societies, and that, where this occurs, small-group political violence is likely to become endemic.

This theory, although controversial, seems clear enough. If put into practice, it would place Marxists-Leninists in direct opposition to terrorism whether the terrorists call themselves communists, fascists, or nationalists. According to most Western analysts, however, a wide gap separates Marxist theory from practice: another example of leftist hypocrisy or double-speak. Even Walter Laqueur, perhaps the outstanding American authority on terrorism, convicts the Marxists of "ambivalence" toward terrorism.[19] Laqueur does not equate Marxism with terrorism in the style of some right-wing critics; in fact, he highlights the opposition of leading Communists to small-group violence, quoting Marx on the anarchism of Johann Most ("childish"), Engels on the Irish nationalists ("stupid fanatics"), and Lenin on the Combat Organization's campaign of assassination ("a specific kind of struggle practiced by the intelligentsia").[20] Nevertheless, he insists, not even Marx and Lenin practiced what they preached. Marx found the Narodnik terrorists attractive, and refused to condemn them publicly. Lenin's objections to SR terrorism were merely "tactical," as demonstrated by the campaign of bank robberies undertaken by the Bolsheviks in 1906–7. Trotsky defended the Red terror during the Russian Civil War, and Stalin used terrorism at home and abroad whenever it suited him.[21] Whatever this evidence proves, it is not ambivalence! Let us see where it leads.

First, the refusal of Communists to unconditionally condemn terrorists like the Narodniki no more bespeaks ambivalence toward terrorism than a refusal to condemn suicide evinces suicidal tendencies. Marx considered the terrorists brave but misguided; condemnation, however, he reserved for the czar. Clearly, one may deplore terrorist violence, oppose it politically, and even take steps to defend its victims from attack without joining forces with the state to crush it. Revolutionary Marxists reject terrorism unambiguously because its effect is to sustain the capitalist order; for them, obviously, capitalism is the greater evil. Conversely, those who participate in state suppression of terrorists thereby demonstrate that they consider their rulers less terroristic than the rebels. The Italian Communist party took this position, for example, when it supported the use of exceptional measures against the Red Brigade, thus confirming in practice the renunciation of Leninism it had already announced in theoretical journals.[22] Similarly, West German Social Democrats, determined to suppress the RAF, found themselves implicated in the creation of an array of counterterrorist institutions, including special secret police and military strike forces, special courts, and new rules against representation of accused terrorists by attorneys.[23] Those who refuse to participate in such counterterrorist campaigns are not for this reason apologists for terrorism. Like Marx, they may simply view the ruling class and its repressive apparatus as the greater danger to society.

In the same way, to describe the Bolsheviks' bitter opposition to terrorism as merely tactical is to miss the point that for Marxists, the difference between sectarian violence and class violence is crucial. Laqueur writes that "in October 1905, at the height of the first Russian revolution, [Lenin] expressed real anguish that his party had merely been talking about bombs but that not a single one had been made."[24] But, of course! This was a revolution—the real thing (even though in this case the insurgent forces were defeated), with the Russian fleet in revolt and whole regiments deserting, workers on strike all over the empire, peasants seizing estates, and revolutionary groups like Lenin's caught completely by surprise. In fact, it was the events of 1905 that convinced the Bolsheviks that they must be ready to use force when the *next* mass uprising occurred—not to trigger a revolution, terrorist-style, but to intersect it and lead it to victory. This strategy Laqueur calls "Blanquism on a higher level," which is something like calling world war a fistfight on a higher level.

The most significant evidence for the "merely tactical" criticism is the undoubted fact that for a short period following defeat of the 1905 revolution, the Bolsheviks robbed banks and attacked other government facilities, particularly in the Caucasus region, where banditry was endemic. Laqueur might well have noted that this campaign is the exception that proves the rule, since it was a temporary expedient designed to procure funds for the party, and was clearly never proposed as a strategy for revolution. This campaign of "expropriations" was the closest the Bolsheviks came to a type of political banditry traditional in Russia; in the end, however, it lacked both the risks and rewards expected by genuine terrorists.

> The Bolsheviks . . . did not face the normal situation in which such robberies would immediately trigger the repressive apparatus of an overwhelmingly powerful and centralized state. Neither did they risk the condemnation of workers who might think they were mere criminals in political garb. Nor did the Bolsheviks maintain these expropriations as a "strategy" to be carried out over an extended period with the likely result of degeneration into lumpen criminal activity.[25]

Bolshevik justifications for this campaign were devoid of the usual substitutionism which leads terrorists to proclaim themselves armed representatives of the people. Lenin did not believe that daring acts of small-group violence could produce a great social chain reaction, or that such acts would transfer strength from the government to the revolutionaries. He believed in doing what was necessary to survive following the 1905 upheaval and defeat, and was in no danger of confusing survival strategy with revolutionary strategy.

Indeed, the episode would hardly be worth discussing were it not for the belief prevalent among Western scholars that the Bolsheviks were soft on terrorism. To an extent, this notion is based on antipathy to revolutionary violence, particularly to the mass terror associated with revolutionary civil war. To an extent, it is based on disapproval of Stalin's crimes—as if Stalinism were not a perversion of Marxism, but its inevitably hideous realization! But even to one free of such preconceptions, the relationship of Leninism to terrorism poses problems that cannot be solved by repeating the classical distinction between individual terrorism and mass revolutionary violence.

Indeed, this contrast is frequently so overdrawn by Marxist theorists as to be useless. When mass organizations have been suppressed or pacified, when a regime is firmly in power, and a few hundred militants begin throwing bombs, it is easy to identify their violence as individual (that is, the work of isolated intellectuals). Imagine, however, that the regime is visibly tottering, or that a new government without mass support has recently been installed. Perhaps the universities are closed and the unions are on strike; perhaps the government has fired on street demonstrators and mobilized troops to prevent peasants from seizing the land. Now, if several thousand rebels, declaring themselves an army of liberation, take the field, the matter seems more complicated. Has revolutionary civil war begun, or is this merely terrorism on an unusually large scale?

We have seen that many analysts attempt to settle this question by counting heads—which really means waiting for history to render its verdict. Does Marxist theory require the same waiting period? Lenin's denunciation of the SR's suggests not, since he described them as isolated intellectuals at a time when the Socialist Revolutionaries were better known and more widely admired than the Bolsheviks. What ultimately isolated them, in Lenin's view, was not their status as members of the intelligentsia; intellectuals played as important a role in the Bolshevik leadership as they did among the SR's. It was their failure to organize the most militant sector of the working class that disabled the SR's from leading a mass revolution. By assassinating hated tyrants bravely, they won great popularity, attracted financial support, and even influenced public policy to an extent. But pleasing the public was one thing and organizing it for revolution quite another. To end the revolutionary intellectuals' isolation it would take an organization so strongly linked to potent mass groups as to be capable of leading—that is, actually directing—the mass movement during a period of turbulence and rapid change.

For Lenin, this meant delaying armed struggle until the masses were ready to engage in it. In May, three months after the revolution of February had deposed the czar and installed the Kerensky-Miliukov government, Lenin wrote, "So far we are in the minority, the masses do not trust us yet. We can wait. . . . They will rush to our side; then, taking account of the new correlation of forces, we shall say: Our time has come."[26] During the subsequent months, as the provisional government became increasingly discredited, the Reds contended for support against other parties in the factories, the army, the representative councils of workers and soldiers (Soviets) and in the parliament. In September, Lenin and Trotsky rallied the Petrograd workers to defend the capital against General Lavr Kornilov's attempt to make himself military dictator of Russia. And finally, in November, when it was clear that they commanded a majority in the Soviets and could count on the troops in the major cities to join them, the Bolsheviks called for an insurrection. To them, this was the antithesis of terrorism. It would have been unthinkable to attack the organized power of the state without overwhelming mass support, expressed through the representative organs of dual power—the Soviets—and without having won over or at least neutralized the armed forces.

"The insurrection was thenceforth able to believe in its success, for it could rely upon a genuine majority of the people."[27] So says Trotsky, in his monumental *History of the Russian Revolution*. At the same time, however, he points out that the Bolsheviks were not a representative party in the formal, parliamentary sense, and that they could not have been, given the nature of popular revolution:

> Parliamentary consultations of the people are carried out at a single moment, whereas during a revolution the different layers of the population arrive at the same conclusion one after another and with inevitable, although sometimes very slight, intervals. . . . The difference in level and mood of the different layers of the people is overcome in action. The advance layers bring after them the wavering and isolate the opposing. The majority is not counted up but won over.[28]

This bears a certain resemblance to terrorist thought. For terrorists and Bolsheviks alike, violence planned and organized by a vanguard organization—by definition, a minority of the people—was a method of drawing wavering layers of the population into open struggle. Indeed, the German Socialist leader, Karl Kautsky, charged that under Lenin's guidance, the Bolsheviks had launched a terrorist assault upon the Kerensky regime.[29] Kautsky did not accuse the Communists of being intellectuals isolated from the working class. Rather, he asserted that *the working class itself* was isolated both in Russia, a predominantly peasant nation, and in Europe as a whole, where the masses were more interested in peaceful reform than in class war. Therefore, he argued, a revolution based on the small, backward Russian proletariat was really little more than a *coup d'état* whose initial success could be sustained only by state terror.

Lenin and Trotsky fired off a salvo of argument in return. Of course, it was clear that the Bolsheviks were not terrorists in the ordinary sense, because they had consistently refused to use political violence as a means of overcoming their previous isolation from the masses. For them, violence was not an organizing tool, a public relations device, or a means of intimidating government officials. It was a mass phenomenon that could be either directed and used or dissipated and wasted. In order to keep the conspiracy subordinate to the insurrection, military action was postponed until the party had become dominant among urban workers and commanded a large following in the peasant-based armed forces. Then, with the people in arms, the Bolsheviks used their authority to direct mass violence against the class in power. Kautsky's criticism implies that to be legitimate and nonterrorist, a revolution must be supported openly, actively, and *immediately* by a clear majority of the people nationwide. Lenin and Trotsky responded that none of the great revolutionary struggles of the past, not even the French Revolution or the American Civil War, met this criterion. Kautsky was clearly thinking in terms of parliamentary majorities, and forgetting that a revolution is decided not by votes, but by winning over the population, layer by layer.[30]

Essential to the revolutionary process, therefore, are the advance layers of workers, soldiers, farmers, and intellectuals who are won to the party's banner *prior* to the beginning of open hostilities. These committed activists can leverage support from an ever-widening circle of participants after the first blows are struck. On the eve of the October Revolution, Lenin's party numbered several hundred thousand, and its influence was dominant among several million workers and farmers—far from a majority of the Russian people, but a force sufficient both in quantity and quality to serve as a pole of attraction for millions more. In declaring this party to be the equivalent of a terrorist gang, Kautsky attempted to play the role of Marx denouncing Bakunin. In this view, Bolshevism reincarnated the spirit of the anarchists who attempted to substitute revolutionary will for the fulfillment of objective economic conditions. The Bolsheviks were trying to rush history, when the truth was that backward nations like Russia could not attain socialism without first undergoing a lengthy period of capitalist development and bourgeois rule. (Interestingly, the Socialist Revolutionaries shared this view.) It was impossible to move further left than Kerensky's mild, patriotic liberalism without savage repression of the peasantry. The October Revolution was therefore premature—hence, an essentially terrorist initiative.

To this, the Red leaders offered a three-part answer: First, the Russian proletariat was not isolated on the European stage. The conditions for revolution were at least as ripe in industrialized nations like Germany as they were in agrarian nations like Russia. Second, it was not isolated in the former czarist empire either, since the poor peasants were already allying themselves with revolutionary workers against the rich. Kautsky misunderstood the role peasants might play in social revolution *if* the proletariat maintained a leading role. Third, and most important, even if the European revolution failed and the alliance with the peasantry foundered, the workers' party would have no choice but to hold power as long as it could, since there was never any possibility of Kerensky and his liberals forming a stable government. For historical reasons, liberal businesspeople in poverty-stricken Russia were no more capable of constructing a democratic capitalist state than are most of their Third World counterparts today. The real choice for the Russian people was therefore between Reds and Whites, forces opposing each other with such intensity that any winner would be compelled to use terror against the unreconciled, overthrown enemy. The alternative to Red rule was not a moderate regime; it was a protofascist dictatorship of capital, the army, and the church.

This was a powerful point. The expectation that a wave of workers' revolutions would soon sweep Central Europe was dashed, but if Lenin's analysis was correct, the class struggle precipitated in the cities would rapidly polarize the Russian peasantry, and poorer peasants would flock to his banner. The vast majority would choose Red socialism over White clerical-fascism, thus insuring the mass character of the struggle, as well as a Bolshevik victory. Lenin admitted that,

> if the Bolshevik proletariat in the capitals and large industrial cen-ters had not been able to rally the village poor around itself against the rich peasants, this would indeed have proved that Russia was "unripe" for the socialist revolution.[31]

But rally they did. In one sense, the outcome of the Civil War was the decisive answer to Kautsky. Obviously, the Bolsheviks were not mere terrorists. They were the party of the urban masses and, increasingly as time went on, of the soldiers ("peas-ants in uniform") and poor peasants as well. Nevertheless, it is undeniable that at the time they seized power in the larger cities, the Reds were not yet the dominant political force in the rural villages. "In the course of November and December," wrote Lenin, "the revolution spread to the entire army and peasantry." It did not reach the remote rural districts, however, until "a year after the proletarian revolution in the capitals."[32] In other words, the Bolshevik workers first seized power in the urban centers, then projected it (via advance layers of peasant-soldiers) into the countryside, where they defended it against the Whites and foreign troops. The peasant masses were won to the Red banner *after* the October Revolution had triumphed in the cities and in the course of a continuous process that included civil war.

While this fact certainly does not prove Kautsky's thesis, it does illustrate the novelty, from a classical Marxist perspective, of a proletarian revolution by stages. A from-the-cities-to-the-countryside strategy had long been accepted by Western Marxists, too, but in the industrialized states, a successful series of urban insurrections *was* the revolution, while in semi-industrial Russia, the workers would win only if they succeeded in persuading or compelling the country people to support them. Now, if this support were quickly mobilized, and an effective peasant army formed rapidly around the proletarian core, the rural civil war could be characterized with justice as a continuation of the urban insurrection. This impression would be strengthened if the rural masses had already been in turmoil (as they had been for some time in Russia) and if they had been moving to the left politically since the urban uprisings occurred.

The Bolshevik-led uprisings of 1917 intersected a rising curve of mass revolt in the countryside; so much so that,

the first Bolshevik decrees of November 8, calling for immediate cessation of hostilities [in World War I] and an end to all private property in land, merely gave a stamp of approval to processes that were already going on in the countryside, and which no political party could have resisted even if it wanted to.[33]

By the end of the year, the Socialist Revolutionary party, formerly the strongest revolutionary organization in the villages, had split into Right and Left wings. The leftists blocked with the Bolsheviks while the rightists, representing the increasingly isolated rural middle classes, flirted with counter-revolution. So rapid and deep was this polarization that the Reds felt justified in refusing to convene the Constituent Assembly, which had been elected several months earlier and would have been dominated by rightist SR's. The rightists thereupon fell into the arms of the White generals, and the issue was settled by bloody civil war.[34]

Kautsky's charge of terrorism would have been sustainable if

the Bolsheviks had not been the party of the Russian proletariat
in October 1917, and it would have been arguable if the October Revolution had not spread like wildfire from the urban core.
As it was, the accusation seemed academic and irrelevant.
Trotsky rejoined that the civil war was terroristic only in the
sense that, like revolution, war is founded upon intimidation:

> A victorious war, generally speaking, destroys only an insignificant
> part of the conquered army, intimidating the remainder and break-
> ing their will. The revolution works in the same way: it kills in-
> dividuals, and intimidates thousands. In this sense, the Red Terror
> is not distinguishable from the armed insurrection, the direct con-
> tinuation of which it represents.[35]

Of course, this did not deprive either war or revolution of
their popular, mass character. All political violence is founded
upon intimidation, even the criminal justice system that seeks
to deter (that is, intimidate) many potential wrongdoers by
punishing a few. But the state terror of a revolutionary class
differs both qualitatively and quantitatively from the terrorism
of groups like the White counter-revolutionaries.[36] The Whites
lost the Civil War because their political weakness and their
inability to inspire and organize the masses was translated into
military weakness on the field of battle. A relatively conservative student of revolution, David Wilkinson, sums up the
reasons for the White defeat as follows:

> The Whites were unable to cope with production collapses, short-
> ages, inflation, speculation, and blind business-as-usual behavior in
> the economy. They failed to overcome official corruption, national
> independentism, and class conflict in politics. The Reds were good
> at organizing, good at repression of harmful behavior, and good at
> managing useful class alliances. The natural political supporters of
> the Whites, who could become willing fighters, were fewer than
> those of the Bolsheviks. The program and propaganda of the Whites
> were less satisfactory than those of the Reds—at least to the peasant
> masses whose bodies and food both sides conscripted for the war.
> Forced mobilization provoked disastrous desertions and guerrilla

insurrections behind the White lines, while providing the Reds with superior numbers at decisive points.[37]

These political weaknesses can, in turn, be traced to changes in social structure that were dissolving the links between Russian peasants and landowners and facilitating the formation of a peasant-worker alliance. For this reason, Trotsky maintained, state terror could not in the long run defeat "a historically rising class," although it might well be effective against "a reactionary class which does not want to leave the scene of operations."[38]

This argument is compelling; the Bolsheviks seem clearly justified in emphasizing the mass character of the struggles they led notwithstanding the essential role (unforeseen by Marx) played by the vanguard party. Still, placing terrorism in direct opposition to revolutionary Marxism seems too simple, especially when one recognizes that a key to the Bolsheviks' success was their ability to synthesize, in practice, the Marxist and terrorist strategies for revolution. From Marx and his western European disciplines, Lenin accepted the distinction between preparing the revolution, a process that excluded premature attacks against the state, and the revolution itself, which was to be an explosion of mass violence organized and led by the workers' party. From the terrorists he adopted the notion that a minority of the people might initiate a struggle that would draw the masses by stages into violent opposition to the existing order. Marxist elements predominate in this synthesis because the minority that initiates the struggle is substantial; because although a small percentage of the total population, it represents a majority of the politically active workers; and because it quickly assembles a national majority. That is, the winning-over of successive layers of the population takes place *rapidly,* as part of a continuing mass struggle to seize and maintain state power.

But what if this is not the case? Recall that, in an important sense, neither the Bolsheviks nor their immediate predecessors in power, the Kerensky-Miliukov liberals, defeated the czar's army. That army disintegrated after more than two and one-half years of world war prior to the February 1917 uprising. In a sense, the war did the job that the SR terrorists had set for themselves: it crippled the military apparatus, tore apart the tattered cloak of czarist legitimacy, and, both literally and ideologically, set the peasantry in motion. Clearly, Lenin's call to "turn imperialist war into revolutionary war" would not have been heeded but for the moral and political isolation of the bureaucracy. As it was, "the dynasty fell by shaking like rotten fruit before the revolution even had time to approach its first problems."[39]

Suppose, however, that a revolutionary movement is not carried to victory Russian-style, by rapid extension of a successful urban insurrection into the countryside. Imagine instead that the urban uprising is crushed (or that it never materializes), driving the insurgents into backward rural areas where they must either continue the fight against superior forces or abandon their struggle altogether. If that struggle were to become extremely protracted, putting the masses in the position of passive supporters, neutral observers, or unwilling victims of the violent movement, then what began as revolution might degenerate into terrorism. Now make a final supposition: imagine that, by one means or another, the terrorists manage to defeat the incumbent forces and seize power. Is this, in fact, what happened in China and Vietnam, in Algeria and Cuba? Is it happening now in El Salvador and the Philippines? Many conservative critics and some leftist celebrants of these struggles think it is, asserting that, contrary to both Marx's and Lenin's ideas, terrorist tactics *can* produce social revolution. I disagree, for reasons that will become clear in part V as we discuss the twentieth-century wars of national liberation.

PART V

TERRORISM
AND NATIONAL
LIBERATION

Chapter 12

Terrorism and

Nationalism

IF the relationship between revolutionary violence and terrorism now seems murky or confused, this is largely the result of the wars of national liberation: violent struggles in industrially backward nations by groups seeking either national independence, social revolution, or both.

The awkwardness of this definition suggests that these struggles correspond to no single model, least of all that of Russia's October Revolution. Some were protracted civil wars, consuming the energies and lives of an entire generation or more. Others took fewer lives and far less time to complete. In certain cases, rebel leaders aimed to dispossess landlords and big capitalists, close their nations to foreign investment, and mobilize their followers for social revolution. In others, their goal was to achieve political independence while leaving existing social structures intact. Most common were the mixed movements

which attempted to combine independence with some degree of
social reform—frequently with surprising results. In 1960,
when an alliance of liberal businesspeople with radical nationalists was shattered in Cuba, Castro joined with the Communists (who had initially opposed his guerrilla adventurism) to
unleash a social revolution on that island. In Algeria, on the
other hand, a regime initially proclaiming itself radical and
Marxist was easily displaced by moderate nationalists who
were more interested in Saharan oil than in class struggle.

The relationship of terrorism to these diverse struggles is
complex, but some confusion can be dispelled at the outset
simply by distinguishing terrorist violence from violence that
terrifies. Assassination, sabotage, kidnapping, and guerrilla tactics have proved as useful to mass movements and established
states as they have to terrorists. Merrill's Marauders, dropped
behind Japanese lines in Burma during World War II, were
guerrilla fighters. So were the irregular forces of the Chinese
People's Liberation Army (PLA), which numbered in the hundreds of thousands and supplemented the PLA's conventional
army. And so, in a much different context, are the Peruvian
rebels of the Shining Path *(Sendero Luminoso)* movement and the
New People's Army guerrillas in the Philippines. Guerrilla
fighters may be terrorists, but terrorism, properly defined, is
exemplary small-group violence. Its function is to *create* the
mass movement, whereas guerrilla war, sabotage, or assassination may simply represent a choice of weapons by the mass
movement. For this reason, it makes little sense to say that
"individual terror has been practiced on a fairly wide scale by
Communist-led movements of national liberation such as in
Vietnam."[1] All this really means is that tactics frequently associated with individual terrorism have been employed by the
leaders of mass struggles as well.

During the 1960s, for example, cadres of the Vietnamese
National Liberation Front (NLF) assassinated several thousand
village officials appointed by the Ngo Dinh Diem regime, and
were themselves assassinated in even larger numbers by hit
teams organized by the CIA in its Operation Phoenix.[2] To call

either campaign individual terror, however, is to ignore the fact that both of them were directed and carried out by highly structured mass organizations. By the time the NLF campaign began, the Communist-led coalition had mobilized millions of followers politically and organized "a hierarchy of committees linking the village to the district, the district to the province, the province to the zone, the zone to the central committee."[3] By the same token, the CIA assassination program, which reportedly liquidated twenty thousand NLF activists and sympathizers, was carried out by the South Vietnamese Army, clearly a mass organization, despite its shrinking political base.[4] Terrifying violence in general—a category that includes assassinations, burning villages, and annihilating cities from the air—has become horribly characteristic of virtually all forms of modern warfare. This is probably because it is impossible nowadays to fight a major war that is not a people's war—a struggle tending to obliterate the line between civilians and combatants. Nevertheless, what we need to know is not whether war is terroristic —because of course it is—but whether terrorism can generate mass movements for national liberation.

The question is surely not whether Ho Chi Minh, as leader of North Vietnam and the southern insurgency, was a terrorist. If the term means anything, it does not apply to him. The issue is whether he became the leader of his nation by somehow converting a small guerrilla band into a mass-based people's army. We understand that successful national liberation struggles generally end by involving the masses actively as fighters and militant supporters; but we suspect that there may be some truth in the idea that these struggles begin as terrorist adventures. Interestingly, both conservatives and terrorist sympathizers share the same scenario: today a bandit gang, tomorrow the politburo. The successful nationalist revolutionary, in this view, is a terrorist who made good. But closer analysis suggests a more complex relationship between terrorism and war.

As a rule, terrorism is most effective when four conditions are present: *1.* The theater of action is a society already disrupted by economic crisis or war. *2.* The activists are supported by fellow members of some ethnic, religious, or national group. *3.* The activists' aims are limited to destabilization of the regime in power or opposition organizations. *4.* Their opponents lack the finances, the will, or the political strength to conduct an extended counterterrorist campaign.

All of these factors were operative, for example, when a few thousand KKK fighters succeeded in "liberating" the American South from rule by blacks and white Republicans after the Civil War.[5] The Klan was a diffuse, decentralized organization composed largely of Confederate veterans, and led by ruined ex-officers. It operated with great freedom in the war-ravaged, chaotic South, and managed fairly easily to prevent freedmen from voting and organizing, to silence their white supporters, and to keep northern occupation troops on the defensive. Klan violence forced the war-weary North to choose between fighting a prolonged antiguerrilla struggle to restructure southern society and acceding to the return of white-supremacist state governments. That choice was debated only briefly. It may, in fact, have been predetermined when Confederate soldiers were permitted to keep their horses and their weapons at Appomattox Courthouse.

Klan terrorism was purely nationalist. Its success was directly proportioned to its localism, negativism, and modesty of aim. It did not challenge the vital interests of the northern industrialists or attempt, even in the South, to set class against class. On the contrary, its goal was restoration—right-wing reform *without* social upheaval—and its success was assured when southern whites of all classes opted for racial solidarity and against social change. Compare the Klan's success with the rise of right-wing organizations like the German Freikorps, the Rumanian Iron Guard, Hungarian Arrow Cross, and Croatian Ustache in Central Europe following World War I.[6] Once again, the setting was a postwar society that was economically devastated, socially chaotic, lacking strong political authority. Once more, calls were heard for political counter-revolution to suppress the threat of social revolution, and war veterans responded to the romance of nationalist terrorism. Governments were weak and discredited; their opponents were unable to act together. In the interwar period, right-wing nationalists took advantage of these conditions and assassinated liberal and leftist leaders, intimidated the moderates, destabilized fragile democratic regimes, and stimulated popular longing for a return to law and order. Clearly, their activities helped soften up a number of nations for eventual fascist takeover.

On the other hand, the terrorists of the European Right could not liberate their territory in Klan fashion, since their opponents were organized on a mass basis by the Socialists and Communists. It would take more than small-group violence to smash the class-based organizations of the Left. Thus, after coming to power, the fascists added a ghastly new dimension to the meaning of state terror. They did not take power as terrorists, however, despite their fondness for street fighting and thuggery, but as leaders of well-funded mass movements. To be sure, Joseph Goebbels's propaganda machine canonized the earlier terrorists of the far Right; pilgrimages were made to the shrine of the assassins of Foreign Minister Rathenau, and martyred killer Horst Wessel was immortalized in song. On the other hand, Adolf Hitler—who had relied on legal methods to become chancellor of Germany—exterminated the radicals in his own party, including most of the surviving ex-terrorists, in the "blood purge" of 1934, which liquidated Ernst Roehm and his Redshirts.[7] This apparent contradiction suggests a profound ambiguity in the relationship between nationalist movements and terrorism. Whatever their political character, successful nationalist struggles involve far more popular participation than the phrase "individual terrorism" implies. Nevertheless, terrorism can play a significant role in the formation and development of nationalist movements, particularly if their political orientation is conservative or moderately liberal.

During the 1940s, for example, conservative Jewish terrorist groups succeeded in driving the British out of Palestine for many of the same reasons that the KKK was successful in expelling northern troops from the South: the four conditions for effective terrorism (postwar disorder, nationalist solidarity, modesty of aims, and opposition weakness) were all present. The Irgun's methods, featuring highly selective violence against the foreign occupiers and more indiscriminate terrorism against the Arabs, were well adapted to the tasks of making Palestine ungovernable by the British and inspiring Palestinians to abandon their homes. Moreover, they could be used effectively *without* mass support (and were, in fact, opposed by the larger Labor party and its military wing, the Haganah). Begin's aim was not to mobilize the masses and transform the social order, but to make the cost of administering the Palestine mandate unacceptable to the war-weary, virtually bankrupt British. The Irgun was a militant right-wing organization opposed to the Labor party's rather pedestrian brand of socialism. Nevertheless, it was clear that the result of its campaign, if successful, would be to help eliminate the British buffer, bring on war with the Arabs, and force the Labor party to participate. Begin's extremism was thus an extreme anti-British and anti-Arab nationalism that left open the question of how the Jewish state would be structured socially and economically after liberation. It succeeded in part because it attempted so little and in part because there *was* a mass organization that had no choice but to fight once the British had been driven out.

The Irgun campaign is important in another respect as well. Begin's memoirs make it clear that he seldom acted without calculating the publicity-effect of his deeds on a variety of audiences, including Palestinian Jews and Arabs, the British public, American Jewry, and world opinion as reflected in the United Nations. Jewish nationalist terrorism was not intended to win friends so much as to influence people. It was calculated to dramatize the Israelis' willingness to fight, to create a new image of the Jew as implacable adversary rather than perennial victim. It was meant also to shatter the Anglo-Jewish alliance forged in World War II, to suggest to the international community that the Jewish right to remain in Palestine was beyond debate, and to make a binational solution to the Palestine problem appear unfeasible. Small-group violence employed in such a calculated and symbolic manner represents a kind of bargaining. It "creates facts" by announcing a cause that can no longer be ignored—a new capacity to make trouble that must figure henceforth in political calculations of great powers, even if it lacks the independent strength to win.

The Algerian nationalists used similar tactics in 1956–57, when they unleased a wave of terrorism against French civilians and native collaborators in the city of Algiers. The Battle of Algiers focused world attention on the FLN fighters' desperate struggle to secure their nation's political independence from France. It did *not* drive the French out of the country; indeed, from a military point of view, the French were the consistent winners in Algeria. But by demonstrating a continuing ability to make trouble, by inducing the French to commit counterterrorist atrocities, and by playing the international political game well, the Algerian nationalists were able to divide French public opinion and, after three more years of fighting, to force French withdrawal from their country.

In one sense, the Algerian movement's political alignment reversed that of the Palestinian Jews. The Battle of Algiers was the work of the internal forces led by Ahmad Ben Bella, a leftist, while the larger, external army led by Houari Boumedienne, which seized power shortly after independence, was more conservative. In both cases, then, terrorism by relatively extreme elements of a nationalist coalition ended by serving the interests of the moderates. "Where are the heroes of Algiers?," asked commentator Eqbal Ahmad, after a public showing of Gillo Pontecorvo's film, *The Battle of Algiers,* in Chicago. "Either dead, or in jail, or in Paris."

The examples provided by Algeria and Palestine suggest a paradox of nationalist terrorism: it is most effective when a nonterrorist army, supported by a broad-based coalition, waits in the wings while terrorists and counterterrorists play out their prologue. No terrorist act has ever mobilized the masses, as the Narodniki had hoped. But terrorist campaigns *have* disrupted normal life, incited the authorities to excesses of indiscriminate violence, and generated states of political emergency. The effect of an extended terrorist/counterterrorist struggle, as Trotsky understood, is to exhaust both the masses and the regime, and to turn popular longing toward a peace-making, authority-restoring savior. Earlier Marxists did not foresee that this order-restoring "man on horseback" might be an external army hostile to the regime. But they were correct to assume that no external force assuming power in an environment of mass exhaustion could remain closely connected to the people. If, on the other hand, there is no external army capable of capitalizing on this exhaustion, the group best able to restore order does so. Most often, as one might expect, that group consists of powerful local interests determined to avoid a profound social upheaval.

The preconditions for successful terrorism are more likely to be present when the struggle pits fighters who represent some self-identified nation against a foreign occupier, than when the contestants for power represent competing social classes. Terrorism may convince a colonial occupier that the game is not worth the candle—or that direct administration of a dependent state is not cost-effective. Rarely has it convinced a local ruling class to renounce its privileges and power. In Lebanon, for example, the success of Shiite extremists in forcing U.S., French, and Italian troops to evacuate Beirut rested primarily on the foreigners' vulnerability, and not (as the American press insisted repeatedly) on the terrorists' religious fanaticism. The Western powers' inability to discover the organizational structure or membership of the Islamic Jihad suggests that that group was as local and decentralized, as capable of disappearing into a mass of ethnic brethren, and probably as socially conservative as the KKK. This is precisely the type of organization that triumphant nationalists later hail as a forerunner, and with cause, even as they persecute its surviving members. Terrorists activity *can* play an instrumental role in promoting nationalist goals, in large part because the support commanded by an effective nationalist movement differs both in quantity and in quality from that essential to the success of a social revolution.

Let me insist on this contrast even at the risk of overdrawing it. Social revolutionaries do not aim merely to expel an occupier or replace an old regime with a new one. They attempt to displace an entire ruling class and to alter the real constitution: the interrelated social and political institutions that vest the power of that class. For them, the passive support of a sympathetic population is not enough. In predominantly nationalist struggles, it is possible for the masses to delegate the war-making function to military specialists. Social revolutions, however, tend to become people's wars because the institutions they attack and seek to reconstruct are those that organize the daily lives of the people. Naturally, this does not mean that, in revolution, every adult and child takes up arms. It does mean that the more the movement attempts to achieve socially divisive, radical goals, as opposed to national independence pure and simple, the more active is the support demanded from sympathizers.

Whether they tilt ideologically to the left or to the right, nationalist coalitions are typically organized *across* class lines. Their leaders, representing both upper- and lower-class groups, agree to postpone their differences in favor of a common effort to liberate the cultural or ethnic nation from an oppressive regime. That is, they agree to hold things in place locally while the struggle against the outsider proceeds. It is this holding in place, above all, that limits mass participation in nationalist struggles to certain relatively passive functions: supply of money and matériel to the fighters, refusal of information to the authorities, and (usually as victory nears) participation in strikes, boycotts, or demonstrations. By contrast, revolutionary coalitions mobilize the lower classes against both the outside oppressor, if one exists, *and* their social superiors. In order to organize lower-class violence (and sometimes to win allies among the middle classes), they may restrain their followers' zeal somewhat, as both Lenin and Mao Tse-tung did by protecting the land of the freeholding middle peasants against seizure by poor peasants. But such a coalition wins, in the end, only by allowing fundamental social relations to be put in question, thus politicizing daily life and extending the front of the struggle into virtually every working-class district and rural province.

In this sense, social revolution is the antithesis of terrorism. It is not small-group violence seeking mass support, but mass activism seeking organized defense. Those held in place socially by a nationalist coalition are asked to lend their support to a violent vanguard that will represent them in battle against the authorities. But when peasants seize plantations and workers occupy factories, when the armed forces mutiny and students take over their schools, the old distinctions between activist and supporter begin to disappear. Indeed, even where mass activism is brought under the operational control of a revolutionary party or coalition (clearly a precondition for success), it remains the sine qua non of social revolution. The history of modern revolutionary movements bears out Trotsky's statement that,

> Without a guiding organization the energy of the masses would dissipate like steam not enclosed in a piston box. But nevertheless what moves things is not the piston or the box, but the steam.[8]

Thus, while terrorism appears in many nationalist struggles as one mode of warfare among others, not necessarily vital but legitimated by the cause, in revolution it appears either as a jumping of the gun or as a refusal to quit after mass activism has collapsed—in other words, as a mistake. Compare the Nazis' sanctification of their terrorist forerunners with the Bolsheviks' insistence that leftist terrorism, however understandable, had always been a mistake.

Now, one might object quite properly that this contrast is overdrawn. Liberation movements in the Third World do not come neatly packaged and labeled "social-revolutionary" or "nationalist." In fact, most have had a mixed character, combining the pursuit of revolutionary goals with powerful drives toward national unification and independence. Even so, the historical evidence suggests, terrorism is rarely effective as a mode of class struggle. On the contrary, its use by the partisans of a mixed movement generally signifies either that a serious mistake of timing has occurred or that nationalist impulses have *replaced* social-revolutionary expectations. This seems clearly to be the case, at present, among partisans of the IRA Provisional wing and virtually all components of the PLO, not to mention the various nominally leftist and rightist militias now rending Lebanon. Terrorism by members of the Sunni Moslem Brotherhood, or by the Shiite Moslem sects professing loyalty to Khomeini, is considered socially revolutionary only by those who have no conception of class struggle. And those African liberation movements that relied on small-group violence to destabilize and replace colonial regimes discovered that their dreams of African socialism had been fatally undermined by the tribal nationalism they helped foment.

In other words, the usefulness of terrorism to a mixed social-revolutionary/nationalist liberation movement seems to vary directly with the components of the mix. Although terrorist fighters rarely take power even under nationalist auspices, predominantly nationalist movements have been able to take advantage of a terrorist phase of struggle. By contrast, liberation movements that are seriously committed to overthrowing capitalism have generally renounced terrorism altogether, or have come to see it as counterproductive to their social aims. In this regard, it is instructive to compare two mixed movements that relied heavily on guerrilla warfare tactics: the Chinese and Cuban revolutions. Both movements mixed nationalist with social-revolutionary aspirations. Both were called terrorist by their enemies, as well as by some misguided friends. But while revolutionary organizations led by Communists in China and Vietnam certainly made use of terrifying violence they did not function as terrorist groups. On the other hand, in Cuba, where Castro came to power as the leader of a two-thousand-man guerrilla army, the struggle against the Batista regime *did* resemble terrorism in its method of organization, strategy, and rationale. Each of these cases, as well as certain recent outbreaks of guerrilla struggle, will be examined in greater detail in the following chapter.

Chapter 13

Terrorism and

Guerrilla War

THAT ENEMIES of the Chinese and Vietnamese revolutionary movements would brand their leaders terrorists is understandable, and not just because of enmity. The first attempt by Communists to lead a revolution in China ended in catastrophic defeat for the Reds.[1] In the 1920s, their main source of strength lay in the large cities, where the Chinese Communist party (CCP) was rapidly becoming the party of the urban proletariat. However, their alliance with Chiang Kai-shek's nationalists, which they entered into at Stalin's urging, collapsed in 1927, when Chiang massacred thousands of worker-militants in Shanghai. Three years later an attempted insurrection in Canton was bloodily suppressed. Driven from the large cities, the Communists attempted to establish a Soviet republic in southern Kiangsi province, but after four more years of civil war they were again defeated and compelled to undertake their Long March to far-off Yenan. There, the workers' party was reconstructed on a mass base of peasants who were schooled in Mao Tse-tung's unique brand of revolutionary warfare. Unlike the Bolsheviks, who in two years extended a successful urban insurrection into the countryside, the Chinese Communists were forced to begin anew in the remote rural provinces of the Northwest and engage in protracted war against superior forces.

In order to secure his base in the rural population and to harness Chinese nationalism to his own cause, Mao adapted Marxist conceptions of class struggle to the reality of Chinese underdevelopment. His "bloc of four classes" allied poor farmers and landless laborers with the small-propertied middle peasantry against the large landowners, warlords, and rural "bullies." Similarly, it sought the active support of urban workers, intellectuals, and the so-called national bourgeoisie (local businesspeople oriented toward Chinese economic development) against foreign-dominated business interests and their Chinese collaborators.[2] Maintenance of this bloc required that the Communists prevent the wholesale seizure of land and business enterprises, at least until the party's power could be projected nationally. At the same time, however, defeat of the Kuomintang Nationalists required a social revolution—the unleashing of violent class struggle against specifically targeted groups. Mao was able to exercise an unusual degree of control over this process because of an equally unusual opportunity: apparently isolated in Yenan province, his movement liberated extensive rural areas from Nationalist or warlord control *before* seizing power nationwide and encircling the cities. The strategy of encirclement of the cities by a revolutionary force based in the countryside has been widely noted and discussed. What deserves more attention is the fact that the liberated territories were governed by the Communists and defended by the PLA for a decade or more prior to the victory of 1949, thus reversing the usual sequence of events (from revolution to administration).

From its inception, the PLA was not so much a hardy band of adventuresome guerrillas as a disciplined force composed of both regular and guerrilla units acting under civilian control. Its tasks were to defend the liberated territories, to harass a temporarily superior enemy, and finally, to defeat that enemy in conventional warfare. This said, it is nevertheless true that military activity in general, and guerrilla warfare in particular, played a much more important role for a longer period of time in China than it had in Russia. Not only was the Chinese Civil War protracted, consuming the energies of an entire generation, but the Communists' struggle against the Japanese enabled them to come forward as the most energetic and patriotic opponents of foreign domination. (In Vietnam, where a similar development brought Ho Chi Minh's Viet Minh to the fore, there was considerably less competition for the national leadership.) It is this militarism, above all, combined with frequent reliance of the revolutionary army on irregular tactics, that has persuaded some observers that revolutionary civil war is a species of terrorism.

The parallel seems especially clear to those who believe that revolutionists use force primarily to intimidate neutral or unfriendly villagers—or as hawkish scholars stated in connection with the Vietnam insurgency, to demonstrate that the authorities are powerless to defend them against guerrilla attacks. Such critics view revolutionary war in a rural setting as a contest between rival elites for the allegiance of an essentially passive population; and hence, as terrorist in nature. The fact that such struggles are frequently protracted, with the result that violence tends to become politicized and politics militarized, seems further evidence of the equation. Even sympathetic analysts of the Chinese Revolution have noted Mao's high regard for the military virtues and his belief in the capacity of revolutionary will to overcome material obstacles to political development.[3] Furthermore, the *style* of rural civil war is reminiscent of terrorism, especially when insurgents engage in irregular activities such as sabotage, robbery ("expropriations"), assassination, and hit-and-run attacks on enemy outposts. The kidnapping of Chiang Kai-shek by Red guerrillas was one of the more dramatic events of the Chinese Civil War, while both sides attempted to make use of the terrorist secret societies that had long expressed violent resistance to foreign domination.[4] On this basis, some analysts conclude that even if Lenin was no terrorist, Mao Tse-tung certainly was, at least in the early stages of his career as a rural revolutionary.

This view is incorrect. It is echoed, ironically enough, by proponents and practitioners of urban guerrilla warfare—those who believe it possible to adapt the strategies of Third World revolutionary movements to the requirements of an advanced industrial society. They too assume that the formation of a Red army begins with the activities of an embryo force (a fraction, brigade, or nucleus) whose attacks are designed to awaken the masses, either by demonstrating the state's impotence or by causing it to overreact. Consider Bommi Baumann's explanation of the theoretical basis for the West German June 2d movement, which he helped organize. In *How it All Began* he states:

> Mao provided our theoretical basis: "On The Mentality of Roaming Bands of Rebels." From the so-called robber bands, he and Chu-Teh had created the first cadre of the Red Army. We took our direction from that.[5]

The myth that Mao built the PLA around a nucleus of robber bands, like most myths, contains a grain of truth. Rural banditry was endemic in China, and some bandits (like some secret society members) were undoubtedly recruited to the Red banner. As Eric Wolf informs us, however, the Chinese Red Army was organized in 1927, following the Shanghai debacle, when a partisan force recruited by Mao in Hunan province from miners, peasant guards, and mutinous Kuomintang soldiers was joined by "several crack regiments of the Kuomintang National Revolutionary Army. . . . These—20,000 strong—revolted at Nanching on August 1, 1927."[6] This was hardly a robber band! Even after this army was decimated in the urban phase of the revolution,

> by recruiting peasants—once the policy of relying on the hinterland had been decided on—the army once more regained strength in its

new redoubts until it numbered once again 200,000 regulars in 1934 [that is, *before* the Long March began]. These were supported by an equal number of Red Guards and guerrillas.[7]

During several such cycles of decimation and resurrection, the PLA's numbers waxed and waned, but the character of the army was determined by its constitution, purpose, and method of organization. It was composed, even initially, of regular troops supported by guerrilla forces (which, Mao wrote, "complement each other like a man's right arm and left arm"[8]). Both "arms" were subordinated to the control of the "head"—the party—which used organized violence not to discover the intentions of the masses or to awaken them, but to mobilize the energies of those already liberated from tradition by the collapse of the old social order in China. When Mao was sent to Hunan province early in 1927 to investigate a wave of spontaneous peasant uprisings, he found that "of all the peasants in Hunan, almost half are organized."[9] Approximately ten million peasants, largely self-organized, were already attacking the "local bullies and head gentry." This was the soil out of which the revolutionary army grew—a rural population that, far from requiring awakening by a violent vanguard, had unleashed mass terror on its own.

Mao was quite clear about his differences with Leninism. In backward China, he wrote,

> The fundamental task of the Communist Party is not to go through a long period of legal struggle before launching an insurrection or civil war. Its task is not to seize first the big cities and then the countryside, but to take the opposite direction.[10]

Nevertheless, this strategy of encirclement retained an essential Leninist assumption: the masses (in particular, the tactically mobile peasants) were already awake. In many parts of the country they were already organized, but even the unorganized could be won rapidly to the revolutionary cause in the course of civil war. Johnson and other analysts are no doubt correct to

stress the importance of the Japanese invasion in drawing unorganized peasants under Communist leadership both in China
and in Vietnam.[11] But neither Communist military prowess nor
the collapse of civil order can explain why Mao's cause grew
progressively stronger during the Japanese occupation while
Chiang's declined. This can be understood only if we recognize
that anarchic social conditions gave the Chinese insurgents the
time and space to govern civilly—that is, to prove the superior-
ity of their revolutionary program and thus win the mass support that neither Japanese nor the Nationalists could command.
As Ahmad has said, successful Third World revolutionaries
do not outfight the regime in power so much as they out-
administer it.[12]

One implication of this idea is that protracted armed struggle *can* advance the cause of social revolution, but only where
it is possible to administer and defend some form of liberated
territory. Variations on the Chinese model are possible; in
South Vietnam, villages controlled by the regime during the
day were governed by the NLF at night. But without opportunity to *govern,* armed guerrillas tend to become a purely military force, compelled by the logic of underground activity to
isolate themselves from the people and increasingly vulnerable to attack by larger forces. Had the Yenan sanctuary been
denied, and had the Japanese invasion not provided further
opportunity to expand the area of liberated territory, revolutionary warfare in China might well have degenerated into
populist terrorism, with Mao playing the role of a latter-day
Azev. Maoist strategy escapes criticism on these grounds because, by establishing an alternative government province by
province, it avoided the kind of "hermetic conspiracy" that
"totally excludes agitational and organizational work among
the masses."[13] On the contrary, the CCP's conduct of the Chinese Civil War clearly maintained the primacy of politics,
broadly speaking, over military technique, and the predominance of social-revolutionary over nationalist goals.

We see, then, that the Chinese Revolution was not a terrorist
enterprise in any meaningful sense. Nor did it grow from a

terrorist seed, as Baumann and certain anarchists have maintained. Long before its resort to arms, the CCP had become a mass party of urban workers, allied (almost suicidally) with the Nationalists; and when that alliance was shattered, the Communist leaders found a rural base of support more than sufficient to make up for previous losses. True, the appeal to the peasantry, the use of the PLA for the political education of rural recruits, the protracted nature of the struggle, and Mao's heroic style—not to mention the irregular tactics of his guerrillas—evoked the shades of Bakunin and the Russian populists. But whatever tendencies toward terrorism may have existed in the Chinese revolutionary movement were countered by the establishment of liberated areas as centers of revolutionary administration and foci for expansion. Modern urban guerrillas have not understood that the strategy of protracted revolutionary war may be exportable, but only where the insurgents enjoy mass support from the start and where local conditions make it possible to win the war piecemeal. And clearly, if piecemeal conquests are to be defended, the war must not become *too* protracted. The revolutionary forces must increase their size and capability quickly enough to overtake the ascending curve of state repression, or else face a slow descent into terrorism.

This being the case, how does one explain the resort to urban guerrilla tactics by a subsequent generation of militants calling themselves Marxist-Leninists? In the city, the piecemeal liberation of territory is impossible unless the organs of public order (especially the military organs) have already broken down. The maintenance of a political organization that links the urban guerrillas to the people and controls their activities is equally impossible unless a popular uprising or defeat in war has already dealt the old regime a mortal blow. But if the urban masses are in arms and the machinery of repression has been crippled, why put a would-be nucleus or Red Army Fraction into the field? Why not simply organize the Red Army itself? One answer may be that in some locales, popular dissatisfaction is high enough and the efficiency of the armed forces low enough to permit urban guerrillas to survive for quite a long time. But this is precisely the situation in which the Marxist critique of terrorism seems most germane, for if public order and confidence have been eroded and no new leadership or vision of order stirs mass support, the revolutionist's task is to develop that leadership and vision, not to intensify calamities. When Marighella predicts the results of urban guerrilla activity in Brazil, one hears the authentic voice of the terrorist:

> The government has no alternative except to intensify repression. The police networks, house searches, arrests of innocent people and of suspects, closing off streets, make life in the city unbearable. The military dictatorship embarks on massive political persecution. Political assassinations and police terror become routine.
>
> In spite of all this, the police systematically fail . . . the general sentiment is that the government is unjust. . . . The political situation in the country is transformed into a military situation.[14]

Marxism became confused with terrorism through a series of transformations: from Lenin's vanguard party to Mao Tsetung's mass-based guerrilla army; from Mao and Ho Chi Minh to Castro, whose small band operating out of the Sierra Maestra astonishingly provoked the Cuban Revolution; from Castro to Guevara, whose attempt to create a guerrilla foco in Bolivia ended in disaster; from Guevara to Marighella, who advocated terrorism in the cities as a way of supporting rural guerrillas; and from Marighella's urban guerrillas, wiped out by the Brazilian police, to the Uruguayan Tupamaros, the Argentinian ERP, and a new generation of European terrorists who saw armed struggle in the cities as a way of winning urban workers and poor people directly to the revolutionary cause. Thus, in one decade (roughly from 1966 to 1976), the evolution of guerrilla doctrine moved from the countryside to the city as the primary area of revolutionary activity; from the peasantry toward the urban poor; from the defense of liberated territory toward the provocation of state repression; and from the primacy of politics (and the revolutionary party) to the primacy of military action (the guerrilla foco or urban nucleus).

With the advantage of hindsight, we can picture this strategic transformation as a response to both victory and defeat: the victory of the Cuban Revolution, and the defeat of those attempting to apply the Cuban model elsewhere. Fidel's success persuaded many young militants that he had found a way to adapt Asian guerrilla warfare techniques to the urbanized, largely industrialized states of the western hemisphere. Perhaps it *was* possible, as Guevara urged, to create "two, three, many Vietnams" in Uncle Sam's own backyard. Had not the Cuban fighters succeeded (after several failures) in securing a following among the farmers, defeating the dictator's army in the hinterland, and descending on the cities as liberators—and after only three years of fighting? To Debray, the most widely read theorist of the revolution after Guevara, this victory represented a step beyond Maoist self-defense. Its essence, he stated repeatedly, was "the more or less slow building up through guerrilla warfare carried out in suitably chosen rural zones, of a *mobile strategic force,* nucleus of a people's army and of a future socialist state."[15]

For a number of reasons (imperialist strength being the most important), it is impossible to liberate, administer, and defend rural territory in the industrialized states of Latin America. Therefore, says Debray, the guerrilla force must be clandestine, independent of the civilian population, and aimed at "destruction of the enemy's military potential," *not* direct defense of popular activism.[16] The guerrilla base is mobile, flexible, and autonomous. It is not under the control of any political party, but does its own political work, which Debray calls "armed propaganda." ("The most important form of propaganda is successful military action."[17]) Unlike the Vietnamese liberation forces, which were organized like a pyramid built from the base up, the Latin American pyramid is to be built from the apex down.[18] Debray compares the guerrilla foco to the "small motor" that sets the "large motor" of the masses in motion. He concludes:

> Under certain conditions, the political and the military are not separate, but form one organic whole, consisting of the people's army,

whose nucleus is the guerrilla army. The vanguard party can exist in the form of the guerrilla *foco* itself. The guerrilla force is the party in embryo.

This is the staggering novelty introduced by the Cuban Revolution.[19]

In reality, there is not much that is novel about the notion of an isolated vanguard of fighters overcoming its isolation through heroic violence. Indeed, Debray's small motor/large motor analogy seems little more than a twentieth-century version of the anarchists' favorite metaphor, the spark and the tinder. The abstract, didactic, handbook-like style of Debray's *Revolution in the Revolution?* is reminiscent in tone as well as in content of the manuals of Nechayev and Most; the advice given is exclusively tactical, and does not describe those certain conditions under which the old terrorist theory allegedly works. Which is to say, it tells us little about Cuba, the politics of the July 26 movement, or the unusual conditions underlying Castro's victory and the subsequent course of the Cuban Revolution. It is not surprising to learn, finally, that after a period of daring participation in Guevara's Bolivian foco, ending with his capture and subsequent release, Debray reconsidered his earlier views and joined the government of Mitterand, France's moderate socialist premier. From anarchism to reformism is a well-trodden path![20]

The Cuban Revolution *was* novel, but for reasons unexplored by Debray. In many respects, Castro's success as a social revolutionary was anomalous. Supplied with weapons by the United States's Dominican ally, General Rafael Trujillo, supported by the Cuban middle classes and opposed by most Cuban Communists, praised by the *New York Times,* and feted by Harvard University as a liberal alternative to right- and left-wing extremists, Castro came to power not as a Communist but as the leader of the liberal nationalist revolt.[21] That he remained to lead a social revolution after the United States attempted to ruin Cuba's economy and overthrow its government reveals much about the limitations of reform in nations that are subject to imperialism. It does *not* establish a meaningful connection between small-group violence and social revolution.

In 1957, Cuba was a highly urbanized nation with a two-crop economy based on sugar and tourism, the former controlled by New York banks and the latter by organized crime. Although Cuban agriculture was dominated by large plantations worked by wage laborers, Castro established his rural base in a region of small farmers who either owned land or wanted to do so. Debray's foco theory expressed the truth of the original isolation of the would-be vanguard from both population centers and essential economic institutions; the guerrilla movement in Cuba actually was built from the apex down. With the urban-based Communist party quiescent and agricultural wage labor virtually unorganized, the regime of General Fulgencio Batista had fastened itself to the country like a monstrous parasite, drafting the unemployed youth into a huge army whose chief task was to maintain order in the cities and on the sugar plantations, and to nip opposition to the dictator in the bud. (It is sometimes forgotten that for months after Castro's ascension to power, the bodies of Batista's enemies were discovered buried under the sidewalks in Havana and Santiago de Cuba.[22]) By the time Castro established his base in the mountains, opposition to the regime was rising both in the cities and on the plantations. Strikes and protests were ruthlessly suppressed, but dissent had spread so far that by 1958, even the Cuban Bankers Association was a hotbed of subversion. Nevertheless, a combination of organizational weakness among opposition groups and state terror by the regime had produced a stalemate.

The great success of Castro's July 26 movement was to break this stalemate. What the guerrilla campaign in remote Oriente province revealed was that, when challenged in the field, the Cuban army would not fight. Batista's military apparatus was riven by the corruption endemic to regimes that exist primarily to sell protection to foreign businesspeople and gangsters; its soldiers were trained to terrorize civilians, not to risk their lives in battle. This weakness—combined with the fact that most Cubans, including the business community and the Church,

hoped for Batista's downfall—counterbalanced the inability of
the guerrilla foco to liberate territory. Fidel did not encircle the
cities of Cuba, where most Cubans lived. His relatively small
force pricked the Batista bubble and it burst, bringing to power
a cross-class coalition whose major common features were
Cuban nationalism, the desire to modernize the country, and
hatred for the deposed dictator. This coalition subsequently
split into left and right wings when economic reforms undertaken by the new regime provoked domestic opposition and
North American intervention.[23]

Thus, the mass mobilization of Cuban workers and farmers
did not take place before guerrilla warfare started; nor, despite
Debray's theory, did the foco generate social revolution in the
course of the guerrilla struggle. Castro's small attack force
played an indispensable role in bringing to power a nonrevolu-
tionary nationalist coalition whose collapse, under pressure
from the United States, opened the door to a genuine social
upheaval. As Clea Silva has written, "The Cuban Revolution
did not, at the beginning, have a socialist character, but it
evolved in that direction."[24]

The lesson drawn from this experience by a generation of
young militants influenced by Guevara and Debray was fatally
optimistic. They saw a handful of rural guerrillas overthrow a
military dictatorship, mobilize their people for social revolution, and successfully resist U.S.-supported counter-revolution
—all without enjoying the principal advantages of the Chinese
and Vietnamese revolutions. But clearly, if one subtracts from
the Chinese formula the factors of prior mobilization of the
peasantry, the party with its revolutionary program, liberated
territory to administer, and a mass army to defend it, all that
remains is heroic small-group violence. The hidden message of
the foco theory, then, was that under certain unspecified conditions, terrorism works to generate social revolution.

What are these conditions? The partisans of Fidelismo initially assumed that a Cuban-style revolution could succeed
almost anywhere in Latin America. After all, the entire continent suffered under the imperialist yoke, and Cuba's history,

problems, and resources were not atypical. In 1966, Guevara established a foco in the Bolivian highlands to demonstrate the Cuban model's exportability.[25] His failure, which was repeated by others in Venezuela, Paraguay, Peru, Ecuador, Colombia, and Brazil, demonstrated that the conditions for mere survival of the foco—not to mention victory and eventual social revolution—were more numerous and particular than had been thought. They included initial acceptance of the guerrillas by small peasant landholders; significant opposition to the regime among all social classes, including business and the Church; a corrupt, ill-trained, and demoralized official army; and perhaps most important, initial nonintervention by hostile great powers.

Simply by learning the lesson of Cuba, the United States and Latin regimes threatened by insurgency could eliminate the last condition and affect the third. Thus, Guevara's foco was destroyed within a few months by a U.S.-trained and -equipped Bolivian Ranger battalion, while guerrilla forces elsewhere were generally liquidated before they could secure rural bases. In certain nations—notably, Colombia, Nicaragua, and Guatemala—fighters based in remote areas managed to hold out against inefficient repression, but they were effectively isolated and unable to link up either with plantation workers or the urban masses. As a result, for two decades after Castro's victory, rural guerrillas elsewhere could not get to stage one of the Cuban struggle (national revolution), much less to stage two (social revolution). Furthermore, where reform-minded coalitions attained power through the electoral process, the armed forces overthrew them before they could evolve in a Cuban direction. It was the domino theory in reverse, as the Right seized power from elected governments in Brazil, Bolivia, the Dominican Republic, and—most spectacularly—in Chile. "In sum," Silva writes,

the Cuban Revolution had the particularity of being the synthesis of unique conditions, combined with the negligence of imperialism and the genius of its leaders. No one can guarantee that these factors will be found in the same combination again.[26]

True, and yet the social and political conditions that generated mass discontent in Batista's Cuba were far from unique. In Central America, as in Cuba, one-crop economies were effectively controlled by a few families allied with North American financial interests; the best land was devoted to plantation farming, using landless peasants as cheap labor; the large cities were filled with the unemployed and the nouveaux riche; and bloated armies were created to suppress rising discontent. During the 1970s, Central American ruling elites found themselves increasingly isolated from their subjects. Unable to make significant economic reforms or broaden their mass political base, they relied heavily on state terror (including the unofficial use of right-wing terrorist organizations) to maintain power, thus driving normally moderate, middle-class groups into opposition along with the trade unions, peasant associations, and student organizations. Furthermore, when opposition in the cities and on the large plantations was initially suppressed, as it had been in Cuba, small numbers of guerrilla fighters took to the hills, and established mobile focos in remote provinces that were not well controlled by government forces. Again paralleling Cuba's experience, the guerrilla organizations encompassed a wide variety of political tendencies united by opposition to the regime, commitment to economic and social reform, and nationalism. As early as 1962, guerrillas of the Sandinist Front of National Liberation (FSLN) began operations in Nicaragua, while in Guatemala and El Salvador a number of guerrilla organizations representing Marxist, Christian-Democratic, and liberal nationalist tendencies were functioning in the late 1960s and early 1970s.

Up to this point, the Central American struggles followed the Cuban scenario quite closely; moreover, the Cuban example clearly inspired the fighters of the FSLN and other guerrilla formations. Nevertheless, the Central American guerrillas did *not* defeat government armies in the field while the masses watched from the sidelines. On the contrary, they were isolated and, in many cases, losing ground until the eruption of independent, massive uprisings in the cities created a revolutionary situation and a mass movement requiring military leadership. Thus, in Nicaragua, groups functioning under the FSLN umbrella were relatively impotent until 1973, when strikes and demonstrations began in Managua and Anastasio Somoza "lost much of the support that he had formerly enjoyed from Nicaragua's economic elite." After that,

> more and more young people with impressive elite backgrounds joined the ranks of the Sandinist Front of National Liberation, and some sectors of the business community began giving the FSLN their financial support.[27]

Even so, it was not rural-based guerrillas who defeated the dictator's forces; Somoza was overthrown by a ferocious civil war that lasted almost two years (from 1978 to 1979), involved virtually the entire population, and took more than fifty-thousand lives.[28] There is no doubt that the guerrillas played an important role in both inspiring and aiding this struggle; recall, for example, the daring Operation Pigpen (22 August 1978), in which the Presidential Palace in Managua was seized and held for ransom. Nevertheless, victory could not be obtained until the FSLN had achieved unity of command and there was a true civil war for it to lead.

El Salvador presents a similar historical pattern. As in Nicaragua (and again, unlike Cuba), guerrilla organizations operating in poorly-defended rural provinces were able to do little more than survive until large-scale protests erupted in the cities, creating a popular movement for revolutionary change. In fact, although five separate guerrilla groups began operations in El Salvador in the early 1970s, it was not until 1977–78, when right-wing generals seized power and massacred urban demonstrators and strikers, that a mass movement was created.[29] In 1979 and 1980, as successive centrist juntas collapsed and right-wing terror spread (claiming, as of 1986, an estimated sixty thousand lives), opposition organizations united in a single Democratic Revolutionary Front which subordinated all guerrilla forces to a common leadership. The

Salvadorean Civil War, which began in earnest with the assassination of Archbishop Romero in 1981, thus became a class war, pitting Right against Left and provoking escalated intervention on the part of the United States.[30] Although the Carter administration had refrained from intervening during the mass uprisings in Nicaragua, the Reagan administration intervened in El Salvador both militarily and politically, building and advising the Salvadorean army while promoting the presidency of the centrist, Napoleon Duarte. Again the lesson of Cuba was apparent, as the United States sought to provide the old regime with popular leadership—no more Batistas!—while attempting to modernize and re-moralize the armed forces. Notwithstanding these efforts, however, the outcome remains in doubt. While the rural civil war seems stalemated, with the guerrillas maintaining control over one-third of the countryside, the urban labor unions have moved left notwithstanding continued efforts by right-wing death squads to stop them. Class struggle continues in El Salvador.

Several observations flow from these events. To begin with, it appears that indigenous guerrilla forces in poor, semi-industrial nations may survive for some time by exploiting the authorities' lack of control over remote rural provinces. (Guerrilla groups in several Latin American nations have been continuously active for more than twenty years.) Since Cuba, however, they have not been able to liberate more densely populated provinces or seriously undermine the regime's military power unless mass uprisings also take place in the cities and larger towns. Small guerrilla groups generally are unable to create or even trigger such upheavals. When they occur, however, and a popular movement with which the armed fighters can link up comes into existence, then (and only then) it is possible for a guerrilla band to become the nucleus of a national-revolutionary army. Central American dictatorships have come to understand all of this very well. The unleashing of large-scale right-wing terror in El Salvador and Guatemala is, above all, a response to the threat posed by mass activism in the population centers. By murdering labor organizers, disloyal middle-class intellectuals, revolutionary priests, and on occasion, whole villages, rightist regimes hope to isolate the guerrillas in their rural redoubts, where time (contrary to romantic belief) will work against them.

For fighters like those of the Guatemalan Revolutionary Armed Forces (FAR) and the Guerrilla Army of the Poor (EGP), this strategy has presented difficulties.[31] For more than ten years, they attempted without much success to follow the Cuban road by creating focos in the countryside, until the rise of an explosive mass movement in the late 1970s seemed to open the door to victory. Successive military governments then set about closing that door by using terror on a previously unheard of scale to drive the urban opposition underground or into exile. Under these circumstances, it has been argued, leftist terrorism (urban guerrilla warfare) in the style of the Algerian revolt is entirely justified. At best, it demoralizes the regime's supporters and compels them to tie down troops in the cities; at worst, partisans of the mass movement go down fighting rather than dying silently and alone. Up to this point, however, the Guatemalan FAR has rejected wholesale terrorism on the grounds that indiscriminate killing is immoral and that it will neither energize nor protect the mass movement. On the other hand, where individuals responsible for massacres, torture, or other acts of right-wing terror can be identified, the guerrillas consider their capture or assassination to be legitimate acts of war.

The claim that it is impossible to build a mass movement under the gun of state terror has been one of the principal justifications for urban guerrilla violence in Latin America. We will return to this theme shortly, after summarizing our findings on the relationship between terrorism and movements of national liberation.

We have found, first, that opposition groups that begin by practicing small-group violence do not grow gradually into guerrilla armies capable of contending for state power. Either they command a high degree of mass support and the capability to undertake large-scale military operations ab initio, as the

Chinese and Vietnamese did, or else they remain on the margin of survival, awaiting the mass uprising that will provide them with recruits, supplies, active coalition partners, and the capacity to wage nationwide civil war. Rural-based groups currently in this position include the Guatemalan guerrilla organizations, the Shining Path insurgents in Peru, and the New People's Army in the Philippines.[32] Second, where mass uprisings *do* occur, ex-terrorists may find themselves leading the columns of a popularly-supported guerrilla army. This is especially likely to happen where the working class and its organizations are too weak to go it alone: where there is no revolutionary party capable of uniting the lower classes, splitting the official armed forces, and seizing control of the largest farms and factories. Under these circumstances, a nationalist coalition may provide formerly autonomous guerrillas forces with resources and a popular base, while the guerrillas provide the coalition with military muscle and leadership.

Finally, unless the guerrillas have succeeded, as the Chinese did, in making a social revolution piecemeal by defending liberated territory, they will come to power, if at all, as leaders of a cross-class, nationalist coalition. The more active and widespread their mass support during the period of armed struggle (that is, the less they have functioned as mere representatives of a passive populace), the more their victory will pose the question of social revolution. But to pose a question is not to answer it; the answer will depend on numerous factors, including the nation's class structure and its state of economic development, the relative organizational strengths and leadership capabilities of the coalition's member groups, and the nature and extent of foreign intervention. Nevertheless, the evidence suggests that guerrilla leaders, once in power, are more likely to attempt to govern as liberal nationalists than to unleash class warfare against their bourgeois allies. Of the long list of Third World nations that obtained their political independence, at least in part, by relying on small-group violence, only Cuba has thus far followed the revolutionary road.

Consistently, observers in the United States have overestimated the social radicalism of guerrilla leaders in power (for example, the Nicaraguan Sandinistas), and underestimated that of their lower-class followers. Only in Cuba did nationalist guerrillas make a revolution rather than being made by one. And even there, Castro acted more as an improviser, responding to internal social pressure and foreign intervention, than as a revolutionary ideologue. In the face of similar pressures, the Sandinista coalition has thus far retained its multiclass, pluralist perspective, leaving most property in private hands, coexisting with the Church, and tolerating a considerable amount of antigovernment organization and activity.[33] The situation, however, is extremely unstable, since foreign intervention (particularly the terrorist campaign waged since 1982 by several thousand U.S.-trained and -supported Contras) has contradictory effects. On the one hand, by increasing the level of misery in the country and fanning the flames of militancy, it intensifies class conflict. (The Sandinistas have on several occasions felt it necessary to break strikes aimed at enterprises protected by the coalition.) On the other hand, the state of siege produced by Contra attacks, U.S. threats and military maneuvers, and the economic boycott compels the maintenance of a government of national unity. As in Israel, a continual state of emergency keeps the society perpetually mobilized while forcing postponement of the resolution of internal disputes.

If Nicaragua were left to her own devices, it is not at all clear how these disputes would be resolved. Certainly, the alternatives generally presented in U.S. congressional debates—either a Stalinist state (a Russian base in Central America) or a Western liberal democracy—do not exhaust the range of possibilities. In fact, I would argue that the Soviet base bogeyman promoted by the Reagan administration is a displacement fantasy. The administration's real fear is that establishment of a healthy, *non*-Stalinized workers' and farmers' state in Central America would prove irresistible by sheer example to others, including the Mexican proletariat. At present, what seems clear enough is that the Contra campaign (notwithstanding its counter-revolutionary label) cannot succeed in overturning the Nicaraguan regime.[34] Terrorism is no more effective in reversing revolutions than it is in making them, although it may strengthen bureaucratic tendencies in the government under attack. These tendencies are strong to begin with in regimes whose principal function is to mediate conflicts among competing interests within a multi-class coalition. Again we discover that the terrorist is the bureaucrat's secret ally.

What lessons can we draw from this discussion of the role of terrorism in national liberation struggles? The primary lesson seems to be that the principles of nationalism and social revolution are ultimately incompatible. Terrorism sometimes has a role to play in national liberation struggles that aim to expel the foreigner, "purify" a national culture, reconcile competing domestic groups, and consolidate power in the hands of an indigenous elite. But it has almost no place in social liberation struggles that depend for their success on mass activism, on refusal to delegate the war-making power to representatives, and on insistence that the main enemy is one's own ruling class.

Probably the most dramatic recent illustration of this contradiction is presented by events in South Africa, not really a Third World country at all, as that term is commonly understood, but an industrial powerhouse with the largest black working class in the world outside of the United States. Here, where apartheid has, in effect, created three or four ethnic nations, and where the white army maintains an effective monopoly of military force, there is enormous pressure on black insurgents to conduct their struggle along nationalist lines, which means delegating its violent component to guerrilla "specialists." Thus, both the ultranationalist Azanian People's Organization (APO) and the more pluralistic African National Congress (ANC) combine rhetorical socialism with pragmatic multiclass politics.[35] Since the 1976 Soweto uprising, mass resistance to the apartheid regime has evolved from spontaneous rioting to organized demonstrations, but it poses no immediate threat to white power. With only 5 percent of the black work force unionized and strikes regularly broken by mass firings, economic resistance has been largely confined to local boycotts of white-owned businesses and appeals to foreign corporations and governments to divest themselves of South African holdings and to curtail trade with South Africa. The armed struggle is in the hands of relatively small guerrilla groups which operate from bases in adjacent nations. Up to now, attacks on white civilians in their own neighborhoods have been rare, although there are signs that the guerrillas are becoming less restrained in their choice of targets.

In some respects, the present South African struggle resembles the Algerian revolution prior to the Battle of Algiers. The difference, of course, is that white South Africans, although a small minority of that nation's total population, are not like the French-Algerian *colons* who could be defeated by terrorizing their families and demoralizing their foreign supporters. White South Africans are more numerous, less isolated, richer, and far more determined to dominate "their" country than were the colonists of Algeria, and they have both the industrial and military capacity to go it alone if foreign support evaporates. (Furthermore, foreign backing is not likely to collapse entirely, considering that the white rulers control invaluable mineral resources and sit astride one of the world's most vital sea lanes.) Therefore, although the national liberation movements talk of political revolution and practice a limited type of guerrilla warfare, their basic strategy has been to ally themselves with the liberal business community and force reforms on the Botha government through international pressure. Should these efforts fail, the ANC and APO could unleash more serious terrorism on white civilians, as the FLN did during the Battle of Algiers. What restrains them, no doubt even now, is the likelihood of genocidal retaliation against a population already concentrated for destruction in black townships and "homelands."

Is there an alternative to the nationalist road, with its emphasis on small-group violence and political bargaining? *Can* one build a mass movement for social revolution in an atmosphere suffused by state terror? Several factors, including the size and strategic position of the black proletariat, the growth and radicalization of the labor movement, the extent of mass participation in antiapartheid struggles, and the development of a class-conscious intelligentsia, suggest that in South Africa the answer may not be as clearly negative as has been thought. Armed and organized on the basis of the class principle rather than on the basis of multiclass nationalism, the black majority (with some white, Asian, and mixed-race participation) might make a serious bid for control of the nation's vast resources. But it is hard to see how this could happen without the development of a strong, centralized political organization that is deeply rooted in the proletariat—a party with international support and a strategy for breaking the white regime's monopoly of force. The appearance of such an organization would clearly juxtapose the strategy of social revolution to that of national revolution. Paradoxically (or so it may appear), terrorism in South Africa could end in the first battles of a revolutionary civil war.

Conclusion

IN a number of public lectures, I have described and defended the principal conclusions of this book. I have argued that terrorism, as opposed to other forms of protest or resistance, is produced by a social and moral crisis of the intelligentsia; that serious terrorist movements have local roots and are not mere products of outside manipulation; that the logic of terrorist action is inherently conservative; and that terrorism has proven more useful to conservative or moderately liberal nationalists than to advocates of social revolution. I have maintained viva voce, as I do here, that most terrorists are not insane fanatics, career criminals, or government hirelings, but normal people driven to extremes by their situation and by mistaken political conceptions. And I have often concluded by asserting that no solution to the problem of terrorism is conceivable that does not reconnect politicized young adults to society by involving them in mass-based movements for change. Where militant political movements are not massive, and where mass movements are not militant, terrorism may seem to be the only way of keeping faith.

The question that follows is virtually inevitable: "Now that we have defined terrorism and discussed its causes and consequences, how should we respond to the terrorist threat?"

The question is natural, but, in a way, dumbfounding. Since serious terrorist movements are locally rooted and politically diverse, there is no unified terrorist threat to discuss, and no possibility of prescribing an all-purpose response. One's reaction to any particular terrorist campaign will depend on the nature of the attacking group, the precise situation presented, and one's own political ideas. Most advocates of retaliation against Palestinian terrorists, say, would not think of retaliating against the Nicaraguan Contras. That's politics. Nor would they favor retaliation, as opposed to infiltration or straight police work, against European anarcho-communists or neofascists. That's common sense. Governments are fond of making broad counterterrorist policy pronouncements, like the U.S. government's recent declarations that the war on terrorism will be fought by all means necessary, including retaliation that causes civilian casualties. But grand policy founders on the rocks of political and factual variety. No government—not even that of Israel, which *negotiated* for the release of its soldiers held hostage in Lebanon—has been able to develop and maintain a consistent counterterrorist strategy.

In part, as I say, this is because the terrorist threat is really a multiplicity of real and imagined threats, each emanating from a different source and each presenting a separate set of political and tactical problems. To illustrate: no sooner had the United States retaliated against Libya for allegedly assisting in the bombing of a Berlin discotheque and the attempted bombing of an El Al airliner, than Israeli intelligence announced that Syria, not Libya, was the culpable supplier. Immediately, the advocates of military retaliation fell silent, or muttered darkly about covert action and eventual punishment. Hafez Assad of Syria, who had helped procure the release of some American hostages in Lebanon and might yet release others, was not Muammar Khaddafi. Moreover, taking out Khaddafi's house was one thing, and taking on Syria's MIG's and SAM-7 missiles quite another, especially during a period of rising tensions in the Middle East. Indeed, one can only wonder what U.S. hardliners would recommend if, say, the government of Iraq were linked to a major terrorist attack on American citizens or U.S. government installations abroad. Should American F–111 bombers join the Iranian Air Force in attacking Baghdad? Should we assist the Ayatollah Khomeini in overthrowing the Iraqi regime, or call for economic sanctions against a nation virtually bankrupted by its war against Iran?

Obviously not. In all likelihood, the evidence of Iraqi complicity in terrorism would be either buried or handed over to the CIA (which amounts to the same thing) with orders to take corrective action against the persons or groups directly responsible for the attack. The real-world constraints on public policy making, combined with the variety of phenomena lumped together under the heading of "terrorist threat," consistently undermine attempts to develop a grand strategy to combat terrorism. As a result, the real winners in debates over counterterrorist policy are the intelligence agencies, which get the entire problem dumped in their laps, together with geometric budget increases for covert activities and general directives to act effectively against selected groups. The difficulty is that intelligence agents are true counterterrorists, whose notions of effectiveness are all but indistinguishable from those of their enemy: infiltrate and disrupt; assassinate this leader and bribe that one; suggest a particularly dangerous operation and then betray it; supply the bomber with a defective bomb; spread dissension and paranoia throughout the enemy organization. So goes the underground war.

How effective are these tactics? I answer that question with another: how effective is terrorism? In either case, killing powerful individuals has a certain effect, as does sabotage, betrayal, and disruption. And there is no disputing the fact that, as Trotsky said, "the state is much richer in the means of physical destruction and mechanical repression than are the terrorist groups."[1] Still, if it is true that "the capitalist state does not base itself on government ministers and cannot be eliminated with them," then it is also the case that terrorist movements cannot be eliminated by a policy of assassination and disruption. We have already seen that European terrorist groups like the RAF and the Red Brigade were shattered in the late 1970s and early 1980s by special police forces working with domestic intelligence agencies; yet the movements that spawned them, based on the disaffected intelligentsia, continue to produce new leaders and new urban guerrilla cadres. Even more dramatically, the Israeli intelligence agency, MOSSAD, subjected PLO operatives in Europe to a devastating campaign of assassination and sabotage, while Israel's military forces conducted punitive raids against Palestinian bases and camps in Lebanon. The effect of this effort, culminating in the invasion of Lebanon, was to weaken the PLO while creating dozens of new terrorist formations that were smaller, more difficult to penetrate, and, if anything, more implacable than Black September. Certainly, there seems little reason to credit Israel's claim that its hard-line policies have been successful in suppressing terrorist violence.[2] It would be more accurate to say that Israel chose to confront terrorism on a more diffused and decentralized level in order to weaken the PLO's claim to be the legitimate Palestinian representative.

But what does it mean to confront a more diffused and decentralized terrorism? Most obviously, it means (as the United States discovered in Lebanon) that the actual perpetrators of violent acts become harder to find. This fact leads policy in two directions at once: back to more conventional intelligence work, and forward to retaliation against the unseen terrorist's visible allies. Indeed, the policy of retaliating against governments allegedly complicit in terrorism is the logical product of counterterrorist tactics that succeed in disrupting and splitting large organizations without mitigating the causes of political violence. Groups like the PLO, IRA, and ANC are vulnerable to physical attack because they have a known structure, an identifiable leadership, public offices, and a mass following . . . because, in short, they aspire to be the state in exile and conduct themselves accordingly. Kill them without killing their cause, and every grouplet with a printing press and some *plastique* sets about competing violently for the mantle of leadership. Then, when you cannot find these invisible, indigenous terrorists, whom do you punish? Why, their suppliers, protectors, sympathizers, and kinsfolk!

This policy can be called deterrent retaliation, self-defense, or anything one wishes, but at bottom it is a policy of revenge. Its primary maxim is, *"Someone* must pay!"—a principle that throws us back to the politics of the blood feud, when killing someone's brother provided just cause to kill the slayer's cousin— when all sanctuary was denied, and tit-for-tat continued until the last member of one family or the other was exterminated.[3] When the latest products of American military technology were used to attack Khaddafi's home, killing and injuring members of his immediate family, the atavism of this policy was plain. "Hitting Home," *Time* magazine called it in a particularly gruesome pun.[4] But attacking third parties is what the authorities do when they *cannot* hit home because of the terrorists' ubiquity and anonymity. Enforcing the principle of collective responsibility is not only barbaric, invoking the tribal bloodlust that lies just beneath the surface of modern nationalism, it also plays into the hands of those who want to intensify and broaden the conflict: the terrorists and the war hawks.

What, then, of a softer response? During the 1970s, before the current fascination with retaliation became epidemic, many studies of counterterrorist strategy bore titles like *Living with Terrorism.*[5] They took the position that terrorism, although inexcusable, sometimes reflected (in a twisted way) legitimate national or ethnic grievances; that it represented a long-range problem, but one posing no serious threat to the security of any Western nation. Therefore, their counsel was calmness. Governments should avoid overreacting either by suppressing civil liberties or by retaliating with indiscriminate force, and citizens should avoid panic. Counterterrorism (clearly, a job for professionals) should be subtle, flexible, and discriminating, should strike at the real perpetrators with surgical precision, and should refuse to pander to the popular thirst for revenge. Meanwhile, we should learn the practical skills needed to survive in a time of terror: how to negotiate in a hostage situation; how to manage the mass media during a crisis; how to harden the target and professionalize the counterterrorist strike forces.[6] Many authors advised building an international consensus to support collective legal and political responses to terrorism, and a few noted that legitimate grievances should be remedied, where possible.

There was nothing much wrong with this advice, but there was nothing much right about it either. Certainly, when compared with the superficial conspiracy theories and outright panic-mongering of more recent works,[7] these earlier studies seem models of reasonableness. Nevertheless, the advice they rendered was largely ineffectual, with the result that a policy of preemption and retaliation replaced a line of action perceived as vacillating and weak. We have already seen that the very successes of conventional counterterrorism made small-group violence more difficult to suppress. Similarly, to recognize the existence of legitimate grievances without remedying them was to heap fuel upon the fire. The liberal analysts' failure to account for the causes of terrorism in any real depth disabled them from proposing long-term solutions to the problem; and considering that neither moderate counterterrorism nor moderate reform *is* a long-term solution, the injunction that we learn to live with terrorism was inevitable. Unfortunately, while good advice for citizens lining up for luggage X rays in airports, the policy of patient coping proved politically suicidal when practiced by President Carter during the Iranian hostage crisis.

Indeed, that crisis was the watershed between the two phases of American policy toward terrorism. Strictly speaking, the seizure of the U.S. Embassy in Teheran was not an act of terrorism (that is, small-group violence) at all, but an excess of the Iranian Revolution. Nevertheless, the dilemma it posed for U.S. policy makers was familiar. Must the United States stand by passively while its representatives were imprisoned, its citizens humiliated, and its flag desecrated? In my own (no doubt idiosyncratic) view, President Carter's refusal to act in such a way as to endanger the lives of the hostages, American servicemen, and Iranians represented a rare triumph of human decency over political "necessity." Moreover, there is no evidence that it encouraged terrorists to take advantage of American weakness, or that the more bellicose policies of the Reagan administration have had the slightest deterrent effect. All this said, however, it remains true that a policy of waiting out terrorism is really no policy at all. Like nature, politics abhors a vacuum; and when liberal moderation fails, as it so often does, to solve deep-rooted social problems, the stage is set for the conservative avengers.

I return, then, to the original question of how we should respond to the terrorist threat. The answer that is implicit in our discussion thus far—indeed, in this study as a whole—is that no effective response is possible within the boundaries set by conventional liberalism and conservatism. Patient coping leaves the problem untouched, and counterterrorism worsens it. There is a reason for the impotence of these policies: terrorism has become endemic to modern society because it is the product of a recurrent social crisis. Large groups—classes, nations, ethnic and religious communities—are oppressed (not just aggrieved) under circumstances that make it difficult or impossible for the intelligentsia to participate in mass movements for change. Oppression is a sine qua non for sustained terrorism, but not its sole cause; terrorist movements appear when, for one reason or another, politically active intellectuals are unable to link themselves effectively either with upper-class rulers or lower-class clients. This combination of oppression and isolation is particularly likely to appear in nations subjected to imperialism, although it may appear anywhere that rapid and uneven economic change pulls society apart, detaching teachers, students, priests, and professionals from the mass groups they wish to serve. When the crisis becomes severe enough—for example, when militant mass movements are co-opted by unequal distribution of rewards or smashed by state terror—action by armed elements of the intelligentsia seems almost inevitable.

We have already seen that this response is usually unproductive. Small-group violence does not generate or inspire mass

movements for social revolution, although under certain conditions it may help more conservative nationalist coalitions free
their territory from foreign domination. Successful or not, however, terrorism persists so long as mass oppression and isolation
of the intelligentsia continue. The first wave of terrorist violence in Europe and North America lasted almost forty years,
from the late 1870s until the eve of World War I, while many
of the organizations that currently concern us in Europe, Latin
America, the Middle East, and Asia have been in operation for
almost two decades. Americans can learn to live with terrorism
or they can involve themselves in blood feuds with a widening
circle of enemies, but anti-American attacks will not cease until
the United States's role in the world has been drastically redefined.

The question, "How should *we* respond to terrorism," is really unanswerable if the subject "we" includes both the U.S.
government and its citizens. American diplomats, soldiers, and
businesspeople are prime targets for terrorist attack because
they are considered representatives of imperialist oppression—
not just by Communists, but by a frighteningly broad array of
groups subjected to American power. Why were U.S. diplomats
and embassy personnel held hostage in Teheran? Because ever
since the CIA overthrew the Iranian government in 1954,
Iranian dissidents by the thousands had been imprisoned, tortured, and massacred by SAVAK, the shah's gestapo—an organization directly and knowingly supported by every American
administration since that of President Dwight Eisenhower. And
why have American tourists now become terrorist targets? Because people the world over thirst for revenge against the financiers of their misery. If, tomorrow, some misguided Guatemalan
student, say, were to blow up an American airliner, would we,
in our anger and revulsion, consider the tens of thousands of
Guatemalans hunted down and destroyed by U.S.-supported
death squads in that stricken land? Prominent among the new
breed of Palestinian terrorists attacking international tourist
facilities are survivors of the Sabra and Shatila massacres in
Lebanon. This does not justify their vengeful actions, but it

makes them comprehensible; and it should make us understand that to stop terrorism, we have to stop financing Sabras and Shatilas.

Of course, this is far more easily said than done. Political leaders committed to defending America's imperial interests by force are unlikely to recognize that terrorism is both a response to their policies and an imitation of their style. Their own belligerent nationalism inclines both Republicans and Democrats to portray terrorist fighters as the dupes of hostile foreign governments, incapable of expressing authentic local aspirations for power and justice. But this caricature of terrorism leads policy makers to behave like cartoon imperialists. On the one hand, they dispatch U.S. gunboats and special strike forces around the globe to punish hostile terrorists, their kinsfolk, and their alleged state sponsors. On the other, they openly sponsor "friendly" terrorist forces from Nicaragua to Cambodia. Thus the cycle of repression and rebellion continues, with no end in sight. Policies supposedly designed to stamp out terrorism end by spreading and intensifying it. The line separating small-group violence from mass violence becomes indistinct, and an unstable world moves closer to universal war.

Whatever policies the U.S. government may favor, therefore, it seems to me that *our* policy must be to uproot the causes of terrorism by putting an end to American-sponsored oppression of classes, nations, and ethnic communities, and by permitting young intellectuals to be reunited through collective action with their people. Clearly, rethinking America's place in the world will take more than an effort of the imagination. Reassessing the costs and benefits of empire will require a political debate that goes far beyond the conventional terms of conservative-liberal discourse. In the current political atmosphere, it may seem utopian even to call for such a discussion. Nevertheless, if we are ever to feel at home on this planet, we have no alternative but to begin.

As a small step in this direction, it is worth imagining how a rational policy toward terrorism might be constructed, assuming that there existed a government capable of formulating and implementing it. Suppose that a political upheaval in some Western nation brought to power a post-imperial regime dedicated to resolving deep-rooted international and domestic conflicts by eliminating their causes. How should such a regime respond to armed attacks on its officials or its nationals by self-proclaimed "freedom fighters"? If consulted, I would offer the following policy recommendations:

First, *separate the issue of short-term response from that of long-term policy.* This is exactly what the governments with which I am familiar, including that of the United States, do *not* do at present. Their long-term policy consists of general statements about terrorism: for example, "The United States will not accede to terrorist blackmail; to grant concessions only invites further demands."[8] Since such statements, made for public consumption, tend to be moralistic and unworkable, only short-term policy—that is, the principles governing responses to terrorist incidents—remains. But a government's reaction to an individual incident necessarily reflects immediate political pressures and military/tactical contingencies. A short-term response must take into account the nature of the attacking group, the damage inflicted on the target, the identity, numbers, and vulnerability of hostages, the availability of counterforce, the negotiability of terrorist demands, and other variables. Conditioned by such particularities, the principles governing short-term responses become oracular, and policy in any sense of the word dissolves. Thus, a document distributed by the U.S. State Department states that while "too soft a response may convey [an] image of weakness," exposing the government to further attacks, "too hard a response may create martyrs or become [the] focus of internal and international criticism."[9] Clearly, however, a "Goldilocks and the Three Bears" policy—one advocating a response that is neither too hard nor too soft, but "just right"—amounts to no policy at all.

The antidote to this dissolution of principle is to formulate long-term policies that make sense. By definition, these cannot be general statements about terrorism, a word that in popular and governmental use has become synonymous with illegitimate political violence. As we saw in the first chapter of this study, the meaning of the terrorist label varies with the perceived source of illegitimacy. Small groups with little mass support, like the European anarcho-communists or neofascists, are considered terrorist because they are small and unrepresentative. Larger groups with considerable mass support, like the IRA or PLO nationalists, are called terrorist because their political aims or methods are deemed unacceptable. Even government-style organizations controlling and administering large areas of territory and population—for example, the Salvadorean FMLN—are branded terrorist because of their political orientation. Little wonder that official U.S. government policy on terrorism resembles the proverbial preacher's philosophy of sin: "He's agin' it."

My second recommendation, therefore, is to declare a moratorium on general statements about terrorism. Instead of pronouncing anathemas, policy makers should *develop long-term policies toward violent groups based on analysis in depth of their history, nature, structure, personnel, and constituents' needs.* Without such policies, it is difficult to see how, in any particular case, a rational short-term response can be formulated.

Realistically, one must assume that the government's reaction to a violent incident will be strongly influenced by immediate political and tactical considerations: how to avoid losing face, how to discourage new attacks, how to save lives, and the like. What alone can rationalize such a response is the counterinfluence exercised by coherent long-term policy. If, for example, certain nationals of State A are held hostage by a group commanding widespread, intense mass support in State B—a group, say, like the Lebanese Hezbollah—political necessity may dictate that the government of State A take a "hard" public position. But if the analysis has revealed that the "kidnappers" in question are actually mass representatives destined, in time, to achieve some sort of official recognition, a rational short-term response should include the possibility of negotiating (perhaps in secret, or through intermediaries) for the hostages' release. By the same token, retaliation that would make perma-

nent enemies of the organization and its mass base should probably be ruled out, even if it seems tactically feasible. Similarly,
although the group may issue a set of "non-negotiable" demands including some that, for State A, are out of the question,
analysis in depth of its personnel, interests, and needs can generate negotiating options potentially acceptable to both parties.

This is not to say that an enlightened government ought
never to meet force with force. It is to assert, however, that
where rational long-term policies are adopted, counterforce
alone will rarely be an acceptable response. Suppose, for example, that the government must deal with a group very unlike
Hezbollah. Imagine that violent attacks are perpetrated by an
organization like the Order, a small, extremely violent neofascist group with little popular support outside a narrow circle
of heterodox Christian churches in relatively isolated rural
areas of the United States. As noted earlier, the U.S. government's response to a campaign of bank robbery and murder by
members of this organization was to pursue, capture, and prose-
cute those responsible for the violence (see pages 129–30). This
is all very well, but what was its long-term policy? It goes
almost without saying that no such policy existed, or yet exists.
Small fascist organizations in the United States are treated precisely like their counterparts on the far Right or far Left in
Europe: that is, as "problems" to be dealt with exclusively by
the police and the courts.

The perspective suggested by this book, however, suggests
that such groups are not the problems; they are the *responses* to
problems that, if unanalyzed and unsolved, will regenerate
them or create new groups of the same type. What were the
social and economic pressures, operating on this particular class
of farmers in the Pacific Northwest, that generated the politics
of the Order and the peculiar religiosity of the churches associated with it? What similar pressures, affecting similar
groups elsewhere, are even now breeding fascism in the United
States? Although scholars here and there may work out the
answers to such questions, their views are not considered
"policy-relevant." Present-day governments believe that they

can contain low-intensity domestic violence of this sort simply by applying counterforce. There is abundant evidence that this is not the case—but, in any event, such a belief cannot be verified without doing the social analysis necessary to formulate an intelligent long-term policy. There is thus another reason for this abstention from policy: the fear that analysis will uncover causes of violence that can be remedied only by redistributing wealth, power, or prestige. It is the subversive (in this sense) potential of dispassionate analysis that leads governments, as presently constituted, to prefer comfortable blindness to painful sight.

A government willing to see, however, might adopt the following policy prescription: *no matter how marginal a violent group may seem, mobilize scholarly resources to define the problem to which its violence is a response.* The practical implications of this recommendation raise certain questions that are outside the scope of this study; in particular, they would involve redefining the relationship of scholarship to government. Even if the recommendation were to be accepted, however, and free-thinking scholars were to replace the current crop of technical advisers and court philosophers relied on by those in authority, this would only begin the process of problem solving. Scholarly experts are as biased and as prone to error as any of their fellow human beings; moreover, the more knowledgeable they are in a particular subject area or discipline, the more blinded they may be by the methodological and substantive truths they take to be self-evident. To discover the problem that generates a particular conflict, one indispensable type of "expertise" is that of the parties themselves. Furthermore, if our hypothetical government is interested not just in containing violent conflicts but in resolving them as well, it will want to involve the parties themselves in efforts to define the problem and to discover means of solving it. This leads directly to my final recommendation:

Whatever action the government may take in immediate response to a violent incident or campaign, it should invite leading representatives of the violent group and its principal enemies to engage in the process of conflict resolution. In the short run, rulers may choose either to punish violent activists or to negotiate with them, but in an important sense, these much-discussed alternatives are really two sides of the same coin. They are both tactics for containing conflict temporarily rather than for resolving it on a permanent basis. Recent work in the new field of conflict resolution suggests that longer-term solutions to the problems that generate political violence can be discovered through processes that bring disputants together in a controlled environment where they can explore (with the aid of expert facilitators and social analysts) the deep-rooted sources of their antagonism.[10] The implications of such processes are radical; in practice, they tend to show that the relationship between violent disputants can be healed only on the basis of significant social and political changes that fulfill basic needs. This comes as no surprise, but it underlines a message that present-day governments are loath to hear: the elimination of political violence requires a political system capable of continuous self-transformation. On the day that government becomes a flexible instrument of its constituents' conscious will, terrorism and counterterrorism will seem nothing more than ugly vestiges of a preconscious past.

NOTES

Chapter 1

1. Lawrence Zelic Freedman, "Why Does Terrorism Terrorize?" *Terrorism: An International Journal* 6(3): 399–400.

2. Henry David, *History of the Haymarket Affair* (New York: Farrar & Rinehart, 1936).

3. William Preston, Jr., *Aliens and Dissenters* (Cambridge: Harvard University Press, 1963). See also Robert K. Murray, *Red Scare* (New York: McGraw-Hill, 1955).

4. Hannah Arendt, *Eichmann in Jerusalem: A Report on the Banality of Evil* (New York: Viking Press, 1963).

5. See, for example, Charles A. Russell and Bowman H. Miller, "Profile of a Terrorist," *Terrorism: An International Journal* 1(1): 17–27.

6. Freedman, "Why Does Terrorism Terrorize?" 390.

7. Paul Galloway, "Red Brigades: Like the guy next door," *Chicago Sun-Times,* 5 June 1978, pp. 7, 16.

8. See Russell and Miller, "Profile of a Terrorist." See also Richard L. Clutterbuck, *Guerrillas and Terrorists* (Chicago: Ohio State University Press, 1980); Ted R. Gurr, "Some Characteristics of Political Terrorism in the 1960's," in *The Politics of Terrorism,* ed. Michael Stohl (New York: Marcel Dekker, 1983).

9. Russell and Miller, "Profile of a Terrorist," 27–33. See also Paul Wilkinson, *Political Terrorism* (New York: John Wiley, 1975); Jillian Becker, *Hitler's Children: The Story of the Baader-Meinhoff Terrorist Gang* (Philadelphia: J. B. Lippincott, 1977).

10. Walter Laqueur, *Terrorism* (Boston: Little, Brown, 1977), 120–32. For obvious reasons, terrorist memoirs are fairly rare, but those available are most revealing. See, for example, Boris Savinkov, *Memoirs of a Terrorist* (New York: Albert & Charles Boni, 1931); Menachem Begin, *The Revolt* (London: W. H. Allen, 1954); Bommi Baumann, *Wie Alles Anfing: How It All Began* (Vancouver: Pulp Press, 1977); Susan Stern, *With the Weathermen: The Personal Journey of a Revolutionary Woman* (New York: Doubleday, 1975); Sean MacStiofain, *Revolutionary in Ireland* (London: Gordon Cremonesi, 1975).

11. Leon Trotsky, *Against Individual Terrorism* (New York: Pathfinder, 1974), 8.

12. Ibid., 9.

13. Sergey Nechayev, "Catechism of the Revolutionist," in *Daughter of a Revolutionary: Natalie Herzen and the Bakunin-Nechayev Circle,* ed. Michael Confino (La Salle, Ill.: Library Press, 1973), 230.

14. Ibid.

15. Erik H. Erikson, *Life History and the Historical Moment* (New York: W. W. Norton, 1975), 204. See also Erikson's *Insight and Responsibility* (New York: W. W. Norton, 1964), 125.

16. André Malraux, *Man's Fate* (New York: Modern Library, 1936), 246–47.

17. Ibid., 250.

18. William French Smith, "Attorney General's Guidelines on Investigations," *Criminal Law Reporter* 32 (1095): 3087ff.

Chapter 2

1. There were numerous such attempts to assassinate Castro. See Senate Select Committee to Study Government Intelligence Activities, *Alleged Assassination Plots Involving Foreign Leaders,* 84th Cong., 1st sess., 1975, Rept. 94–465, 75ff. See also Warren Hinckle and William Turner, *The Fish Is Red: The Story of the Secret War Against Castro* (New York: Harper & Row, 1981).

2. J. Bowyer Bell, *Transnational Terror* (Washington, D.C.: American Enterprise Institute for Public Policy Research, 1975), 6.

3. For example, the proposed "Antiterrorism Act of 1985," S. 275, 99th Cong., 1st sess. (1985) defines terrorism as criminal acts intended "to intimidate or coerce" a civilian population or a government.

4. See North American Congress on Latin America, *Argentina in the Hour of the Furnaces* (New York: North American Congress on Latin America, 1975); Eduardo Crawley, *A House Divided: Argentina, 1880–1980* (New York: St. Martin's Press, 1984); Jacobo Timerman, *Prisoner Without a Name, Cell Without a Number* (New York: Knopf, 1981).

5. Bell, *Transnational Terror,* 6.

6. See, for example, Rand Corporation, *International Conference on Terrorism and Low-Level Conflict* (Santa Monica, Calif.: Rand Corporation, 1982); Institute for the Study of Conflict, *Political Violence and Civil Disobedience in Europe, 1982* (London: Institute for the Study of Conflict, 1983).

7. See Anthony M. Burton, *Urban Terrorism: Theory, Practice and Response* (New York: Free Press, 1975): "The Algerian insurgents opened their military campaign for independence on 31 October 1954, with a mere five hundred men" (p. 134). The relationship of vanguards to mass movements is discussed herein, in chapters 10 and 11.

8. See, for example, Albert Parry, *Terrorism from Robespierre to Arafat* (New York: Vanguard Press, 1976): "At all times the root of the terrorists' so-called idealism is a deep psychological disturbance. . . . such terrorists usually are not oppressed or terrorized; they only imagine themselves victims of hostility" (pp. 23–24).

9. On the French Resistance, see David Schoenbrun, *Soldiers of the Night: The Story of the French Resistance* (New York: Dutton, 1980).

10. This is nowhere better illustrated than in Marcel Ophuls's film masterpiece, *The Sorrow and the Pity.* See also Bertram M. Gordon, *Collaborationism in France During the Second World War* (Ithaca: Cornell University Press, 1980); Milton Dank, *The French Against the French: Collaboration and Resistance* (Philadelphia and New York: J. B. Lippincott, 1974).

11. Vo Nguyen Giap, *The Military Art of People's War* (New York: Monthly Review Press, 1970), 101ff.

12. Marvin E. Gettleman et al., eds., *El Salvador: Central America in the New Cold War* (New York: Grove Press, 1981), 62–65, 86–89.

13. Cf. W. E. B. DuBois, *John Brown* (1962; reprint, Millwood, N.Y.: Kraus-Thomson, 1973); and Stephen B. Oates, *To Purge This Land With Blood* (New York: Harper, 1970).

14. Albert Parry, *Terrorism from Robespierre to Arafat* (New York: Vanguard Press, 1976), 274, 281.

Chapter 3

1. Mark N. Hagopian, *The Phenomenon of Revolution* (New York: Dodd, Mead, 1974), 200.

2. Albert Parry, *Terrorism from Robespierre to Arafat* (New York: Vanguard Press, 1976), xi.

3. Boris Nicolaejewsky, *Aseff the Spy* (1934; reprint, Hattiesburg, Miss.: Academic International, 1969).

4. Albert Camus, *The Rebel: An Essay on Man in Revolt* (New York: Vintage, 1956), 173 *n.* 6.

5. Ibid., 169.

6. Ibid., 172.

7. A good example is Hannah Arendt, *On Revolution* (New York: Viking, 1963).

8. See Theodore Draper, *Castro's Revolution: Myths and Realities* (New York: Praeger, 1962); Warren Hinkle and William Turner, *The Fish Is Red: The Story of the Secret War Against Castro* (New York: Harper & Row, 1981).

9. J. Bowyer Bell, *A Time of Terror: How Democratic Societies Respond to Revolutionary Violence* (New York: Basic Books, 1978); Jan Schreiber, *The Ultimate Weapon: Terrorists and World Order* (New York: William Morrow, 1978).

10. Bernard Avishai, "In Cold Blood," *New York Review of Books,* 8 March 1979, 41.

11. Ibid., 43.

12. Ibid., 44.

13. Ibid., 41.

14. Walter Laqueur, *Terrorism* (Boston: Little, Brown, 1977): "As experience shows, societies with the least political participation and the most injustice have been the most free from terrorism in our time" (p. 220).

15. Hugh D. Graham and Ted Gurr, *Violence in America: Historical and Comparative Perspectives* (New York: Bantam Books, 1969); Richard E. Rubenstein, *Rebels in Eden: Mass Political Violence in the United States* (Boston: Little, Brown, 1970).

16. Schreiber, *The Ultimate Weapon,* 26. See also discussion of the Chinese Revolution herein, pages 206–212.

17. Edward Hyams, *Terrorists and Terrorism* (London: J. M. Dent, 1975), 13.

18. Leon Trotsky, *Terrorism and Communism: A Reply to Karl Kautsky* (1920; reprint, London: New Park, 1975), 78.

19. Leon Trotsky, *Against Individual Terrorism* (New York: Pathfinder, 1974), 7.

20. V. I. Lenin, *What Is to Be Done? Burning Questions of Our Movement* (1902; reprint, New York: International Publishers, 1981), 74–77. See also Lenin's *Collected Works,* vol. 9 (New York: International Publishers, 1927), in which he defines terrorism as "a specific kind of struggle practiced by the intelligentsia" (p. 130).

21. Trotsky, *Against Individual Terrorism,* 22.

22. Geoffrey Pridham, "Terrorism and the State in West Germany During the 1970's," in *Terrorism: A Challenge to the State,* ed. Juliet Lodge (New York: St. Martins, 1981), 11ff.

23. Ibid. See also Marx's comparison of the assassination of Czar Alexander II with "the earthquake of Chios," in Karl Marx and Friedrich Engels,

Selected Correspondence, 1846–1895 (Westport, Conn.: Greenwood Press, 1975), 391.

24. Trotsky, *Against Individual Terrorism,* 37.

Chapter 4

1. A. Chalmers Johnson, "Perspectives on Terrorism," in *The Terrorism Reader: A Historical Anthology,* ed. Walter Laqueur (New York: New American Library, 1978), 278.

2. Walter Laqueur, *Terrorism* (Boston: Little, Brown, 1977), 120.

3. Office for Combatting Terrorism, U.S. Department of State, "Document: Current Trends in Terrorism," *Terrorism: An International Journal* 7(1): 81–84.

4. Ibid., 83–84

5. Network theory is represented in Claire Sterling, *The Terror Network: The Secret War of International Terrorism* (New York: Holt, Rinehart, & Winston, 1981); Christopher Dobson, *The Terrorists* (New York: Facts on File, 1982); and Ray S. Cline and Yonah Alexander, *Terrorism: The Soviet Connection* (New York: Crane Russak, 1984); among others. Permissive society theories are offered in Laqueur, *Terrorism;* Paul Wilkinson, *Terrorism and the Liberal State* (New York: John Wiley, 1977); J. Bowyer Bell, *A Time of Terror: How Democratic Societies Respond to Revolutionary Violence* (New York: Basic Books, 1978); and Jan Schreiber, *The Ultimate Weapon: Terrorists and World Order* (New York: William Morrow, 1978).

6. Sterling, *The Terror Network,* 10.

7. Ibid.

8. There is unfortunately no definitive work as yet on the "Black network(s)." But see Edward S. Herman, *The Real Terror Network* (Boston: South End Press, 1982). See also Hans Josef Horchem, "European Terrorism: A German Perspective," *Terrorism: An International Journal* 6(1): 27ff.; Bruce Hoffman, "Right-Wing Terrorism in Europe," *Conflict* 5(3): 185ff.; "The Contra/Nazi Connection," *Workers Vanguard,* 1985, no. 377: 1, 14–15.

9. See John Dinges and Saul Landau, *Assassination on Embassy Row* (New York: Pantheon, 1980).

10. Claire Sterling was again in the forefront of the "Soviet Plot" theory: see the March–April 1984 issue of *Problems of Communism* for a skeptical review by William Hood (of the CIA) of Sterling's *The Time of Assassins: Anatomy of an Investigation* (New York: Holt, Rinehart & Winston, 1985) and Paul Henze's *The Plot to Kill the Pope* (New York: Scribner, 1985).

11. In Argentina, for example, right-wing terrorists denounced the Pope and attacked Catholic bookstores during the "dirty war" of the mid-1970s. The American KKK has long been fanatically anti-Catholic, and the Grey Wolves, the terrorist arm of the Turkish fascist National Action party, follow in this tradition.

12. House Select Committee on Assassinations, *Investigation of the Assassination of President John F. Kennedy,* 95th Cong., 2d sess. (Washington, D.C.: Government Printing Office, 1979).

13. Department of Defense, *Report of the DOD Commission on Beirut International Airport Terrorist Act, October 23, 1983* (Washington, D.C.: Government Printing Office, 1984). The *Report* refers to "indirect involvement in this incident by Syria and Iran" without offering any evidence of such involvement (p. 122).

14. Thomas L. Friedman, "State Sponsored Terror Called a Threat to U.S.," *New York Times,* 30 December 1983, p. A6, col. 1.

15. Ibid.

16. Ibid., p. A6, col. 2.

17. Ibid., p. A6, col. 1.

18. Charles R. Babcock and Bob Woodward, "Antiterrorist Plan Rescinded After Unauthorized Bombing," *Washington Post,* 12 May 1985, p. A1. See also Babcock and Woodward, "CIA Denies Part in Bombing: Agency Criticizes Post Article on Beirut Attack That Killed 80," *Washington Post,* 23 June 1985, p. A4.

19. Terence Smith, "Israeli and Arab Agents Go on Killing Each Other," *New York Times,* 16 January 1977, p. E4.

20. Karl Marx and Friedrich Engels, *Collected Works,* vol. 10 (New York: International Publishers, 1975), 318.

21. See, for example, Walter Laqueur, "The Continuing Failure of Terrorism," *Harper's,* November 1976, 69ff.

22. See, for example, Paul Wilkinson, *Political Terrorism* (London and New York: Macmillan, 1974); Richard Clutterbuck, *Living With Terrorism* (London: Faber, 1975).

23. See theories summarized in Paul Wilkinson, "Social Scientific Theory and Civil Violence," in *Terrorism: Theory and Practice,* ed. Yonah Alexander et al. (Boulder, Colo.: Westview Press, 1979), 45–72. The most useful causal theory, which has influenced my analysis of terrorism's origins, is the "relative deprivation" theory originally outlined by Ted Gurr in *Why Men Rebel* (Princeton, N.J.: Princeton University Press, 1970).

24. Screiber, *The Ultimate Weapon,* 27.

25. Laqueur, *Terrorism,* 144.

26. Schreiber, *The Ultimate Weapon,* 148ff.

27. Alan O'Day, "Northern Ireland, Terrorism, and the British State," in *Terrorism: Theory and Practice,* ed. Yonah Alexander et al. 127.

28. Schreiber, *The Ultimate Weapon,* 198.

Chapter 5

1. Regis Debray, *Revolution in the Revolution? Armed Struggle and Political Struggle in Latin America* (New York: Grove, 1967), 109.

2. Carlos Marighella, "Appendix: *Minimanual of the Urban Guerrilla,*" in Robert Moss, *Urban Guerrilla Warfare* (London: Institute for Strategic Studies, 1971), 20.

3. Ernst Halperin, *Terrorism in Latin America* (Beverly Hills, Calif.: Sage, 1976).

4. Ibid., 51–52.

5. Ibid.

6. See, for example, Richard Gillespie, *Soldiers of Peron: Argentina's Montoneros* (New York: Oxford University Press, 1982).

7. J. Bowyer Bell, *Transnational Terror* (Washington, D.C.: American Enterprise Institute for Public Policy Research, 1975), 52. On the Tupamaros, see Alain Labrousse, *The Tupamaros: Urban Guerrillas in Uruguay* (Harmondsworth: Penguin, 1973); Anthony M. Burton, *Urban Terrorism: Theory, Practice and Response* (New York: Free Press, 1975), 94–104.

8. Ernest Mandel, "In Defence of Leninism, In Defence of the Fourth International" (Typescript, 1973), 5–6.

9. Maria Esther Gillo, *The Tupamaro Guerrillas* (New York: Saturday Review Press, 1970), 101–33.

10. Bell, *Transnational Terror,* 52.

11. Andrew Graham-Yool, *A Matter of Fear: Portrait of an Argentinian Exile* (West-

port, Conn.: Lawrence Hill, 1982); Jacobo Timerman, *Prisoner Without a Name, Cell Without a Number* (New York: Knopf, 1981).

12. Robinson Rojas, *The Murder of Allende and the End of the Chilean Way to Socialism* (New York: Harper & Row, 1976).

13. Walter Laqueur, *Terrorism* (Boston: Little, Brown, 1977), 124.

14. W. Vance Grant and C. George Lind, *Digest of Educational Statistics: 1973 Edition* (Washington, D.C.: Government Printing Office, 1974), 7.

15. Daniel Singer, *Prelude to Revolution: France in May, 1968* (New York: Hill & Wang, 1970), 198–200; Allan Priaulx and Sanford J. Ungar, *The Almost Revolution: France, 1968* (New York: Dell, 1969), 122–24.

16. Sergio Romano, "The Roots of Italian Terrorism," *Policy Review,* 1983, no. 25: 25–27. See also Vincent E. McHale, "Economic Development, Political Extremism and Crime in Italy," *Western Political Quarterly* 31 (March 1978): 59–79.

17. See, for example, Roderick Aya and Norman Miller, eds., *The New American Revolution* (New York: Free Press, 1971).

18. Nelson Blackstock, *COINTELPRO: The FBI's Secret War on Political Freedom* (New York: Vintage, 1976); Paul Chevigny, *Cops and Rebels: A Study of Provocation* (New York: Pantheon, 1972); Gilbert Moore, *A Special Rage* (New York: Harper & Row, 1971); National Commission on the Causes and Prevention of Violence, *Rights in Conflict* (Walker Report) (New York: Bantam, 1968).

19. Harold Jacobs, ed., *Weatherman* (Berkeley, Calif.: Ramparts Press, 1971); Susan Stern, *With The Weathermen: The Personal Journey of a Revolutionary Woman* (New York: Doubleday, 1975); Peter Collier and David Horowitz, "Doing It: The Inside Story of the Rise and Fall of the Weather Underground," *Rolling Stone,* 30 September 1982, 19ff.

20. Sergey Nechayev, "Cathechism of the Revolutionist," in *Daughter of a Revolutionary: Natalie Herzen and the Bakunin-Nechayer Circle,* ed. Michael Confino (La Salle, Ill.: Library Press, 1973).

21. Yehoshofat Arkabi, "Al Fatah's Doctrine," in *The Terrorism Reader: A Historical Anthology,* ed. Walter Laqueur (New York: New American Library, 1978), 151.

22. Don Sassoon, *The Strategy of the Italian Communist Party: From the Resistance to the Historic Compromise* (New York: St. Martin's, 1981); R. Grant Amyot, *The Italian Communist Party: The Crisis of the Popular Front Strategy* (New York: St. Martin's, 1981).

23. See Philip G. Cerny, "France, Non-Terrorism, and the Politics of Repressive Tolerance," in *Terrorism: A Challenge to the State,* ed. Juliet Lodge (New York: St. Martin's, 1981), 91ff. See also Georges Marchais, *La Politique du Parti Communiste Français* (Paris: Editions Sociales, 1974).

24. Quote is from Gramsci's *Prison Notebooks,* in James Joll, *Antonio Gramsci* (New York: Viking, 1979), 79.

25. M. A. Farber, "Behind the Brink's Case: Return of the Radical Left," *New York Times,* 16 February 1982, p. 1, cols. 2, 3, p. B4ff.

Chapter 6

1. See Gene Marine, *The Black Panthers* (New York: New American Library, 1969); Geoffrey Pridham, "Terrorism and the State in West Germany During the 1970's," in *Terrorism: A Challenge to the State,* ed. Juliet Lodge (New York: St. Martin's, 1981), 11ff.; Senate Committee on the Judiciary, Subcommittee on

Criminal Laws and Procedures, *West Germany's Political Response to Terrorism* (Washington, D.C.: Government Printing Office, 1978); Alan O'Day, "Northern Ireland, Terrorism, and the British State," in *Terrorism: Theory and Practice,* ed. Yonah Alexander et al. (Boulder, Colo.: Westview Press, 1979), 121–35; James J. Eisenhower, "The British Constitution in Northern Ireland," *Temple Law Journal,* In press.

2. Urban guerrilla theory borrows heavily from ultra-left theoreticians of the 1960s—e.g., Regis Debray (*Revolution in the Revolution?* [New York: Grove, 1967] and *Strategy for Revolution: Essays on Latin America* [New York: Monthly Review Press, 1970]); Che Guevara (*Guerrilla Warfare* [New York: Vintage, 1969]); Franz Fanon (*The Wretched of the Earth*); Abraham Guillen (*Philosophy of the Urban Guerrilla* [New York: William Morrow, 1973]); and Herbert Marcuse (*One-Dimensional Man: Studies in the Ideology of Advanced Industrial Nations* [Boston: Beacon, 1964] and *An Essay on Liberation* [Boston: Beacon, 1969]). The Red Brigade has the strongest theoretical interests of the modern guerrilla groups. See Richard Drake, "The Red Brigades and the Italian Political Tradition," in *Terrorism in Europe,* ed. Yonah Alexander and Kenneth A. Myers (London: Croom Helm, 1982).

3. Vittorfranco S. Pisano, "Terrorism in Italy: the 'Dozier Affair,' " *Police Chief* 49 (April 1982): 38–41; and "War Without Boundaries: West Germany Takes the Offensive Against Skyjackers and Kidnappers," *Time,* 31 October 1977, pp. 26–41.

4. Steven J. Dryden, "Car Bomb Damages U.S. Army Building in Brussels Suburb: Terrorist Group Seen Escalating Attacks," *Washington Post,* 16 January 1985, p. A17; "Leftists Claim Mortar Attack in Lisbon Port," *Washington Post,* 29 January 1985, pp. A1, A12; and "European Terrorist Groups Believed Cooperating: Attacks May Be Planned on NATO Targets, Defense Firms, Government Facilities," *Washington Post,* 29 January 1985, p. A12.

5. Hans Josef Horchem, "European Terrorism: A German Perspective," *Terrorism: An International Journal* 6(1): 27ff.

6. Ibid.; Bruce Hoffman, "Right-Wing Terrorism in Europe," *Conflict* 5(3): 185ff.; Anti-Defamation League of B'nai B'rith, *Extremism on the Right: A Handbook* (New York: Anti-Defamation League of B'nai B'rith, 1983).

7. Walter Laqueur, "International Terrorism: It's an Irritant, But Not a Mortal Danger," *Washington Post,* 29 April 1984, p. B8. See also Laqueur's "The Continuing Failure of Terrorism," *Harper's,* November 1976, 69ff.

8. Fyodor Dostoyevsky, *The Possessed* (New York: New American Library, 1962). Mark Slonim, in the afterword of the Signet (1962) edition of *The Possessed,* is surely correct to say that, "Historical accuracy in *The Possessed* is sacrificed for the purpose of political denunciation and polemical intent" (p. 697).

9. See Bommi Baumann (of the German June 2d Movement), *Wie Alles Anfing: How It All Began* (Vancouver: Pulp Press, 1979); "Before I get transported to Auschwitz again, I'd rather shoot first, that's clear now" (p. 31). Patty Hearst, as "Tanya" of the American Symbionese Liberation Army, stated, "The SLA terrifies the pigs because it's called all oppressed people in this country to arms, to fight in a united front to overthrow this fascist dictatorship" (Marilyn Baker, *Exclusive! The Inside Story of Patricia Hearst and the SLA* [New York: Macmillan, 1974], 229).

10. Carlos Marighella, "Appendix: Minimanual of the Urban Guerrilla," in Robert Moss, *Urban Guerrilla Warfare* (London: Institute for Strategic Studies, 1971), 23.

11. Walter Laqueur, *Terrorism* (Boston: Little, Brown, 1977), 22–25.

12. André Malraux, *Man's Fate* (New York: Modern Library, 1936). Camus quotes the terrorist Ivan Kaliayev as follows: "How can we speak of terrorist

activity without taking part in it?" (*The Rebel: An Essay on Man in Revolt* [New York: Vintage, 1956]), 166.

13. See Jillian Becker: *Hitler's Children* (Philadelphia: Lippincott, 1977). See also, Schura Cook, "Germany: From Protest to Terrorism," in *Terrorism in Europe,* ed. Yonah Alexander and Kenneth A. Myers (London: Croom Helm, 1982), 154ff.

14. Daniel Berrigan, "Letter to the Weathermen," in *The Berrigans,* ed. William Van Etten Casey and Philip Nobile (New York: Praeger, 1971), 203–13.

15. Valerio Morucci and Adriana Faranda, authors of "To the Editorial Staff of *Lotta Continua,* " in *Autonomia: Post-Political Politics,* ed. S. Lotringer and C. Marazzi (New York: Semiotextes, 1980), 278. See, more generally, Robert Katz, *Days of Wrath: The Ordeal of Aldo Moro* (Garden City, N.Y.: Doubleday, 1980).

16. This support is not discussed in the available English-language literature on German terrorism. My observation is based on conversations with a well-informed West German official.

17. Marighella, *"Minimanual,"* 28.

18. Pridham, "Terrorism and the State."

19. Nechayev, 229.

20. Fanon, *Wretched of the Earth.*

21. Nechayev, 232.

22. See Marcuse, *Essay on Liberation,* 58–62. The doctrine that youth is a revolutionary "class" was given formal expression by the Revolutionary Youth Movement (RYM) faction of Students for a Democratic Society in the United States. RYM became the Weather Underground. See Kirkpatrick Sale, *SDS* (New York: Random House, 1973).

23. Daniel and Gabriel Cohn-Bendit, *Obsolete Communism: The Left-Wing Alternative* (Harmondsworth: Penguin, 1968), 256.

24. Marcuse, *One-Dimensional Man,* 22–34. See also Marcuse's *Counter-Revolution and Revolt* (Boston: Beacon, 1972), 1–42.

25. Fanon, *Wretched of the Earth.* See also the discussion by Henry Bienen in *Violence and Social Change: A Review of Current Literature* (Chicago: University of Chicago Press, 1969), 72–74.

26. Marcuse, *One-Dimensional Man,* 1–57.

27. Says Regis Debray: "This minority [the foco] establishes itself at the most vulnerable zone of the national territory, and then slowly spreads like an oil-patch, propagating itself in concentric ripples through the peasant masses, to the smaller towns, and finally to the capital" in *Strategy for Revolution* (New York: Monthly Review, 1970), 39.

28. See, for example, Rick Atkinson, "European Terrorist Groups Believed Cooperating," *Washington Post,* 29 January 1985, p. A12.

29. A symptom of this development is the rise to prominence of influential right-wing "think tanks" like the Heritage Foundation and the American Enterprise Institute.

30. The wave of bombings of abortion clinics in late 1984 and early 1985 resembled American anarcho-communist terrorism in its focus on property damage and its effort to avoid causing personal injury. Should the attacks continue, however, it is likely that this line will be blurred.

31. Omega 7 has shifted its main attacks from Cuban diplomats to members of the Cuban-American community who are sympathetic to the Castro regime. Eduardo Arocena ("Omar"), one-time leader of the organization, was indicted in December 1984 on three charges of anti-Castro terrorism (including a plot to murder the Cuban ambassador to the United Nations) and eleven counts of

terrorism against local sympathizers. "Castro Opponent Indicted in N.Y., Miami Bombings," *Washington Post,* 29 December 1984, p. A6.

32. Brian Jenkins, *International Terrorism: A New Kind of Warfare* (Santa Monica, Calif.: Rand Corporation, 1974).

Chapter 7

1. See Hans Josef Horchem, "European Terrorism: A German Perspective," *Terrorism: An International Journal* 6(1): 27ff.

2. Quoted in Walter Laqueur, ed., *The Terrorism Reader: A Historical Anthology* (New York: New American Library, 1978), 148.

3. Yehoshafat Harkabi, "Al Fatah's Doctrine," in *Terrorism Reader,* ed. Laqueur, 151.

4. In Yemen, for example, a similar struggle in the mid-1960s resulted in the destruction of the Front for the Liberation of South Yemen (FLOSY) by the rival NLF, aided by the South Arabian Army. See Anthony Burton, *Urban Terrorism: Theory, Practice and Response* (New York: Free Press, 1975), 172–76.

5. The OPEC kidnapping was a multinational enterprise led by Carlos, but its purpose does not seem nearly as obscure as some commentators have maintained. See, for example, Walter Laqueur, *Terrorism* (Boston: Little, Brown, 1977), 215–16.

6. John F. Devlin, *Syria: Modern State in an Ancient Land* (Boulder, Colo.: Westview Press, 1983), 81–83.

7. See Julen Agirre, *Operation Ogro: The Execution of Admiral Luis Carrero Blanco* (New York: Quadrangle/New York Times, 1975); Pierre Vallières, *White Niggers of America: The Precocious Autobiography of a Quebec "Terrorist"* (New York: Monthly Review, 1971).

8. See Raymond Aron, *The Century of Total War* (Boston: Beacon, 1955).

9. Cf. J. Bowyer Bell, *Terror Out of Zion: Irgun Zvai Leumi, LEHI, and the Palestine Underground, 1929–1949* (New York: St. Martin's, 1977); and Thurston Clarke, *By Blood and Fire: The Attack on the King David Hotel* (New York: Putnam, 1981). See also William R. Polk, *The United States and the Arab World,* rev. ed. (Cambridge: Harvard University Press, 1969):

> On April 10 [1948] the Irgun with the help of the Haganah attacked and took the village of Deir Yasin. After the Haganah left, the Irgun, in a deliberate attempt to promote terror among the general Arab population, massacred all the village inhabitants and widely publicized its action (p. 184).

10. The use of U.S. weaponry in the Lebanese war is documented in *Reason Not the Need: Eyewitness Chronicles of Israel's War in Lebanon,* ed. Franklin P. Lamb (London: Bertrand Russell Peace Foundation, 1984), 419–535.

11. Anti-Defamation League of B'nai B'rith, "International Terrorism—Europe," *ADL International Report* 2(1): 8–9, documents training of German neo-Nazis by the PLO as well.

12. Gerard Chaliand, *The Palestinian Resistance* (Harmondsworth: Penguin, 1972).

13. V. I. Lenin, *Lenin on the National and Colonial Questions: Three Articles* (Peking: Foreign Languages Press, 1970), 8.

14. Ibid., 26–27.

15. Ibid., 27, 33.

16. See Patricia G. Steinhoff, "Portrait of a Terrorist: An Interview with Kozo

Okamoto," *Asian Survey* 16(9): 830–45. The synthesis of pseudo-Leninist philosophy is derived from numerous sources, and is my own.

17. V. I. Lenin, *Imperialism: The Highest Stage of Capitalism* (New York: International Publishers, 1939), 126. Emphasis added.

18. Ibid., 125.

19. Joseph Seymour, *Lenin and the Vanguard Party* (New York: Spartacist, 1978), 107.

20. See, for example, Ernest Mandel, ed., *Fifty Years of World Revolution: An International Symposium* (New York: Pathfinder Press), 1970.

21. Leon Trotsky, *Problems of the Chinese Revolution,* 3d ed. (New York: Paragon, 1966), 23–72. The same approach led the Soviets to sponsor armed repression of social revolutionaries (anarchists, POUMists, Trotskyists, etc.) during the Spanish Civil War.

22. Other nationalist groups might also be added to this list—for example, the KKK and the Black Liberation Army. See Kenneth F. Englade, "Terrorism in the Name of God and Country," *Liberty,* January–February 1981, 2ff.

23. See, for example, Steven J. Dryden, "Car Bomb Damages U.S. Army Building in Brussels Suburb," *Washington Post,* 16 January 1985, p. A17; and "French, German Terrorists Reported to Join Forces," ibid.

24. Quoted in Rick Atkinson, "European Terrorist Groups Believed Cooperating," *Washington Post,* 29 January 1985, p. A12.

25. See J. F. Pilat, "Research Note. European Terrorism and the Euromissiles," *Terrorism: An International Journal* 7(1): 67: "The extreme right has also targeted the U.S. and NATO since 1981, not only to express its traditional hostility to the U.S. and NATO presence in the FRG, but in apparent hopes of benefiting from the peace movement's popularity."

26. See Walter Laqueur, *Germany Today: A Personal Report* (Boston: Little, Brown, 1985), 57–59.

Chapter 8

1. J. Christopher Herold, *The Age of Napoleon* (New York: American Heritage, 1963), 215–22.

2. Menachem Begin, quoted in Walter Laqueur, ed., *The Terrorism Reader: A Historical Anthology* (New York: New American Library, 1978), 143.

3. Bruce Hoffman, "Right-Wing Terrorism in Europe," *Conflict* 5(3): 194, 208.

4. Ağca's trial during the summer of 1985 only increased the confusion, particularly when the would-be assassin claimed to be Jesus Christ.

5. See Anthony Burton in *Urban Terrorism: Theory, Practice, and Response* (New York: Free Press, 1975): "In the first week of May [1962] there were 203 murders. It was no longer 'OAS' but fury and sadism, a blind nihilistic destruction of property and life. It was the day of the psychopath" (p. 205).

6. Hoffman, "Right-Wing Terrorism," 197–99.

7. Edward S. Herman, *The Real Terror Network* (Boston: South End Press, 1982).

8. Hans Josef Horchem, "European Terrorism: A German Perspective," *Terrorism: An International Journal* 6(1): 40–41; Hoffman, "Right-Wing Terrorism," 188–92.

9. Thomas Sheehan, "Italy: Terror on the Right," *New York Review of Books,* 22 January 1981, 25.

10. Ibid., 23.

11. See, for example, Nelson Blackstock, *COINTELPRO: The FBI's Secret War on Political Freedom* (New York: Vintage, 1976). The FBI collaborated with Cook County sheriff's police in the 1969 raid that killed Fred Hampton and Mark Clark of the Black Panther party; the Greensboro, North Carolina, police collaborated with the KKK and Nazis in the 1979 attack that killed five members and sympathizers of the Communist Workers party.

12. "Fugitive White Supremacist is Seized Carrying Arsenal: 'Turning Point' Seen in Federal Probe," *Washington Post,* 28 March 1985, p. A18.

13. Bob Woodward and Carl Bernstein, *All The President's Men* (New York: Simon & Schuster, 1974).

14. On 7 June 1985, a jury in Winston-Salem, North Carolina, brought in a verdict in the thirteen-week civil suit brought by survivors of the Greensboro victims. Five Nazis and Klansmen, two Greensboro policemen, and one police informer were found liable for the wrongful death of Dr. Michael Nathan and were ordered to pay $355,100 to his widow. Smaller awards were made to two wounded victims, and all charges of conspiracy were dismissed against forty-five defendants, "including some thirty-six Greensboro cops, two FBI informers and an ATF (Alcohol, Tobacco and Firearms) agent named in the civil suit" ("No More Greensboro Massacres!" *Workers Vanguard,* 12 July 1985, 4).

15. Hoffman, "Right-Wing Terrorism," 90–92. See also Hans Josef Horchem, "Rightist Extremism in the Federal Republic of Germany, 1977," *Conflict* 1(3): 171ff.

16. Hoffman, "Right-Wing Terrorism," 187.

17. William Drozdiak, "German Bombers Shift to Civilian Targets: Escalation Seen as Sign of Desperation," *Washington Post,* 9 March 1985, p. A13. (In fact, the killing of military-industrialist Ernst Zimmerman near Munich by the RAF on 1 February 1985 did not necessarily imply desperation.)

18. Wilhelm Dietl, *Holy War* (New York: Macmillan, 1984).

19. See Fouad Ajami, *The Vanished Imam: Musa al Sadr and the Shia of Lebanon* (Ithaca, N.Y.: Cornell University Press, 1986).

20. The Air India disaster is widely believed to have been the work of Sikh terrorists. For background on the Sikh movement, see Surjit Singh Gandhi, *The Struggle of the Sikhs for Sovereignty* (New Delhi: Gur Das Kapur, 1980).

21. See, for example, Moshe Arens, "Terrorist States," in *Terrorism: How the West Can Win,* ed. Benjamin Netanyahu (New York: Farrar, Straus, 1986), 93–97.

22. Christopher Hill, *Intellectual Origins of the English Revolution* (Oxford: Clarendon Press, 1965).

23. See, for example, Michael M. Fischer, Jr., *Iran: From Religious Disputes to Revolution* (Cambridge: Harvard University Press, 1980).

24. See Imam Khomeini, *Islam and Revolution: Writings and Declarations of Imam Khomeini* (Berkeley, Calif.: Mizan Press, 1981).

25. Aleksandr Solzhenitsyn, *Press Conference on the Future of Russia,* Zurich, November 16, 1974, ed. D. Prospielovsky (London, Ont.: Zaria, 1975); Stephen Carter, *The Politics of Solzhenitsyn* (New York: Holmes & Meier, 1977).

26. Hans Rogger and Eugen Weber, eds., *The European Right: A Historical Profile* (Berkeley, Calif.: University of California Press, 1965).

27. Hisham Melhem, "The Case for the Lebanese Resistance," *AAUG Mideast Monitor* 2(3): 3.

28. Ibid.

29. Ibid., 2.

30. See, for example, Gerard Chaliand, *Report from Afghanistan* (New York: Viking, 1982), 47–61.

31. Walter Laqueur, *Terrorism* (Boston: Little, Brown, 1977), 71–77.

32. J. Bowyer Bell, *Terror Out of Zion: Irgun Zvai Leumi, LEHI, and the Palestine Underground, 1929–1949* (New York: St. Martin's, 1977).

33. Robert Payne, *The Life and Death of Mahatma Gandhi* (New York: Dutton, 1969).

34. Franz Fanon, *The Wretched of the Earth* (New York: Grove, 1967), 134.

Chapter 9

1. Paul Avrich, "Preface," *Bakunin on Anarchy,* ed. Sam Dolgoff (New York: Knopf, 1972), xv.

2. Sam Dolgoff, ed., *Bakunin on Anarchy* (New York: Knopf, 1972); G. P. Maximoff, ed., *The Political Philosophy of Bakunin: Scientific Anarchism* (Glencoe, Ill.: Free Press, 1953). See also Eugene Pyziur, *The Doctrine of Anarchism of Michael Bakunin,* 2d ed. (Chicago: Henry Regnery, 1968), 29.

3. See Michael Bakunin, *God and the State* (New York: Dover, 1970).

4. Sergey Nechayev, "Catechism of the Revolutionist," in *Daughter of a Revolutionary: Natalie Herzen and the Bakunin-Nechayev Circle,* ed. Michael Confino (La Salle, Ill.: Library Press, 1973), 230. Bakunin expressed similar views. See Mikhail Bakunin, "Revolution, Terrorism, Banditry," in *The Terrorism Reader: A Historical Anthology,* ed. Walter Laqueur (New York: New American Library, 1978), 65–68.

5. Mikhail Bakunin, "The Reaction in Germany," in Dolgoff, *Bakunin on Anarchy,* 57.

6. Paul Avrich points out that Bakunin *was* a nationalist of sorts: a pan-Slavic enthusiast who disliked Germans and Jews ("Preface," xxiv).

7. Quoted in K. J. Kenafict, *Michael Bakunin and Karl Marx* (Melbourne [privately publ.], 1948), 89.

8. Quoted in Dolgoff, *Bakunin on Anarchy,* 10.

9. This quotation, from the memoirs of Debogori-Mokrievishc, appears in Kenafict, *Michael Bakunin and Karl Marx,* 296.

10. Nechayev, "Catechism," 229.

11. Ibid., 230.

12. Ibid., 224.

13. Ibid., 223–24.

14. Julius Braunthal, *History of the International,* vol. 1, trans. Henry Collins and Kenneth Mitchell (New York: Praeger, 1967), 175–85 (other reasons for abandoning the organization are discussed on p. 64).

15. This theme was replayed a century later by Franz Fanon in *The Wretched of the Earth* (New York: Grove, 1967).

16. Karl Marx and Frederick Engels, *Selected Works In One Volume* (New York: International Publishers, 1968), 43–44.

17. Ibid., 170.

18. Ibid., 428–32.

19. Karl Marx, "On Bakunin's *Statism and Anarchy,*" in *Karl Marx: Selected Writings,* ed. David McLellan (Oxford: Oxford University Press, 1977), 561.

20. Marx and Engels, *Selected Works,* 62–63.

21. Ibid., 43–44.

22. Karl Marx, "Address to the Communist League," in *Karl Marx: Selected Writings,* ed. David McLellan (Oxford: Oxford University Press, 1977), 282.

23. Ibid., 285.

24. Quoted in Shlomo Avineri, *The Social and Political Thought of Karl Marx* (Cambridge: Cambridge University Press, 1968), 201. See also Karl Marx and

Friedrich Engels, *Collected Works*, vol. 10 (New York: International Publishers, 1975), 318.

25. Avineri, *Social and Political Thought of Karl Marx*, 185ff., 201.

26. Karl Kautsky, *Terrorism and Communism* (Westport, Conn.: Hyperion Press, 1973).

27. Walter Laqueur suggests that Marx and Engels "exaggerated the strength of the Narodnaya Volya and overestimated the weakness of Tsarist despotism." It would be more accurate to say that they overestimated the revolutionary temper of the Russian masses. See Laqueur's *Terrorism* (Boston: Little, Brown, 1977), 64–65. Engels believed that the Narodniks could trigger a revolution, but that they could never hold power: "Let them only make the breach which will destroy the dike, then the flood will swiftly put an end to their illusions" (quoted from a letter to V. I. Zasulich, 1885, in Laqueur, *Terrorism Reader*, 208).

28. Stewart Edwards, *The Paris Commune* (Chicago: Quadrangle, 1971), 313–50. See also Roger L. Williams, *The French Revolution, 1870–1871* (New York: W. W. Norton, 1969).

29. Marx and Engels, *Selected Works*, 292.

30. Ibid., 295.

31. Ibid., 288.

32. Karl Marx, "To Ferdinand Domela Nieuwenhuis," in *The Letters of Karl Marx*, ed. Saul K. Padover (Englewood Cliffs, N.J.: Prentice-Hall, 1979), 334. See also Marx's "To Ludwig Kugelmann," in ibid., 280.

33. Marx and Engels, *Selected Works*, 295.

34. Ibid., 259.

Chapter 10

1. See Mark Twain and Charles Dudley Warner, *The Gilded Age: A Tale of Today* (1874; reprint, New York: Trident, 1964).

2. Peter Gay, *The Dilemma of Democratic Socialism: Eduard Bernstein's Challenge to Marx* (New York: Collier, 1962).

3. Ibid., 141ff.

4. See James Joll, *The Anarchists* (London: Eyre & Spottiswoode), 1964.

5. An excellent discussion is James H. Billington, *Fire in the Minds of Men: Origins of the Revolutionary Faith* (New York: Basic Books, 1980), 386–418.

6. Paul Avrich, *The Russian Anarchists* (Princeton, N.J.: Princeton University Press, 1971). See also Boris I. Nikolaejewsky, *Aseff the Spy* (1934; reprint, Hattiesburg, Miss.: Academic International, 1969); Boris Savinkov, *Memoirs of a Terrorist* (New York: Albert & Charles Boni, 1931).

7. The relative isolation of many terrorist groups does not mean that they operate in a vacuum. On the contrary, survival generally requires some support among client groups. Antiterrorist analysts frequently minimize the extent of this support.

8. Walter Laqueur, *Terrorism* (Boston: Little, Brown, 1977), 123.

9. See Avrahm Yarmolinsky, *Road to Revolution: A Century of Russian Radicalism* (New York: Collier, 1962).

10. See Ted R. Gurr, *Why Men Rebel* (Princeton, N.J.: Princeton University Press, 1970); James C. Davies, ed., *When Men Revolt and Why?* (New York: Free Press, 1970).

11. Nikolai Morozov, "The Terrorist Struggle," in *The Terrorism Reader: A*

Historical Anthology, ed. Walter Laqueur (New York: New American Library, 1978), 73–74.

12. Ibid., 75.

13. Ibid., 74; see also Ibid., 78.

14. Eduard Bernstein, *Evolutionary Socialism: A Criticism and Affirmation* (New York: Schocken, 1961), 204–5.

15. Gerasim Tarnovski, "Terrorism and Routine," in *The Terrorism Reader: A Historical Anthology,* ed. Walter Laqueur (New York: New American Library, 1978), 84.

16. Ibid., 82.

17. Ibid.

18. Serge Stepniak-Kravchyinsky, "Underground Russia," in *The Terrorism Reader: A Historical Anthology,* ed. Walter Laqueur (New York: New American Library, 1978), 89.

19. Nikolaejewsky, *Aseff the Spy.*

20. Karl Marx and Friedrich Engels, *Selected Works In One Volume* (New York: International Publishers, 1968), 37.

Chapter 11

1. V. I. Lenin, *What Is to Be Done? Burning Questions of Our Movement* (1929; reprint, New York: International Publishers, New World, 1969).

2. Ibid., 74–75.

3. Ibid., 131–39.

4. Ibid., 133–34.

5. Ibid., 134–39.

6. V. I. Lenin, "Revolutionary Adventurism," in *The Terrorism Reader: A Historical Anthology,* ed. Walter Laqueur (New York: New American Library, 1978), 211.

7. Leon Trotsky, *History of the Russian Revolution,* vols. 1–3 (New York: Simon & Schuster, 1932), vol. 2, 223–49.

8. V. I. Lenin, "Why the Social Democrats Must Declare War on the SR's," *The Terrorism Reader: A Historical Anthology,* ed. Walter Laqueur (New York: New American Library, 1978), 208.

9. Lenin, "Revolutionary Adventurism," 213.

10. Leon Trotsky, *Against Individual Terrorism* (New York: Pathfinder, 1974), 7.

11. Ibid., 12.

12. Ibid., 4.

13. Ibid., 7.

14. Ibid., 11.

15. Ibid.

16. Ibid., 12.

17. Ibid., 20.

18. Ramy Nima, *The Wrath of Allah: Islamic Revolution and Reaction in Iran* (London: Pluto Press, 1983). See also Shaul Bakhash, *The Reign of the Ayatollahs: Iran and the Islamic Revolution* (New York: Basic Books, 1984).

19. Walter Laqueur, *Terrorism* (Boston: Little, Brown, 1977), 63.

20. Ibid., 63–66.

21. Ibid., 67–68.

22. Don Sassoon, *The Strategy of the Italian Communist Party: From the Resistance to the Historic Compromise* (New York: St. Martin's, 1981). See also C. Grant Amyot,

The Italian Communist Party: The Crisis of the Popular Front Strategy (New York: St. Martin's, 1981).

23. Geoffrey Pridham, "Terrorism and the State in West Germany During the 1970's," in *Terrorism: A Challenge to the State,* ed. Juliet Lodge (New York: St. Martin's, 1981), 11ff.

24. Laqueur, *Terrorism,* 67.

25. Spartacist League, *Lenin and the Vanguard Party* (New York: Spartacist, 1978), 63–64.

26. V. I. Lenin, *Collected Works,* vol. 20 (New York: International Publishers, 1929), 275.

27. Trotsky, *History of the Russian Revolution,* vol. 3, 177.

28. Ibid., 178.

29. Karl Kautsky, *Terrorism and Communism* (Westport, Conn.: Hyperion Press, 1973), 31, 37.

30. Trotsky, *History of the Russian Revolution,* vol. 3, 178.

31. V. I. Lenin, *The Proletarian Revolution and the Renegade Kautsky* (1952; reprint, Peking: Foreign Languages Press, 1970), 103.

32. Ibid., 102.

33. Eric R. Wolf, *Peasant Wars of the Twentieth Century* (New York: Harper & Row, 1969), 90–91.

34. Lenin, *The Proletarian Revolution,* 49–59; Trotsky, *Terrorism and Communism: A Reply to Karl Kautsky* (London: New Park, 1975), 63–68, 80–84.

35. Trotsky, *Terrorism and Communism,* 78.

36. Ibid.

37. David Wilkinson, *Revolutionary Civil War: The Elements of Victory and Defeat* (Palo Alto, Calif.: Page-Ficklin, 1975), 12.

38. Trotsky, *Terrorism and Communism,* 78.

39. Trotsky, *History of the Russian Revolution,* vol. 1, 78.

Chapter 12

1. Walter Laqueur, *Terrorism* (Boston: Little, Brown, 1977), 68.

2. Frances FitzGerald, *Fire in the Lake: The Vietnamese and the Americans in Vietnam* (Boston: Little, Brown, 1972), 411–14. See also Stephen T. Hosmer, *Viet Cong Repression and Its Implications for the Future* (Lexington, Mass.: D. C. Heath, 1970).

3. Eric Wolf, *Peasant Wars of the Twentieth Century* (New York: Harper & Row, 1969), 205. See also Douglas Pike, *Viet Cong: The Organization and Techniques of the National Liberation Front of South Vietnam* (Cambridge: MIT Press, 1966).

4. In *Fire in the Lake,* FitzGerald states that the government of South Vietnam reported 19,534 Viet Cong "neutralized" in 1969 alone. The U.S. government figure was 13,668 enemy dead. All figures are rough estimates, given that "the program in effect eliminated the cumbersome category of 'civilian'; it gave the GVN [Government of Vietnam], and initially the American troops as well, license and justification for the arrest, torture, or killing of anyone in the country, whether or not the person was carrying a gun" (p. 413).

5. On the first KKK, see Stanley F. Horn, *Invisible Empire: The Story of the Ku Klux Klan, 1866–1871* (Boston: Houghton Mifflin, 1939); David M. Chalmers, *Hooded Americanism* (Chicago: Quadrangle, 1968).

6. Laqueur, *Terrorism,* 71–77. See also Hans Rogger and Eugen Weber, eds., *The European Right: A Historical Profile* (Berkeley, Calif.: University of California Press, 1965).

7. Conan Fischer, *Stormtroopers* (Boston: Allen & Unwin, 1983). See also Eliot B. Wheaton, *Prelude to Calamity: The Nazi Revolution, 1933–1935* (Garden City, N.Y.: Doubleday, 1968).

8. Leon Trotsky, *History of the Russian Revolution,* vol. 1 (New York: Simon & Schuster, 1932), xix.

Chapter 13

1. See Leon Trotsky, *Problems of the Chinese Revolution,* 3d ed. (New York: Paragon, 1966).

2. Stuart R. Schram, *The Political Thought of Mao Tse Tung,* rev. ed. (New York: Praeger, 1969), 134–35, 210–14.

3. Ibid., 72–73.

4. Wolf, *Peasant Wars of the Twentieth Century* (New York: Harper & Row, 1969), 111–13. See also A. Chalmers Johnson, *Peasant Nationalism and Communist Power* (Palo Alto, Calif.: Stanford University Press, 1962), 88–89.

5. Bommi Baumann, *Wie Alles Anfing: How It All Began* (Vancouver: Pulp Press, 1977), 40.

6. Wolf, *Peasant Wars,* 151–52.

7. Ibid., 152.

8. Stuart R. Schram, ed., *Quotations from Chairman Mao Tse-Tung* (New York: Bantam, 1967), 49.

9. Mao Tse-tung, *Selected Works of Mao Tse-Tung,* vol. 1 (Peking: Foreign Languages Press, 1967), 24.

10. Quoted in John E. Rue, *Mao Tse-Tung in Opposition, 1927–1935* (Palo Alto, Calif.: Stanford University Press, 1966), 283.

11. Johnson, *Peasant Nationalism and Communist Power.*

12. Eqbal Ahmad, "Revolutionary Warfare and Counterinsurgency," in *National Liberation,* ed. N. Miller and R. Aya (New York: Free Press, 1971).

13. Leon Trotsky, *Against Individual Terrorism* (New York: Pathfinder, 1974), 12.

14. Carlos Marighella, "Appendix: *Minimanual of the Urban Guerrilla,*" in Robert Moss, *Urban Guerrilla Warfare* (London: Institute for Strategic Studies, 1971), 40.

15. Regis Debray, *Revolution in the Revolution? Armed Struggle and Political Struggle in Latin America* (New York: Grove, 1967), 24. See also Debray's *Strategy for Revolution* (New York: Monthly Review Press, 1970).

16. Debray, *Revolution in the Revolution?,* 41.

17. Ibid., 47ff.

18. Ibid., 51.

19. Ibid., 106.

20. See, for example, David Stafford, *From Anarchism to Reformism: A Study of the Political Activities of Paul Brousse, 1870–1890* (London: Weidenfeld & Nicholson, 1971).

21. Leo Huberman and Paul M. Sweezy, *Cuba: Anatomy of a Revolution* (New York: Monthly Review Press, 1960); Theodore Draper, *Castro's Revolution: Myths and Realities* (New York: Praeger, 1962). I witnessed Castro's appearance at Harvard University in May 1959, at Soldier Field, and was permitted to ask him a public question: "What works of political philosophy have influenced you the most?" (Laughter.) His answer: "The works of Thomas Jefferson and Simon Bolivar."

22. Terence Cannon, *Revolutionary Cuba* (New York: Crowell, 1981), 108–10.

23. K. S. Karol, *Guerrillas in Power: The Course of the Cuban Revolution* (New York: Hill & Wang, 1971). See also Maurice Zeitlin, *Revolutionary Politics and the Cuban Working Class* (New York: Harper & Row, 1970).

24. Clea Silva, "The Errors of the Foco Theory," in *Regis Debray and the Latin American Revolution,* ed. L. Huberman and P. Sweezy (New York: Monthly Review Press, 1968), 24.

25. Debray, *Strategy for Revolution,* 179–227.

26. Silva, "Errors of the Foco Theory," 24.

27. Thomas W. Walker, *Nicaragua: The Land of Sandino* (Boulder, Colo.: Westview Press, 1981), 32.

28. George Black, *Triumph of the People: The Sandinista Revolution in Nicaragua* (London: Zed Press, 1981).

29. Marvin E. Gettleman et al., eds., *El Salvador: Central America in the New Cold War* (New York: Grove, 1981), 59–89.

30. Ibid., 108–210.

31. See Jonathan L. Fried et al., eds., *Guatemala in Rebellion: Unfinished History* (New York: Grove, 1983).

32. Carol Barton, "Peru: 'Dirty War' in Ayacucho," *NACLA Report on the Americas* 17(3): 36ff.; Philip Bennett, "Peru: Corner of the Dead," *The Atlantic,* May 1984, 28ff.; William Branigin, "Filipino Communists Shift 'People's War' to Cities," *Washington Post,* 25 June 1985, pp. A8–9.

33. Walker, *Nicaragua,* 41–63.

34. See Reed Brody, *Contra Terror in Nicaragua* (Boston: South End Press, 1985).

35. See, for example, Robert Fatton, Jr., *Black Consciousness in South Africa: The Dialectics of Ideological Resistance to White Supremacy* (Albany, N.Y.: SUNY Press, 1986).

Conclusion

1. Leon Trotsky, *Against Individual Terrorism* (New York: Pathfinder, 1974), 17.

2. See Rex B. Wingerter, "Eye for an Eye Causes Blindness," *In These Times,* May 7–13, 1986, pp. 16–17.

3. An unforgettable description of feudal behavior among civilized people is Mark Twain, *The Adventures of Huckleberry Finn* (Berkeley, Calif.: University of California Press, 1985), chap. 18, 142–55.

4. See *Time,* 28 April 1986, cover, 16–33.

5. Richard Clutterbuck, *Living with Terrorism* (London: Faber, 1975).

6. J. Bowyer Bell, *A Time of Terror: How Democratic Societies Respond to Revolutionary Violence* (New York: Basic Books, 1978).

7. See esp. Benjamin Netanyahu, ed., *Terrorism: How the West Can Win* (New York: Farrar, Straus & Giroux, 1986).

8. U.S. Department of State, "National Policy on Terrorism (Strategy and Tactics in Handling Terrorist Incidents)" (privately distributed, n.d.), 4.

9. Ibid., 1.

10. See John W. Burton, *Deviance, Terrorism & War: The Process of Solving Unsolved Social and Political Problems* (New York: St. Martin's, 1979), and his *Resolving Deep-Rooted Conflict: A Handbook* (Lanham, Md.: University Press of America, 1987).

INDEX